CHOOSING EROS

JULIE HAGERTY

NEWMAN SPRINGS PUBLISHING
320 Broad Street
Red Bank, NJ 07701

First originally published by Newman Springs Publishing 2019

ISBN 978-1-64531-261-1 (Paperback)
ISBN 978-1-64531-262-8 (Digital)

Printed in the United States of America

With gratitude for the love of my beloved Bill and my dear children

Part I

Chapter 1

"Hello, Father Bill. I'm a widow." As my words coursed through the phone to the other side of the Atlantic, I realized this was the first time I had spoken them aloud.

"I'm a widow." It hadn't sunk in yet. The past few days had been a terrifying maelstrom from which I'd struggled desperately to escape. I was still in shock. I glanced at Chris, whom, for one moment, I expected to contradict me, but instead she mouthed, "I'll leave you to it," as she headed toward her living room.

"Oh, Julie, I've been praying for you and have just written you a letter. Thank God you're not harmed." His comforting voice calmed me as I considered my new status. Thirty, with four small children now solely dependent on me. *It's real*, I thought to myself. *I'm a widow.*

On March 17, 1969, Father Bill had appeared on our doorstep as my parents were getting ready to attend a St. Patrick's Night Dance in the Grendon Underwood Prison Officer's Club. He was thirty-five, and I was eleven. My mother, resplendent in her emerald-green dress splattered with sequins, breezed past me and answered his confident knock on the door. Smiling warmly and reaching for his suitcase, she announced, "Hello! You must be Father Hagerty. Come on in. You are *most* welcome!" This was her way. It would have made no difference had the person standing before her been selling encyclopedias, asking for directions, or trying to win converts for the Jehovah's Witnesses; the welcome would have been just as sincere. In this instance, however, she was expecting a Jesuit priest, here by invitation.

7

"Oh, thank you," he said in his distinctly American accent as he was ushered into the hall. "Please, call me Father Bill."

We had been eagerly anticipating his visit. For my parents, devout Irish Catholics, hosting a priest in our home was viewed as a sacred privilege. Living in "pagan England," as my father deemed it, made the visit even more significant. And so, for the next week, we pretended that we had a spare room as the five children squeezed into small beds together to provide our guest with privacy.

"Would you like to come to the dance with us, Father?" enquired my dad after the formal introductions were over. We were all gathered curiously gazing at this tall man, dressed head to toe in black, standing like an apparition in our living room.

"Thank you, Danny, but I'm pretty done in after my journey. If you don't mind, I'll pass."

"Not at all, not at all. Please, make yourself at home," said my dad, directing him to the "comfy" armchair.

My mother summoned me into the kitchen as she dabbed a final dusting of Max Factor powder on her flawless complexion. "Take care of Father Bill," she directed.

"Yes, Mammy."

"Make him a cup of tea. Use the good cups, not the mugs, and he might want a sandwich."

"Yes, Mammy." I knew the script by heart. All guests were to be afforded our best hospitality. I waited for her to remind me to heat up the teapot.

"And heat up the pot first—there's nothing worse than a cold teapot."

"I will. And I'll put some biscuits on a plate too. Maybe those chocolate digestives?" The chocolate biscuits were reserved for special guests, but it would be rude to have Father Bill eat alone. I planned on one for each of us and two for the priest.

"Mm, mmm." She nodded, her lips pressed together over a folded tissue to ensure the lipstick stayed put. And so, with Pagan by Picot perfume wafting in the air, off to the dance went my parents, calling to us their final reminder, "Remember your manners!"

We did as we were told. We had been brought up to be in awe of the clergy, who were, by their ordination, elevated to a status well above our own, and it seemed somehow disrespectful not to address Father Hagerty by his full title and surname. But as he had invited us to dispense with the formalities, we soon got used to calling him Father Bill. I felt like a member of an exclusive, privileged group. For the next few hours, I, as the eldest, engaged Father Bill in conversation, made him tea, and introduced him to my brothers and sisters. I felt very grown up. It was the beginning of a friendship neither of us had any inkling would become so vital.

My father took a spiritual retreat once a year for a week or so, and it was after one such hiatus that he returned to his work as a prison officer and approached the governor with a suggestion that maybe the prison inmates would benefit from a similar experience. The governor agreed that if Dad provided food and accommodation for the priest, then the retreat could go ahead. This was how Father Bill Hagerty came into our lives. He spent the days working in the prison and then the evenings relaxing with us. If my younger brother Sean is asked (though he was only two at the time), his memory is of Father Bill landing in our back garden in a helicopter. Such was the impact he had on us all. From him, we learned how to make popcorn, improve at hangman, create Spirograph designs, and best of all, hold conversations.

"Julie, sweep down the stairs before Father Bill gets home. This house looks like a gypsy's caravan!" my mother called out, somewhat flustered, to the back garden where I was playing with my younger siblings. "I don't know why I bother cleaning this house at all."

"All right, Mammy," I called back, letting her know I'd heard her. "I'll be back in a few minutes. So play nicely," I told Vincent and Edel, who were squabbling over a ball while Sean, the "baby," amused himself by reaching into the sack of potatoes, almost as big as he was, propped up against the wall, throwing them one at a time onto the grass. "Sean, put those back like a good boy."

"Outside! Stay outside!" ordered my mother as I stepped into the kitchen and on to the wet tiles. "Can't you see I'm washing the floor?"

"Oh, sorry, Mammy. I was just coming to get the dustpan and brush to sweep the stairs like you asked." I waited by the door until the floor was almost dry, then tiptoed carefully across it to the broom cupboard. Mam was wringing out the mop in the sink, the bucket of water mixed with pine disinfectant still in the middle of the floor. I opened the cupboard door, and the sweeping brush that had been leaning against it fell out. Startled, I stepped backward, knocking my leg against the bucket, sloshing water onto the almost dry floor.

"Julie! For goodness sake, watch where you're going!" my mother scolded. "I've just washed that floor."

"I'm sorry, I'm sorry. It was an accident. I'll mop it up." I hated upsetting her.

"If there was an elephant in the middle of the room, you'd trip over it! Why do you have to be so clumsy?"

"Sorry." I sighed before heading off to sweep the stairs.

A few minutes later when I returned to the garden, Mam and Sean were in the throes of battle.

"Pick it up!" Mam demanded of Sean as she pointed to one of the many potatoes strewn around the grass. "And put it in the sack." Each word was spoken with calculated emphasis—a pause between each one.

"No!" he stated emphatically as only a two-year-old could.

"Don't you say no to me, little man. Now pick it up!"

"No!"

"Sean, do as you are told. Pick up the potato!"

"No!" he replied defiantly.

Annoyed by his stubborn disobedience, Mam took his hand and, bending down, wrapped his chubby little fingers around the potato, her own hand covering his, holding it in place. When she removed her hand, he released his grip, and the potato fell back to the ground. She smacked the back of his hand, and he let out a wail.

"We'll stay here all day if we have to. But you are going to pick up every single one of the potatoes," she told him.

"No!" was still his retort.

She smacked the back of his legs, hoping to gain his submission, but Sean was just as stubborn as she was.

"I'll pick up the potatoes, Mammy," I offered, wanting the standoff to end, knowing that Sean would be the loser.

"No!" she stated as she smacked the back of his legs again. "Sean will pick them up. I'll see to that if it's the last thing I do."

"Please, Mammy. Don't smack him. I'll do it," I cried, tears welling in my eyes.

"No, Julie. He *has* to learn obedience."

"Sean, be a good boy and do as Mammy says," I urged, but it was no use. He would not relent.

The standoff continued for about half an hour, till Mam was close to exhaustion; and Sean, his face blotchy from tears, eventually and reluctantly surrendered as each potato was first forced into and then, with equal effort, prized out of his closed hand.

"Now why couldn't you do that in the first place?" Mam said gently. Sean just sobbed in reply as he was led into the house, all the potatoes back in their sack.

"Hello, Ena. How was your day?" asked Father Bill on his return from his work in the prison.

"Oh, exhausting, Father. The house looked like the wreck of the Hesperus before you came in," she said with a touch of humor.

"Hello, Father Bill!" I said, happy to see him home, the mood in the house already brighter. "Father Bill's home!" I called out to my siblings, who rushed to greet him.

"Hello, Julie, have you had a good day?"

"Yes, we've been busy tidying up."

"Well, you've probably earned a break—hasn't she, Ena?" he asked cheerfully.

"Yes, she's a good girl—most of the time."

I was being reminded of the water spill.

"Well, maybe the kids and I will take a walk before dinner, if that's okay," he suggested.

"Yes, that's fine, but not the little ones. Sean is too much of a handful anyway."

"Okay, so, Stephen and Julie, are you up for a walk? How far is it into the village, Ena, or some shops?"

"Yes, yes!" we said with undiluted enthusiasm.

"You could do the triangle. It's about a three-mile stroll to Marsh Gibbon and back. Be careful, though, there's no footpath."

"That sounds perfect. Okay, let's do it."

"Stephen knows the way. Don't trust Julie. She'll get you lost," she added, teasing me.

So off we set, excited to be away from the house, the tension, and the chores.

"We're like the three musketeers!" said Stephen as we strode out.

"Yes, indeed," said Father Bill. "Which one are you, Stephen?"

"I'm d'Artagnan!" he replied, piercing the air with his imaginary sword. "Which one are you, Father Bill?"

"Hmm, well, I think I must be Aramis. What about you, Julie? Which musketeer are you?"

"I'm not a musketeer. They're all men! I'm Joan of Arc."

"A very strong woman, good choice," he said, congratulating me.

I felt respected and affirmed in his simple remark, void of scolding. Here was a person who saw me, who heard me, and who liked me.

When we got to Marsh Gibbon village shop, Father Bill invited each of us to select our favorite treats. I felt irritated by how "hungry" Stephen seemed as he left the shop with his pockets stuffed with gobstoppers, toffees, and sherbet dib-dabs while I, using restraint (though secretly jealous of his assertiveness), picked out one packet of something or other to share. It was tough trying to be a good and holy person.

The rest of the week was a joyful interlude in our routine as we grew closer to Father Bill. In him, we had someone who listened, who valued our ideas, who enjoyed our company, who took walks with us, who prayed with us, and with whom we had fun! The joy he brought our family only exceeded by the sadness at his leaving.

The day of his departure came, but I was ill prepared for how emotionally taxing it was going to be. As an avid writer of letters, I drew some consolation knowing that I could add Father Bill to my list of pen friends from around the globe. It was my practice to scour magazines looking for compatible and exotic people with whom to correspond. Bandula from Sri Lanka was most constant. Now Father

Bill would receive letters from me in America, in the hopes that he would write back.

The family gathered on the front lawn as Father Bill plopped his case into the trunk of the taxi. I watched from my bedroom window, too distraught to go down and see him leave. My mother glanced around at her brood and might have done a head count, for a moment later, she called up the stairs, "Julie! Don't be so ignorant! Get down here and say goodbye to Father Bill."

"I'm *never* saying good bye to that man!" I called back defiantly. It was the first time in my life that I had intentionally disobeyed my mother. I watched as the taxi pulled away from my parents and as my younger siblings jumped up and down shouting and waving till it turned the corner, just a disappearing speck in the distance. "Bye-bye, Father Bill. We'll miss you. Bye!"

"I'm never saying goodbye," I whispered stubbornly, staring down at the empty street. Then I wept.

I was immensely sad at his going. We had bonded in a way that was mysterious, sacred, and profound. I didn't understand it but felt sure that just as the sun rises in the east and sets in the west, whether we ever saw each other again or not, Father Bill and I were friends and would remain so for life.

March 26, 1969

Dear All—

Just a note of sincere thanks for your wonderful hospitality and kindness. Really—in spite of the various ailments, I have never spent a more enjoyable week in my life. The atmosphere of love that exists in your home is truly marvelous—and a great tribute to Irish Catholicism. Thanks too for the many gifts but above all for your friendship and love which I will remember and treasure always. Please remember me and my work in your prayers—I will count on them and keep you always in mine. May God bless you always.

Love,
Bill

I was delighted then, when only a few weeks later, my mother informed me that she had secured Father Bill as my traveling companion after a visit to my granny in Ireland.

"So Aunty Theresa will take you to Granny's, and Father Bill will bring you home."

"Father Bill? Really? Are you sure, Mammy?" I might have misheard, or she might have made a mistake.

"Yes, Father Bill. He'll be traveling to Berlin and France to judge films in a festival, I think," she explained.

"Oh, I'm so happy!" I said giddily. "*So* happy!"

"Well, take your happiness away with you and set the table for dinner."

As I placed the salt and pepper shakers on the dining-room table, I looked forward excitedly to the next time I would see Father Bill as a guest at my granny's table.

I cherished the times spent in Tuam with my grandparents, Willie and Bridie McGrath. For a blissful brief interlude, I was the "only" child. Although they had raised a family of eleven children, they also took me in as an infant to help out my struggling parents, who were finding it very difficult to care for their young family of four. So this summer visit was the first time I was back staying with them since I was a toddler.

The small house was as I remembered it. Three bedrooms and one main living area, where the black-topped range, the only source of heat and upon which all meals were prepared, was the focal point. Each morning, I woke to the sounds of clattering iron as Granny pried open the hungry heavy mouth of the range to top it up with turf. It was just another demanding child needing to be fed. But in its turn, it provided warmth and sustenance. As the fuel burned behind the scorching door on one side, on the other, an "almost-ready" rhubarb or apple tart, or loaf of soda bread taught us patience. The anticipation of fresh-from-the-fire soda bread with a big dollop of butter plopped on it and melting before it reaches your mouth is deliciously tantalizing.

Above the range, with its well-worn kettle and pots simmering away, was a mantelpiece on which two chipped china spaniels did sentry duty, guarding the elusive biscuit tin, well out of reach of greedy little hands and only opened by Granny or Grandad when we had earned a reward. Granny, at only four feet ten, had quite a challenge to reach that tin. Even on tippy-toes, she was always just a tipple away from toppling into the range. I can see her now, like a champion gymnast preparing to reach for the horizontal bars, securing her lit cigarette between her lips before sliding both palms down her flowered apron to remove any moisture. A deep intake of breath out of one side of her mouth before stretching her arm up…up, her tiny toes the only part of her grounded. A slight shifting of weight to steady the wobble. Reaching, reaching—"You can do it, Granny," I said encouragingly. "You're nearly there…be careful!" Her fingertips were feeling their way to the edge of the mantle. But it was all too much. The convulsive giggling began, interrupted by choking and coughing brought on by the captive cigarette.

"Agh! Stop making me laugh, girly!" she scolded as she caught her breath and then took one long drag on the cigarette, as though somehow it would extend her reach, ready for round two.

Granny might have been rewarding me for taking my granddad his packed lunch. He worked at the Shell garage on the Galway Road, which was about two miles from their home in Demesne Cottages, Tuam. I enjoyed the walk and the trust placed in me to deliver the lunch. Some days, Granddad would be waiting at the garage, happy to see me and ready with a three-penny bit to buy sweets on my way back. Other days he was not at the garage when I got there. These were my favorite days. I would have to find him by spotting his bicycle—the cleanest, shiniest black bicycle in town—leaning against a pub wall.

"Ah, here she is. Sister Julianna!" announced my granddad. "Let's have a look here. What have ye brought me?"

I handed over the brown paper package secured with twine and the flask of hot, milky, sweet tea. He opened the parcel to reveal two thick wedges of bread stuffed with boiled bacon and slathered in Colman's hot mustard. After ritually smoothing out the creases of the paper, he took a swig of his Guinness, leaving half a pint in the glass. Then, without ceremony, he unscrewed the top of the flask and added its contents to the Guinness in his glass. No one else I know drinks such a concoction—half Guinness and half sweet milky tea!

I sipped on some lemonade as the men in the pub bantered good-naturedly with one another, elbows on the bar, chins resting on their knuckles, their eyes peering into the contents of their glasses, as though some truth lurks in the depths of dark stout—the sound of their voices a low, comforting drone. Granddad scribbled down the names of horses on the back of a ripped Players cigarette packet; then he handed me some money for myself and more for the bookies. No one in the betting shop seemed to care that an eleven-year-old-girl was in line to place a few wagers on the day's races. They knew I was Willie McGrath's granddaughter and that was sufficient reference. Now, looking back, I see it was a routine that included me and which I thoroughly enjoyed. It was a sacred time.

And so it was, to these people, into this home, that Father Bill was welcomed, eager to experience real Irish hospitality before escorting me back to England. It proved to be yet another opportunity to deepen our friendship. My granny was keen to get him settled and explain to him how things worked. If he was surprised at the fact that there was no bathroom in the house, he didn't show it. Granny assured him that the toilet outside was scrubbed down daily with Jeyes fluid disinfectant and that she would provide him with a china potty at night in case he was "caught short."

There were two rainwater barrels. The one in the front was newer, so the water from that one was used for cooking and drinking. The one in the back had specks of rust floating on the surface of the water, revealing its age. This water was for washing with or, on occasion, much to my distress, for drowning newborn kittens. I remember one time when the cat had given birth to about six kittens, and Granny had to dispose of them. I felt it was cruel to drown them, but she was not at all sentimental about such things and viewed it as a necessary, if unpleasant, task. I watched, horrified, as she stuffed each of the kittens, one on top of the other, into one of her old nylon stockings. Their pitiful high-pitched squeaks called out feebly as though anticipating their fate as she tied a secure knot in the top of the mesh. I cried out in their defense, "Please, please, Granny, don't kill them—I'll look after them. Pleeease, oh, please…" My persistent pleading was acknowledged, and in her pity for me, I think, she let me save one of the tiny creatures. Only one. The rest were lowered into the back barrel—oblivious, submerged, and silenced.

Father Bill was well taken care of by Granny, who rose first each day, drew water from the barrel, heated it on the range, and kept it there till he needed to wash or shave. She then poured it into a large blue pitcher and from that into the matching bowl on his nightstand. He was fed well too, at least as well as Granddad, with boiled bacon and cabbage, potatoes with their skins on waiting for a coat of butter, and of course, a seemingly limitless supply of rhubarb tart. With no refrigerator, food was prepared fresh daily, and the word *leftovers* had no place in the vocabulary.

We took a few day trips; something new to me. Father Bill had made inquiries and discovered a sightseeing tour company in Galway, twenty-two miles away. We headed out to join one such tour of Connemara and Kylemore Abbey and were disappointed to find there was no bus that could get us there. So we did what many others did at that time: we hitchhiked. It was more common then for people in Ireland, imbued with a natural optimism, to trust that they would get a lift from some passing driver. Being American, Father Bill did not share this optimism, however, and persuaded me that our chances of getting a ride quickly would increase if I stood on the roadside alone. I walked ahead and stuck out my thumb, looking back to see Father Bill crouching behind a low stone wall. Within a few minutes, a kindly couple had pulled up beside me. Father Bill emerged, telling them a story about needing a wee, and we arrived in Galway in time for the tour. I told him that I felt somewhat dishonest using that strategy. So I did it only once.

By the time we returned to England a few days later, our friendship had grown; and this time, the parting was not so sad. I knew in my heart that we were part of each other's lives in a way that defies understanding but was nevertheless real and true. I pledged to add him to my pen-friend list and had every intention, in that moment, of corresponding with him. He promised he would answer all my letters.

HOTEL AM ZOO
1 Berlin 15

Kurforstendamm
June 1969

Dear Julie,
   Just a note to thank you for being such wonderful company during our week together. We really managed to have a lot of fun in spite of the rain. If I had married instead of becoming a priest, my one wish would have been to have a daughter like you.
   Write me sometime in care of my Chicago address. May God bless you always.

                                        Love,
                                        Fr. Bill

Father Bill kept his promise. Every letter I wrote received a response. When I asked for a photo, he sent me a passport shot. As I got older, I wrote fewer letters but always remembered to send him a birthday card. He also remembered mine. My mother, who was much more dedicated to her writing, maintained a regular correspondence with him, keeping him up to date with all our news: the marriages, the births, the milestones. Being only a year apart in age, they had much in common and cultivated a close and lasting friendship.

In high school, I became keenly interested in boys and lost interest in practically everything else, including writing letters. Free moments were spent daydreaming about Peter, or Simon, or Jeremy, or whichever boy had deigned to shoot a friendly glance in my direction. I practiced writing my first name with a variety of last names, testing out what my signature might look like if I were to become Mrs. [Insert name of latest crush here]. I was a typical naive teenager, very immature and easily entertained by unoriginal romantic fantasies. My friends and I would carefully plan walking routes around the school grounds during lunch break to increase the likelihood that we would bump into one of the boys. Then, when we did, suddenly overcome with shyness, we would turn and rush away in the opposite direction. Even with all of this silliness going on, Father Bill had secured a place in my life and was close in thought often.

When I was about fourteen, I instructed my friends Angela and Carol to make a note of his name and put it somewhere safe. I explained that when I became famous (I didn't say *if* but *when*) and appeared on the television show *This Is Your Life*, which ambushes celebrities and then presents them with all the significant people in their life, they were to make sure that the last person presented, the *big surprise* guest who held the most cherished place in my soul, was to be Father Bill Hagerty.

Chapter 2

Bristol, 1974

By 1974, my parents had moved to Bristol. I had left school and was keen to become independent. My O level results had been good enough to continue on and prepare for university, but there had been no discussion of that in our family; and even if there had been, I'm not sure I would have chosen to follow that course then. Like many sixteen-year-olds who had also just left school, I was eager to stride out on my own.

I met no resistance or interference from my parents, who had adopted two children by this time and were immersed in the day-to-day challenges of life with a family of nine. I wonder now whether they even thought about how to direct me with regard to career or whether they were simply giving me time to figure things out for myself. I'm grateful to them for allowing me to create my own labyrinthian path, as it turned out. They had established a firm moral foundation rooted in their Catholic faith, which I embraced; and with the exception of a few peculiar and harsh disciplinary practices, which they both later apologized for, they managed to raise, without exception, children who developed an extraordinary capacity for compassion and social justice.

My father was a strict authoritarian. To instill respect for the commandments, he engaged the use of "the rod of retribution," which rested menacingly on the mantelpiece. He had no tolerance for disobedience, answering back, or bad manners. "Instant obedience" was demanded. I learned quickly how to avoid punishment. It was simple: obey and be good. So I was a good girl.

I loved my dad. I saw beyond his need to control, maybe because I had so much more time with him as he practiced being a good parent on his first child. When we were small, he read to us nightly from the classics such as *Black Beauty*, *Little Women*, and *Little Men*, books then way beyond our years. But he read to us. He also gave us catechism lessons, expecting us to memorize the text, and then tested us on it a few days later.

"You don't need to understand it now. You just need to know it by heart," he insisted. I can still recite from memory the seven deadly sins, the seven gifts of the Holy Spirit, the Ten Commandments, the corporal works of mercy, etc. He took us to Black Acre, a field across the road to do military drills—for fun, perhaps a nod to his time as a sergeant in the British Army. He took us to the Odeon to see silly Saturday-morning films like *Old Mother Riley*, and best of all, he made me a skipping rope.

I was five, and we were poor. There was no money to spare for skipping ropes. When Olivia Casey came over to play with her skipping rope, other girls from the street joined in with *their* skipping ropes, and I felt left out. My dad must have been watching from the window and noticed the dejection in my face when I couldn't join in. I was summoned into the house, wondering what trouble I was in, but was greeted instead with, "Would you like me to make you a skipping rope?"

"Oh yes, Daddy, *yes*! Thank you!" I squealed. I was overjoyed and giddy with excitement as he braided strand over strand of kitchen twine. I fidgeted impatiently, urging him, "Hurry, Daddy, hurry!" afraid that my friends would go home before I could join in. Eventually, he handed me my very own handmade skipping rope. This was love in action. So my father's misguided reliance on corporal punishment, I forgave.

My mother had to manage the children and my dad. She had to be strong. She was the anchor, the one to whom we went for everything. It was she who taught us the difference between venial and mortal sins, though for a long time I was under the terrifying impression that a certain number of venial sins converted to a mortal sin. It was very worrying for me as a six-year-old. Later, once I had made my first confession, Mam made me keep a sin diary, which she inspected weekly to ensure I had recorded my sinfulness accurately. If I had not, that was another sin: the sin of omission. It was so distressing trying to be holy, not out of fear of hell but out of love for Jesus. But I persevered.

Our mother, through her example, also cultivated in us a deep concern for those less fortunate. In spite of being desperately poor for many years, relying on others to house us, spending time in a homeless shelter, surviving dangerous pregnancies, she stayed constant and never turned away a person in need. Most of the time, she was also frustrated and exhausted. It was important to her that we kept our dignity. It didn't matter that we were poor; we could be clean. We were to give people *nothing* to talk about with regard to our behavior or appearance. So we were expected to be always clean, courteous, kind, and speak in complete sentences.

While living temporarily with our great-aunt Mai and uncle Martin in Tuam, in a house on the same street and almost identical to my grandparents' home (Mai had an open fire, not a range, on which to cook), we were asked to donate supplies for the missions and to those poor black babies in Africa. My mother, whose pride prevented her from allowing anyone outside the family to know how badly off we were, purchased rolls of two-ply toilet paper, some Lux soap, Colgate toothpaste, and other sundry toiletries, which were neatly boxed up and handed to me to deliver to Mrs. Kennedy in the big house as she was in charge of collections.

"Make sure she knows it's from Ena Manning née *McGrath*," she instructed. "The *McGrath* name is the important one," she emphasized. The McGraths had lived in Tuam for generations; it was imperative that the family name be associated with good works and kept in good regard.

As I trundled up the road towards Mrs. Kennedy's imposing house, perusing the fragrant treasures in the box, I harbored a secret wish that *I* was the black baby in Africa. Back in Aunty Mai's outside toilet for me to use were scraps of old newspapers surreptitiously lifted by my mother from the doctor's office, cut into squares and hanging on a nail. No two-ply toilet paper for us! No Lux soap either.

That was reserved for much posher people, those who occupied the front rows in church. We were scrubbed raw in the tin bath with a heavy pink brick of Lifebuoy carbolic soap, sometimes in the back garden as neighborhood boys peeped over the wall. To my eight-year-old self, life just didn't seem fair. So as I had been taught to do with all suffering, I offered it up for the souls in purgatory.

My mother's generosity and compassion were unmatched. It was from her we learned to put others first. One Christmas morning, this lesson was reinforced when, on our way back up the hill from Mass with Daddy, my brother Stephen and I saw a young gypsy boy appear over the top of Tullinadaly Road. He was leaping in the air with happiness as he shot his cap gun and yelled, "Bang! Bang!"—the hero of his own cowboy film. Behind him was a gypsy girl, lovingly cradling her doll. Stephen and I looked at each other in pained disbelief yet knowing the horrible truth. While we were at Mass, Mammy had given away our Christmas presents to the gypsies. When we got home, I asked, "Mammy, did you give our toys to the gypsies?" half-hoping that we had *not* seen what we had seen.

"I did," she replied, not needing to explain.

"But, Mammy," I pleaded, "those were *ours!*"

"I know that. But tell me this. If *you* had opened the door to two poor little children and knew they had no Christmas presents, would you have given them your doll?"

"Yes, I would," I admitted reluctantly. And I would have. But somehow, arguing with my mother that giving away what was mine should be *my* choice and not hers seemed pointless.

"Well then," she concluded, and the discussion was over.

It was from these two people that I got my faith, my morals, and my courage; and I couldn't wait to become the arrow shot from that bow.

"So what will you do with your time now you've left school?" my mother enquired.

"Work with children," I announced confidently. And so began the hunt for a job. I checked the classified ads in the social work magazines and in the newspapers and quickly discovered that there were plenty of openings all over the country, for which I was not qualified.

I concluded that since I want a job, then the person hiring should know that I'm available. So I made an appointment with Mr. Cole at the health center and headed off on the bus to secure my future. I had no understanding of protocol with regard to getting a job. Apart from a paper round, I'd never had one before. I knew nothing of résumés, or references even. It was not arrogance but ignorance and innocent confidence in the goodness of life and people that had me knocking so boldly on his door, expecting to get hired on the spot.

"Come in," called a cheery voice. I entered the room where a middle-aged man sat behind a dark wooden desk. He continued with the standard greeting, "Hello. Please have a seat. What can I do for you?"

"Hello, my name is Julie Manning, and I'd like a job working with children, please." Some part of me expected him to say, "We've been waiting for you," or at least flip though his files to find exactly the position for me. Instead, he said, "Hmm, how old are you?"

"I'm sixteen. I'll be seventeen in September," I added encouragingly.

"Well, Julie, can you tell me what qualifications or experience you've had in the field?" He had obviously decided to indulge me, though I naively believed he was seriously considering hiring me.

"Well, I'm the oldest of seven children, and," I added, "I've been a Girl Guide leader of the Swallow Patrol." *What other experience could I possibly need?* I thought to myself.

"Oldest of seven. Well, that's quite a responsibility, but unfortunately, Julie, without more qualifications or experience, we can't use you right now."

I felt disappointed and asked, "How do I get experience or qualifications if I don't have a job?" It was a genuine enquiry, not a challenge. I was remembering my manners.

"Well, I suggest you take some social-work courses at Filton College and come back in a couple of years. I can help you get that set up," he added helpfully.

"Oh no. I'm finished with school. I need experience."

He was either amused by my argument or impressed by my determination, for he then asked, "Would you be willing to volunteer in a children's home for a few months to gain experience? You wouldn't be paid, though."

"Oh yes, yes!" I replied enthusiastically.

"That way, we can assess how you do and take it from there. In the meantime, here's a reading list of novels that will help you better understand the problems some young people face."

"Thank you very much, Mr. Cole. I'll start reading them today." I carefully folded the list, which was later transferred to the back pages of my diary, where it wouldn't get lost.

Ecstatically, I headed off to join Kingswood Library before heading home on the bus and drew out the first four books on the list:

Banks L. R. *The L-Shaped Room*. PENGUIN, 1960, 25p PB
Behan B. *Borstal Boy*. CORGI, 1970, 30p PB
Boswell S. G. *Story of a Gypsy Man*. GOLLANCZ, 1970, 2.10p HC
Burgess A. *Clockwork Orange*. PENGUIN, 1972, 25p PB.

As I stepped onto the bus to go home, my newly acquired library card and reading materials in hand, I felt not only smarter, but also confident that I was going to make my parents proud.

A few weeks later, I was volunteering at 1 Barnwood Road, Gloucester, with Ms. Penny Sweet, who was "mother" to six children in the care of Social Services. For the next three weeks, I caught a bus from Pucklechurch to Gloucester every Sunday evening, returning to my home on Friday, working in a grocery store in Staple Hill on Saturday to earn my bus fare back to Gloucester, on Sunday. It was worth it! Not only did I grow to love the children in my care; I also learned how to nurture children who are not part of my family. As a result of this experience, I was invited to interview at Glebe House Children's Home in Dursley and, along with a birthday message from Father Bill, received a letter from Mr. Nichols at Social Services on Friday September 13, 1974 (three days before my seventeenth birthday), confirming that I had secured a full-time position as a junior housemother. My pay would start at twenty-seven pounds a week, and I would get six weeks holiday a year. It was time to open a bank account!

Jesuit Community
Schott Residence
Xavier University
Cincinnati, Ohio, 45207

Dear Julie,
I just arrived back after a trip to Detroit (for class reunion) and Chicago (to see my mother), so I hope this arrives on time to wish you a VERY HAPPY BIRTHDAY! Seventeen years old, right? My goodness— you'll be getting married soon (not for a few years, though, I hope)!
I hope your plans for the job are going well— you should make an excellent teacher or counselor. My best to all—have a great year, and may God bless you always.
Love,
Fr. Bill

This was to be one of the last letters from Father Bill that I responded to, even though he faithfully remembered my birthdays. Life was taking me in a new direction, and it would be thirteen years before I wrote to him again.

Chapter 3

It was at Glebe House that I met the man who was going to marry me. Adrian Kenneth Long, a private in the Light Infantry and son of my boss, Sybil. On a weekend visit to see his parents, who lived in a private wing of the children's home, he asked his father, Den, about me. I noticed the cheeky grin directed at me and smiled back but couldn't hear the conversation.

"Who's that girl?"

"You leave that girl alone," warned his dad.

"I'm going to marry her," Adrian replied confidently. And he did.

I was thrilled to be working full-time as a residential house-mother to seventeen children. There was a junior housefather, Miles, a house-father, Mr. Wells and the officer in charge, Sybil, my future mother-in-law. Between us, we were to care for the children as parents should. As "live-in" staff, we were there twenty-four hours a day, the first to wake them in the morning and the ones who tucked them in at night. We also helped with homework, took walks, played games, and escorted them to church.

I was in my element. I loved the daily interactions, the banter, the playfulness, the cajoling and coaxing that seemed such a big part of my role. I had a lot of responsibility and the authority that was innate to the role. At first, I found it difficult to assert my authority, particularly as Valerie, one of the "children," was older than me. They were not told my age, and I knew better than to reveal it. It naturally took some time to gain their trust, but eventually they realized I was sincere, trustworthy, and genuinely wanted to like them. I was determined to do well in this position.

I felt so adult. It's incredulous, looking back, to realize that Social Services hired teenagers for such sensitive and important work. We were entrusted with the emotional and psychological health of fragile children who had experienced trauma and rejection and whose parents had been deemed unfit to care for them by the courts. It proved much more daunting than minding my siblings or leading a Girl Guide troop.

Sybil and Den were kind to me, inviting me into their flat in a wing of the home during my free time. I was grateful to have somewhere to go as my room was tiny and held only a single bed, a small wardrobe, and a sink. They included me in their family meals, and I felt as though I had another set of parents, even more so when I received my first Christmas card from them signed "Mum and Dad number 2." Sybil and I worked opposite shifts and alternate weekends. But it was on *my* duty weekends that the children attended church. All of them.

The vicar must have been bracing himself as we spilled up the aisle each fortnight to take our seats in the front two pews. I wouldn't be surprised to learn that some of the congregation also went to church fortnightly, but not on our schedule. I was about as authoritative as Mrs. Santa Claus and looked like one of the kids, so Sunday mornings were particularly stressful for me. I had been brought up going to Mass and had great respect for the occasion, but it seemed no one had fostered that same reverence in these children. A sense of dread and helplessness swept over me during each service, trapped in my seat and sitting beyond arm's length from the most in need of a whisper in their ear or a gentle arm squeeze to encourage them to be still. Before church, I would pay close attention to the moods and interactions of the children to see which two were most likely to be disruptive and then sit between them. They weren't naughty, just restless and overflowing with youthful exuberance. There wasn't much to engage them in a typical Sunday service either, where even some of the most pious in the parish fell asleep. Church, apparently, is no place for youthful exuberance. I could hear my mother's voice warning me, as she so often did, to "avoid occasions of sin." And there were Sundays with this motley crew that would have qualified.

The only respite in the service, from what must have seemed like interminable captivity, was going up at communion time to receive a blessing. It was an opportunity to move without getting into trouble, unless of course you and your buddy had tied the strings of your anoraks together during the sermon and then tried to wrestle free in the communion line, oblivious to the consternation of those behind you. Oh, Sunday afternoons couldn't come quickly enough.

Adrian, who was stationed in Colchester, visited his parents at Glebe House about once a month—until, that is, we began "going out" with each other, when the visits became more frequent. He was funny, attentive, playful, and persistent in his pursuit of me, and he had also inherited his dad's mischievous side, especially regarding practical jokes, like the time Den sent me to the hardware store to purchase a glass hammer and skyhooks. I felt terrible coming back empty-handed only to witness him chuckling at my innocence as he explained that there's no such thing as a glass hammer.

I was flattered by the attention Adrian lavished on me and surrendered willingly. My parents had been very strict about most things and about dating in particular.

There had been only one "serious" boyfriend before Adrian who had to face my parents and gain their approval before we were allowed to "date." It helped a great deal that Peter was Catholic, from the same parish, the son of an Italian (not an English) dairy farmer, and exquisitely shy. What helped most, though, was my parents getting transferred to a prison estate in Bristol, about ninety miles away, leaving me behind with a neighbor for three months to finish my high school education, take my O level exams, and go out with Peter.

Peter's mother adored me, and the feeling was reciprocated. She called me "La Bella Julia!" and treated me like the daughter she never had. She actively encouraged our relationship though we were both very shy and inexperienced when it came to romance. We didn't have a clue, really. We were "going out" for weeks before we got up the courage to hold hands, and it took even longer for our first long-anticipated and excruciatingly awkward first kiss, leaning against each other's faces, our breath held, and our eyes and lips tightly closed. It was such an innocent time. Peter's mother, though, was growing impatient. She seemed eager for us to move forward in our relationship and created opportunities for us to be alone.

On one occasion, she instructed us to "go inta da woods and picka da bluebells. I want lotsa bluebells!" So off we went, hand in hand, and gathered up "lotsa bluebells." We returned, our arms full, expecting his mother to be delighted with our offering, but instead she threw her arms in the air with exasperation while muttering something in Italian, which I didn't understand but which made Peter blush. How were we supposed to know that "picka da bluebells" was her code for something much more intimate?

Time was our enemy. I had to join my parents in another town, and the looming separation was all too much for us to bear. I suggested that we stay close through letters, but Peter couldn't be persuaded. For days, I cried myself to sleep listening to the voice of Ringo Starr singing "You're Sixteen" after Peter, the first boy to buy me a record and the first boy to say "I love you," to whom I gave my heart, broke up with me.

I was still sixteen when Adrian took an interest in me. This time, since I no longer lived at home, I did not need, nor did I seek, my parents' approval. Adrian was twenty, not a shy teenage boy but a man. His kisses revealed that he was experienced, and I was ready to learn. His mother supported our dating, though we didn't actually go on any dates. We hung out together at Glebe House on my free weekends, or when Sybil switched shifts with me if Adrian was home on my duty weekend. She was very accommodating, making it all so easy. The Longs had a much more relaxed attitude towards dating and sex than my parents. I found it refreshing and liberating to be able to cuddle with Adrian on the couch in front of the TV and in front of his parents. They all gently teased me about my timidity and modesty, so over time I grew less self-conscious when Adrian made suggestive comments or slapped my bottom playfully, much to everyone's amusement.

There was to be no cuddling on the couch at my parents' home, however. That would have fallen into the "occasion of sin" category. So when I brought Adrian home to meet my family for the first time, I was particularly anxious. I desperately wanted them to like him. I saw through his rough veneer and his confident, casual manner to an attentive, funny, outgoing person, who was liked instantly by most who met him. He promised me that he would refrain from making any inappropriate comments that would offend my parents' Catholic sensibilities. He would avoid any smutty jokes, and at no time would he grab me or kiss me in their presence. I reminded him that this was a strict Catholic home where we were all expected to remember our manners. He was on his best behavior and did nothing to embarrass me, for which I was grateful. My parents were welcoming, hospitable, and curious; and though they made no comments expressing it in front of Adrian, I sensed mild disapproval, especially when my mother noticed the watch I was wearing.

"That's new. Where did you get that?" she asked accusingly when we were alone together.

"It's a present." Her look told me my reply was unsatisfactory. "From Adrian," I added.

"You shouldn't have accepted it," she scolded, shaking her head disapprovingly.

"Why not?" I was puzzled by her annoyance at the gift.

"Girls should not accept gifts of jewelry from men unless they are engaged to them," she declared as though it were the eleventh commandment.

"Oh, I didn't know that," I answered innocently, wondering if Adrian knew this rule. Her protective instincts were revealed in her remarks, though her real concern was not that I had been given a watch by my boyfriend but that my boyfriend was a Protestant, and worse, an English Protestant.

I noticed that Adrian was sometimes disrespectful towards his mother, which bothered me at first; but as I got to know her and witnessed her impatience and unkindness to the children, I accepted that his snapping at her was justified. So I made allowances for most of his errant behavior, understanding better now what is meant by the saying "Love is blind."

Before running Glebe House, Sybil had been one of the cleaning ladies there. She had no credentials other than her high school diploma. She had not studied child development or psychology, though she did have six of her own children and may have taken a few social-work classes in a day release program after assuming the role of officer in charge. Nevertheless, she was seriously unqualified to hold such an important position. But so was I, and perhaps too, the housefathers. But here she was in frequent meetings with Ms. Trask and Ms. Pulford and various other representatives from Social Services, winning them all over with her charm. Her charm soon lost its gloss for me after witnessing how she disciplined some of the children.

One little boy who came to us reminded me of the children in the stories of Romulus and Remus, Mowgli, and Little Tree— all raised away from society. His family lived roughly in the woods, foraging for food and without modern amenities. Once they were discovered by the authorities, they were deemed derelict; the children promptly removed from the distraught parents.

I was there the day he arrived, ready to welcome this frightened seven-year-old and shower him with love. "Hello, I'm Aunty Julie," I said gently. "What's your name?"

"Denny FUCKIN' Ruffin!" was his sharp reply.

"Oh!" I was shocked hearing such strong language delivered so confidently from such a little person, but recognized the fear he was trying to disguise. I chose to respond to the frightened boy, not the angry one. Denny and I soon bonded. His feistiness reminding me of my own brother Sean when he was small.

"Denny, please use the cutlery," I urged one dinnertime as he picked up the slice of gammon from his plate with his fingers.

"What's cullery?" he asked.

"Cut-lery, Denny. Your knife and fork. Use your knife and fork, like a good boy."

"Don't know how."

"Here, let me help you." I attempted to give him a lesson on how to hold the utensils, but he had only ever eaten with his fingers. Hunger won out that day. I would try again tomorrow.

Denny missed his parents and his brothers and sisters, often crying himself to sleep at night and also wetting his bed. I felt very sorry for him and did all I could to cheer him during the daytime, but I couldn't comfort him at night as I was in charge of the girls' wing, not the boys'.

His habitual bed-wetting became a source of annoyance and a challenge to Sybil, who was determined to put a stop to it, even though the dirty sheets went off to the laundry. I was appalled by the "lesson" she was about to teach him.

"Julie, tell the children and the staff to gather in the hallway, please," she directed.

"Okay." Instant obedience, no questioning, just do as you're told. I had taken to heart the respect for authority that my parents had instilled and set off immediately to fetch everyone. I had no idea why she wanted us all gathered; maybe we were having a special visitor or going on a day trip or getting a new resident. Curious, I ran the different possibilities through my mind as I rounded up the children and the cleaning ladies.

"Line up, either side of the hall," said Sybil once we were all assembled.

"Why? What's happening?" the children asked as they shuffled into position. They could always be counted on to ask the right questions.

"You'll see. Just wait."

She left us there squirming with anticipation, wondering what was coming next as she disappeared down the end of the boys' corridor. We waited like devoted subjects, eager for the queen to pass by.

Then I saw him. Running down the corridor towards us. Little Denny stark naked with Sybil following behind. "Go on! Go on! Keep moving!" she scolded, clapping her hands together as though she were chasing chickens. I tried to process what I was watching. My heart cried for him. The pain of humiliation etched on his innocent face.

"This is what you get for wetting the bed!" she continued, seeming to revel in the punishment. The children, now taking their cue from her, started to laugh and point at the helpless exposed child who had nowhere to hide.

"He's bleeding!" cried out one boy, shocked. "Look at his willie!"

"He's not bleeding," corrected Sybil. "It's tomato sauce." She wasn't trying to frighten the other children, just Denny.

Another round of nervous laughter as the children, relieved it wasn't blood but ketchup daubed on his penis, became a sneering mob.

I was a coward. My silence sickened me. Why was I not standing up for Denny in this moment? Why was I not calling my boss—my future mother-in-law—a bully? Why were all the women witnessing this horror with me not speaking out? Were we all waiting for someone else to step in and speak out for the victim? I profess to love God, and yet I can't even speak out for a defenseless child. Would I too have lined the route to Golgotha and watched silently as Jesus carried his cross to his crucifixion? I knew I was complicit in my silence.

"That's mean," said the courageous little voice of one small girl sadly.

"Yes, it's very mean," I whispered in her ear, putting my arm around her shoulder and drawing her close to me. Maybe that whisper could be a step towards exonerating me from my guilt.

For the next two years, Adrian and I grew closer. Probably, in part, because of the long enforced separations which included a three-month spell with the British Army in Belize. Our letters became the conduit for expressing our growing affection for each other. Somehow, in his absence, the idea of Adrian forged a new yearning within me. I fell in love with him through the letters we exchanged, where it was easier to write on paper what was too private or personal to say face-to-face. Each morning I kept vigil by the front door in anticipation of the postman's arrival. There was always mail, but not always for me. When the postman spotted me, he would either keep walking towards the door to deliver the post to Glebe House, or he would pause and sort through the letters in his hand and place any for me on the top of the pile. I used to pray silently for the postman's pause. It was no accident that "Please, Mr. Postman" by the Carpenters was the first record I ever bought for myself.

Adrian's letters were very distinct. In addition to putting my name and address on the front, he smothered the back of the envelope with romantic acronyms that became so familiar. Everyone knows the standard SWALK (sealed with a loving kiss). But there were so many more. Some reminiscent of time spent in Northern Ireland, like BELFAST (be ever loving faithful and stay true), ARDOYNE (another rotten day of your nonexistence), SOLDIER (should our love die, I'll ever remember). There were also other geographical and horticultural acronyms: HOLLAND (hope our love lasts and never dies), TULIP (to us, love is precious), ITALY (I trust and love you), and NORWICH (kNickers off ready when I come home). I requested that the last one, NORWICH, not be added to future letters as, besides being incorrect, it was also not going to happen. Adrian had disclosed that he slept with a girl when he was sixteen, and I appreciated his honesty, but I also made it clear to him that as a practicing Catholic, it was important that when I marry, it be in white, in a state of grace, and as a virgin.

I was devout and sincere in my faith and had been taught to expect others to misjudge or misunderstand me because of it. The one aspect of their faith that my parents had passed on to us was the conviction that Christ had died for all of us because of love. That God is Love, and since God is in us, we, as his agents, must be love too: without discrimination or prejudice, always willing to work towards understanding the other person's perspective. We should avoid committing any sin that would contribute to His suffering. The rod of retribution on hand to reinforce the lesson.

So I expected to be teased about being Catholic, and I was. Even Adrian's family, who were baptized Methodists, attributed any reluctance on my part to join in with certain activities or hesitation to laugh at dirty jokes as being prudish because of my upbringing when, in fact, I was simply trying to discern what the right course of action in that instance should be. I was figuring out how to navigate the river of moral dilemmas I was so often adrift on. I got tired of hearing, "Loosen up. Have some fun. Relax." I was happy and confident, loved life and people, and when accused of being "uptight," was actually tuning in to my conscience, or wrestling with it, as it alerted me to truth.

I should have listened more intently to that inner voice.

Eventually, the frequent heartwarming letters, brimful of loving declarations, and read over and over till they could almost be recited from memory, were put aside. Adrian was home from his interminable three months in Belize. I was smitten, and so, it seems, was he.

To celebrate his return, we accompanied his parents to a dance at Lister's club. Everyone was in a jolly mood setting out and only got jollier as the night wore on, the mood intensifying in tandem with the rising degree of intoxication. Not yet eighteen, I was too young to drink alcohol, but as it was a special occasion, Adrian's mother said it wouldn't hurt me to have one or two.

"Have some fun. Relax!" she suggested. I wasn't used to drinking. I may have had a sip of something bubbly as a toast on St. Patrick's Day, but that was it.

"Oh, all right then, as it's a special occasion," I agreed. "But I don't know what to have," I added.

"Have a pint of Guinness," teased Den. But his joke was lost on me as an embarrassing memory from a few months earlier flashed into my mind.

I had been asked to be godmother to my cousin David by my aunty Theresa and uncle Terry. What an honor. It meant a visit by train to their home in the north of England, followed by a reception to "wet the baby's head." While in a pub after the baptism, Aunty Theresa turned from the bar and called over to the table, "What do you want to drink?" I was going to ask for a Britvic orange, which was my usual response to that question, no matter who asked it. But this time, considering the weighty role I had assumed as David's spiritual guide, I felt grown up enough to have a "proper" drink. I recall my sophisticated and elegant friend Karen, younger than me, but who looked much older, partly due to her long legs and womanly curves, telling me she drank Port and lemon. In that moment, I wanted to be as sophisticated as Karen, so I called back, "I'll have a Port and lemon, Aunty Theresa." There was a noticeable hush in the room as my aunt dashed over to admonish me. "Only whores in Hull drink Port and lemon!" she whispered loudly.

"Oh! Sorry. I didn't know." I was dismayed that I had embarrassed her. "I'll have a Britvic orange, please," I said apologetically, resigned to never ask for alcohol again.

"Well, what's it to be?" Sybil asked.

"Anything. Just *not* a Port and lemon," I answered.

Well, it seems that I can get drunk on anything, and a small amount of anything at that.

The next morning, I remembered everything. I remembered Sybil putting me to bed. I remembered her holding her well-manicured hand against my cheek because her hand was cold and my head was hot. I remembered crying that the ceiling was spinning and making me feel sick. I remembered Adrian, also drunk, dancing with me to the Carpenters' "Top of the World" and asking me to marry him, and I remembered saying yes.

As I brushed my teeth, staring blankly into my bathroom mirror, a part of me hoped that Adrian had forgotten about asking me to be his wife. I planned on avoiding the topic until he broached it. I sat dejectedly on the side of my bed, delaying going into the flat as I felt so ashamed of my behavior, imagining how mortified my parents would be if they knew what state I had been in the night before. But when I eventually emerged, it was to smiles, back slaps, and "How are you feeling?" I felt like I had been through an initiation and survived and should be proud. "It's always best to get drunk with family or friends the first time," consoled Den.

"First time? Oh, I'm *never* doing that again," I pledged. I was relieved that there had been no finger-pointing or lectures about responsible behavior. But they didn't need to do that as I was already berating myself and examining my conscience in preparation for my next confession, relieved that my mother no longer had access to my sin diary.

Later, snuggled on the couch, Adrian and I discussed the previous night. "Do you remember what I asked you and what you said to me?" he asked as he tucked a strand of my hair behind my ear.

"Yes, I remember."

"Did you mean it?" he asked nervously.

"Yes, I meant it. I don't say things I don't mean, Adrian." I was trying to sound more convincing than I felt. I was disappointed that his proposal had been so unromantic. Had I been sober when he asked me, I would have refused to answer until he asked me properly, and the answer would still have been yes. As it was, I could hardly be annoyed with him for being drunk; how hypocritical would that have been?

"We can't tell my parents until I'm eighteen, though," I insisted.

"Absolutely. I wasn't planning on asking your dad before then anyway."

I kissed him. I was grateful that he would follow convention when speaking with my parents. I wanted them to approve. I could forgive a few lapses, but they were more demanding, expecting only the most worthy spouses for their children.

There was no engagement party. In fact, for many months, there was no ring. I didn't mind waiting, though, until after we had shared the news with my parents. That way, it felt more honest.

A few months later, we arrived at my home to share the good news with my family. Adrian was understandably anxious as my father could be an intimidating figure. But we were ready. We had figured that the best time for Adrian to speak to Dad would be right after watching his favorite American TV cop *Kojak*.

"Whatever you do, don't interrupt when *Kojak* is on," I urged. He nodded.

Mam and I went into the kitchen to make tea once Dad's program had ended. I glanced encouragingly at Adrian as I left the room. Mam had an inkling about what was happening. She had admitted to reading my diary and had also noticed our nervousness during the evening.

"Um, excuse me, Mr. Manning. Can I talk to you a minute?"

"Hmmph, what is it?"

"Well, as you know, Julie and me have been going out for about a year."

"Have you now?" Dad wasn't making this easy.

"Yes, and we love each other," Adrian continued.

"Do you even know the meaning of the word?" Dad asked, unconvinced.

"I think so. We are… I mean, I am hoping that you will allow me to ask for your daughter's hand in marriage," he stammered.

It was done. The request had been made, but the dreaded encounter was far from over. Adrian had followed the rules and now awaited my dad's response.

Dad would have expected to be asked for his blessing as a courtesy and conventional formality and, regardless of his thoughts on our readiness for such a commitment, would not have objected to the marriage out of respect for our right to make our own decisions as adults. He was keen to caution us though.

He may have been reminded of his own courting days with my mother while he was serving in the British Army. Their short four-month courtship, which they originally thought would be a "fleeting acquaintance," turned into a lifelong partnership. They too had forged their love through letters from places like Korea, Japan, and the Suez. So the rather gruff exterior presented to Adrian in this encounter may have concealed a more sympathetic attitude such as the romantic one revealed in all his love letters to my mother.

When Mam and I returned to the living room with a tray of tea and plain biscuits, Dad had some questions for us. Well, mostly for Adrian. So in his familiar Dickensian manner, he began the litany. "So how do you intend to provide for my daughter?"

"Do you understand that you will be bringing up your children as Catholic?"

"Why the rush?"

"Don't you think you're a bit young for such responsibility?"

"Where will you live?"

"When are you planning to marry?"

"Do you intend to stay in the army?" And so the interrogation continued until all questions had been exhausted and answers provided. The questions were over, for now at least. All my father had left to say was, "We will be praying for you."

October 25, 1975
"Popping the Question" by Julie Manning

You worried and wondered, what will I say?
I'm hoping to marry their daughter one day.
Would they object? Would they agree?
Only one way to find out, just ask them and see!
The moment soon came, the time was just right.

I must ask now while Julie's out of sight.
Feeling quite nervous and very afraid,
You popped the question while tea was being made.
I came back into the room with the tea tray,
Thinking, "Have they been talking? What did Ade say?"
I soon knew the answer and what had been said,
You had remarked that we wanted to wed.
I thought they'd be angry and perhaps even mad,
But to my surprise, they were almost glad.
The asking's now over, it wasn't in vain,
You'll be thankful that you won't have to ask again.
I'm so very happy that they did agree,
As dear Darling Adrian, you mean everything to me.
Now we must be thankful to God up above,
For letting us share in his great gift of love.
Adrian, my Darling, you know I love you.
I can't wait for the time when we both say, "I Do"
I've no more to mention, but this I will say,
It will not be long now till our Wedding Day.

It was now official. Both sets of parents had been told of our intentions, and it was time to buy a ring.

"All right me, 'andsome?" Adrian's now familiar greeting, delivered in an appealing Cornish accent, always elicited a smile in return.

"We need to go shopping!" he announced triumphantly.

"Ooh, when?"

"In a couple of weeks—next time I'm home. I need to save up to buy you the ring you deserve."

"Aww, thank you, sweetheart. I'm so excited."

"I'll have about one hundred pounds to spend on it. You're worth it!" He drew me close and kissed me gently on the lips. I sighed contentedly. *Life is good*, I thought to myself. *Life is good.*

Every female in Glebe House—Sybil, the cleaning ladies, the cook, Adrian's two younger sisters, and the girls who called it home—shared in the buildup of excitement. I became suddenly curious about jewelry, flipping through catalogues, asking to inspect the rings on the fingers of all married women I knew, and inviting opinions on what type of ring might suit me.

"How about a sapphire? It's your birthstone," suggested Sybil. "Wouldn't that be lovely?"

"Hmm. My mam has a sapphire and diamond ring. I don't want to copy her."

"That's fair enough. What about an emerald? You're Irish—forty shades of green and all that," she offered enthusiastically.

"Yeah, I like that idea. I was thinking an emerald in the middle and diamonds on each side."

"Sounds beautiful. Oh, I'm so excited for you both," his mother declared proudly. "Whatever Adrian gets you will be perfect."

"Oh, I know. Any ring will be perfect," I said, looking down at my left hand and visualizing the twinkling emerald that would soon adorn it.

The couple of weeks turned into a month, but the shopping day finally arrived. Mandy, one of the teenagers in the home who was keen on fashion, offered to be my "stylist" for the day.

"You should let me do your hair, Aunty Julie."

"Oh, thanks, Mandy. That'll be lovely."

"Can I watch? Can I watch? Me too!" called out a chorus of younger girls.

"Of course you can," I said cheerfully. I had been in a happily distracted state since the visit to my parents, Adrian's letters and regular phone calls sustaining me in his absence.

"You can watch so long as you keep your mouths shut," warned Mandy.

"They'll be good. Won't you, girls?" They nodded to me mischievously. "Thanks, Mandy, you're so kind for doing this."

"It's fun! Besides, it's good practice for when I'm a hairdresser."

"You'll make a great hairdresser someday," I affirmed.

"Yes! And you can be one of my clients. And your friends too."

And so the seemingly insignificant conversation went on as Mandy fussed with my hair and chatted casually about her dreams for her future. It was ordinary moments such as these that helped build trust and forge bonds so absent in these children's lives.

"I think your hair looks better down," mused Mandy after tugging, pulling, and braiding for almost an hour, then brushing it all out to its original state. The style session was over.

"I agree, but I'm glad you showed me how different I can look. It gives me ideas for my wedding day," I said.

"Do you want to borrow my shoes?" she offered as she kicked off her three-inch platform sandals and handed them to me.

"I'm not sure I should wear these, Mandy. My eyesight's bad, and I'm so clumsy."

"They suit you!" She beamed as I finished buckling the strap.

"Hmm, I'm not sure," I repeated. I was concerned more about keeping my balance than being in vogue. So I did a test run down the stairs and along the carpeted hallway, managing to stay upright. In my mind, I was more elegant, somehow, now that I was three inches taller, though my tentative steps contradicted that notion.

"They look really good on you."

"Thanks, Mandy. I'll wear them."

I caught the bus from Dursley and greeted Adrian off the train in Gloucester. He looked tired.

"Hello, sweetheart. I'm so happy to see you."

"Hello, me 'andsome," he replied as he gave me an affectionate squeeze. Then glancing at my feet, he asked incredulously, "What on earth are you wearing?"

"Mandy lent me her shoes," I explained.

"You better be careful in those," he cautioned. "You'll break your bloody neck!"

"I'll be fine. I'll lean on you if I need to. I'll be fine."

"Well, don't expect me to scrape you off the pavement when you come a cropper," he teased. "Why d'ya want to be taller than me anyway?" I hadn't given that a thought when setting out; but at five feet five and a quarter inches (as was stated on his passport), Adrian, called Shorty by his army pals, felt self-conscious about his height.

"Well, now you have to look up to me."

He just shook his head dismissively as I linked arms with him and headed towards the exit.

"I'm gagging for a cup a tea," he announced.

44

In my eagerness, I hadn't given a thought to his needs. I didn't know that the mention of tea was a delaying tactic.

"Let's have one here in the station before we go shopping…for the…engagement riiiiing!" I sang out the last two words in a mock operatic voice.

He made no remark as he lit a cigarette.

After drinking our tea, we set out to gaze in the windows of jewelers. I didn't want to be greedy so decided to look at rings that were sixty pounds or less. I was discovering quickly that our tastes were vastly different.

"Oh, look, Adrian, the one with the emerald in the middle."

"Nah, don't like it," he said, hardly looking at it.

"Really? Why not?"

"Too showy." He seemed subdued.

"Oh, I like it," I persisted, hoping that my excitement would liven him up. "It reminds me of Ireland."

"Let's keep looking—there's loads of shops," he argued as he guided me away from the glass. Some version of this conversation was repeated shop after shop, ring after ring, until my feet went on strike.

"Adrian, my feet are killing me. We've looked in about seven shops already, and you don't like any of the rings I like." I groaned.

"I know, I know!" He was trying to be patient with me, but the agitation in his voice betrayed him. "Look, Julie, the truth is…," he confessed, "I don't have a hundred pounds to spend on a ring."

"Oh!" It took me a moment to process what he had told me. I was silent.

"I'm sorry, love." His tone shifted to apologetic. "I should have told you. I wanted this to be such a special day. Please forgive me. I'll make it up to you somehow, I promise."

"It's okay, Adrian. I'm only looking at rings under sixty anyway." I tried to appear nonchalant.

"Well, the thing is, I don't have sixty pounds either," he said, mumbling into his shirt, obviously embarrassed.

"How much do you have?" A knot was forming in my chest as my heart rate quickened.

"Thirty quid," he mumbled.

"Thirty? What happened to the money you were saving?" I needed to understand.

"Look, I'm sorry, all right? My mate had a leaving do last night, and we all had to chip in to buy him a barrel."

I looked at him, bemused.

"It's the tradition when someone is getting out of the army to buy a barrel of beer," he explained. I was thinking that a barrel must be awfully expensive or that Adrian was exceptionally generous. I chose to believe the latter. He didn't have a credit card or a bank account and had opted to be paid in cash. That cash, as I was learning, never stayed in his wallet long.

"Don't worry. It's okay. I just wish you had told me sooner 'cause my feet hurt." I feigned cheerfulness to hide my disappointment for his sake.

"I told you those shoes were a stupid idea," he scolded, changing the subject.

"I know. You were right. Come on, let's find a ring you can afford," I coaxed.

"Well, if you lend me the money, sweetheart...," he began, "we'll go back and get the green one in that first shop, and I'll repay you. Honest." He was softer now, less agitated, as he had assuaged his guilt with his confession.

"No. No. I'd rather you bought one with your own money. It's not about the green ring, Adrian. Besides, I can't lend you any money as I've just about enough for bus fare back," I explained.

So we found an engagement ring for thirty pounds that didn't have an emerald. I was happier now. "It's beautiful, Adrian. Thank you," I said as I admired the delicate square of platinum resting on the gold band, four tiny specs of glinting diamonds, one in each corner, saluting the ruby in the center.

"I love you, Julie." His voice was tender as he slid the ring on my finger and kissed me. "Now everyone will know you are taken."

I held my hand at arm's length, looking at my engagement ring admiringly, tilting it from side to side to catch a splinter of sun dancing on its surface. *I'm a fiancée*, I thought to myself. *Soon I'll be a bride.*

"I love you too, Adrian." I sighed. "My heart is full."

"Well, my pockets are empty. I'm skint now. Can you lend me the bus fare home?"

Adrian was a most attentive fiancé. He phoned regularly, clogged the mailbox with love letters, and often appeared unannounced, just to surprise me. We had limited opportunities to spend time alone as we were either at my parents' house where cuddling on the couch was frowned upon, or at his parents' flat, where there was always someone hovering. So we took long, secluded walks where we had deep discussions about our expectations of marriage and our beliefs and stole kisses on Stinchcombe Hill while lying on a grassy slope or leaning against an old tree.

"Thank you for coming to Mass with me and for agreeing to bring the children up Catholic, Adrian. It's so important," I said as I focused on threading daisies into a chain while on one such outing.

"Of course, love. Wouldn't have it any other way," he assured me as he drew on his cigarette and blew smoke rings into the air. I was grateful that the person I fell in love with was so amenable. I was also impressed with his willingness to entrust the responsibility of the spiritual well-being of our future children to me.

"In fact, I was thinking of becoming a Catholic myself," he went on, sitting up and handing me a freshly plucked daisy.

"Why?" I asked.

"To make you happy. I thought you'd be pleased?" He couldn't fathom why I questioned him.

"Oh, Adrian, it would please me, of course, but—"

"But what?" he interrupted.

"Well, that's not reason enough to convert."

"What do you mean?"

"Well, you've got to have the conviction that this is right for you—not for me," I explained.

I was flattered that he thought so much of me that he wanted to share my faith but knew too that we all have our own spiritual path to travel in our own time and in our own way.

"If you feel that God is calling you to become a Catholic down the road, then I'll be your biggest supporter. But to do it now, just to please me, is not a good enough reason."

"Fair enough," he said, taking a drag on the cigarette before exhaling not only smoke but maybe even a tinge of relief.

We planned on getting married soon after my nineteenth birthday, but the date was brought forward a few months when the threat of a military posting to Hong Kong interfered. The truth was irrelevant to the gossips and curtain twitchers who wagged their tongues in sordid speculation. But they didn't know that I had taken to heart the warnings from my mother about occasions of sin, which, by her definition, included the entire engagement period. "It's the good girls that get caught, Julie," she cautioned. "The bad girls know how to avoid getting into trouble." Her voice lowering in case any younger siblings were within earshot. "The good girls get swept up in the passion of the moment, and then it's too late." She was trying to fulfil some parental obligation by discussing the delicate topic.

"I know, Mam, we're waiting till we're married," I reassured her, willing the conversation to be over.

"Well, don't become too familiar with him. You should always keep the mystery alive. Do you hear me?"

"Mam, we'll be married in a few months." I so wanted her to drop the subject.

"Your father has never seen me without my teeth. It's so important to keep the mystery alive." I smiled at the image she presented. *Maybe, she'll go off on a tangent*, I thought.

"Don't worry, Mam. We're being good," I assured her.

She wasn't convinced. "Well, men have urges, you know…," she went on.

"Mam! Please. I know," I interrupted, wanting the lesson to end, but she was deaf to my protests.

"And women too. Sexual urges that are hard to control. You mustn't put yourself in a vulnerable position by being alone with him. Do you understand what I'm saying?" She looked straight at me, waiting for an answer.

"Please, Mam, stop. I do get it," I pleaded, but it was no use begging. My mother always had the last word.

Adrian and I had both been managing our "urges," and I was uncomfortable discussing it with her. He respected my wish to be a virgin on our wedding day, though made it clear that it was becoming a mammoth feat of self-control.

"Well, just make sure you're not putting yourself into an occasion of sin." She was having the last word.

I was asked by Social Services to spend a week in Barnwood Road so that Penny Sweet could take a holiday. I was happy to oblige. It was a treat to see the children again and assume full responsibility for them even for such a short spell. They were so well behaved and, as there were only six of them, easy to manage. I stepped into the roles of caregiver, cook, cleaner, and gardener with gusto. If my success was judged solely on my enthusiasm and love, I'd have earned a trophy. My attempts at cooking, however, ensured that a trophy was as elusive as butterflies in the arctic.

Penny was an avid gardener and had an impressive vegetable plot, from where much of the produce ended up on the dinner table. I felt like a pioneering earth mother, taking the offerings of the land to feed my hungry brood as I strolled up and down the rows of potatoes, lettuces, radishes, and spring onions before snipping a few sweet pea from the trellis to adorn the windowsill and side table with their delicate paper-thin flowers and exquisite fragrance. Then I filled a bowl with peas picked from the fence and headed in to make dinner.

I imagined women in times past bonding over food preparation, chatting merrily as they peeled potatoes or laughing heartily at some story a wife shared about her husband's amorous efforts as they shucked corn. I surrounded myself with these phantom ladies as I settled down to work. I had heard the expression "as easy as shelling peas," but as I used my thumbnails to pry open the pods, I began to wonder if I had misunderstood that expression. After a while, I stared into the saucepan where I had been depositing the peas and felt defeated. "How is this going to feed all of us?" I must have said that out loud as one of the children came over to look in the pot too.

"We've never eaten green beans like this before!"

"Green beans? Aren't these peas?"

"No." The child chuckled. "They're green beans, silly!"

"They look like peas," I stated, but I was talking to the air as the child had already left the kitchen. There was no recrimination, no tut-tutting or disapproving looks, just a seven-year-old calling me silly.

Once the children were fed, which sometimes took longer than it should with me in charge, the nighttime rituals were completed cheerfully and predictably. Bath, books, prayers, and bed by eight o'clock. Then I plopped into an armchair to watch television after saying my own quiet prayer of thanks, that in spite of my incompetence in the kitchen, all my little chicks were safe.

One evening, after they were all tucked in, I heard a knock at the front door. There on the doorstep, wearing his uniform and a broad cheeky grin, was Adrian.

"What are you doing here?" I whispered anxiously.

"Well, that's a nice way to greet your future husband, I must say," he replied, stepping into the hall. "Don't I even get a kiss?"

"Shhhh! Adrian, you can't be here." I gave him a peck on the lips to hush him. "I don't have permission to have company."

"I won't stay long, I promise. I'm going to Glebe House after. I've missed you and just hitchhiked all the way from Colchester to see you," his voice mimicking a whiny child. "I thought you'd be pleased."

"Of course, I'm glad to see you, but I wish you had told me so I could ask Penny if it was okay."

"Oh, for God's sake, Julie! She's not going to mind if you make me a cup of tea!"

"I know, I know. I'm sorry. I'll go put the kettle on. But you can't smoke in the house."

He followed me through to the kitchen and out onto the back step to smoke his cigarette while I made the tea. The thought of him hitchhiking all that way just to surprise me warmed my heart and made me feel guilty about how I had greeted him. I joined him on the step, leaning in close for warmth, linking my arm through his before cradling the hot mug of tea in my hands. "Ooh, it's chilly out here. Let's go in the warm. But be quiet, please." He turned and kissed my cheek as I realized we were alone for the first time. Now *this* was an occasion of sin.

The television was on, but we were not watching it. Thoughts of the sleeping children upstairs retreated to the back of my mind as we sank into the couch. This was not my mother's couch. This was not his parents' couch. For now, it was *our* couch. It did not take long for us to go from sitting next to each other sipping tea, Adrian's arm draped casually over my shoulder, to lying down together and fumbling nervously with buttons and zips.

"Adrian! Stop, stop!" I pleaded, grabbing his wrist as his hands glided up between my thighs. We had never gone this far before. He exhaled loudly as he drew his hand away and dropped his head onto my shoulder, grunting in frustration. "Julie, you're killing me. I can't wait much longer."

I wanted to apologize. I hadn't anticipated things moving so fast. "I'm sorry, sweetheart. It won't be long now." I felt like one of those girls who earn bad names for themselves because they lead boys on. I felt responsible for his suffering and wished I was back on my mother's couch. I was keen to join the ranks of other married Catholics who could engage in an abundance of guilt-free sex.

My parents offered to pay for the wedding reception, and Adrian and I agreed to share responsibility for the rest of the expenses. My mother assumed the role of wedding planner, and I was content to hand it all over to her. She was in her element. Each time I visited, I gave her an envelope with cash for the photographer, the DJ, the cars, the flowers, the church, etc. so that she could pay all the bills as they arose. Adrian contributed too, but as I had fewer living expenses, I absorbed most of the burden.

The wedding date coincided with my grandparents' golden wedding anniversary, so that influenced all choices from dresses to decor and, most importantly, the guest list. I had certainly surrendered control to my mother.

"This will be an international affair," my mother said triumphantly. "There'll be people from America, Ireland, South Africa, Wales, and maybe even New Zealand if Uncle PJ comes. You can invite five friends each," she went on. "We're already at over a hundred with just family."

"Only five? I was hoping to invite some of the children from Glebe House."

"They can come to the do in the prison club in the evening. I don't care how many come to that," she added. I was relieved. I was beginning to see that this wedding was a great excuse for my mother to organize a gathering of the McGrath clan. I was happy to share our celebration.

The day was glorious with sunshine outside and within. Adrian had shown great generosity in inviting my dear friend Miles, with whom I had shared many work shifts at Glebe House, to be the best man. Adrian had two brothers whom he could have asked, so this departure from tradition to honor my request filled me with joy. My mother's impeccable attention to detail was evident in every aspect of the occasion. St. Augustine's Church in Downend, Bristol, was decked out in exquisite white and yellow roses that coordinated with my bouquet. My dress reflected the Spanish influence in the west of Ireland with its lace mantilla instead of a veil, my five bridesmaids glowed in peach, and I wore silver shoes that were flat so that Adrian could be taller than I am.

When Father Daly asked us to "repeat after me," I knew that in minutes I would become Adrian's wife. In our premarriage conversations with the priest, I had requested that the word *obey* be dropped from the vows and replaced with *respect*. I had been a child who obeyed. I obeyed my parents. I obeyed the nuns. I obeyed my church. Now, as a married woman, I was asserting my independence, which seems somewhat contradictory, but it was important that I made it clear that obeying was a thing of my childhood. So facing Adrian and looking into his eyes, I pledged with absolute sincerity, "I, Julie Manning, do solemnly swear to love, honor, and respect you, in sickness and in health, for richer, for poorer, for better, for worse, till death do us part."

Chapter 4

For better or for worse.

Married life as an Army wife brought a new set of challenges, so I was grateful that there were plenty of young women close in age to befriend. We all bonded in the same way people bond in a crisis. We created support groups and wives' clubs to fill the emptiness when our men were away on a military exercise or on a posting, which seemed far too frequent. Older wives gave unsolicited advice about how to behave when the men were gone to preserve our marriages and our reputations. "You need to switch washing powder if you use OMO," warned one woman. "If you leave OMO on your window ledge in full view, you're asking for trouble." Apparently, a box of OMO laundry detergent sent a message to the single soldiers that the lady of the house needed company and fun. OMO stood for "old man out" or "on my own." I listened to her advice and used Persil, hoping that I wasn't inadvertently advertising anything more than "clean clothes worn here."

Adrian had transferred to the Royal Corps of Transport to avoid a posting to Hong Kong, his new squadron often called on to escort regiments abroad. He earned an HGV license to drive the heaviest trucks on the road, so his services were often in demand. Unless the squadron was going to be away for more than a year, the families could not accompany the soldier, which left a lot of women lonely. I was one of them. In our first four years of marriage, we were together only twelve months.

The separations were heartbreaking, but the reunions were sublime. It was as though we were given repeated false starts. Just as we were falling into a routine, Adrian would be called on to accompany another regiment to a new posting in Germany or Denmark or Cyprus. Each separation was harder to bear than the one that preceded it, and each reunion was more passionate. It eventually became an exhausting cycle of recurring honeymoon with little time to move to the next stage of the relationship.

We settled into our army quarters in Colchester, which looked exactly like all the other homes right down to the cups we used. The carpets, curtains, furnishings, appliances, linens, and housewares, were all army-issue: functional but with dubious aesthetic appeal. We had been through "march in," where a military housing representative walked through the house with us to create an inventory and note any damage so that we would not be liable on "march out," an excruciating, nail-biting, brow-furrowing experience where it seems a deeper scrutiny is given to the inspection and from which few families escape without a fine.

Wives competed to be the most creative homemaker by displaying quirky knickknacks brought back from exotic places: a wall hanging from South America, an exquisite Asian doll in national costume from Japan, a sombrero from Mexico, a tribal mask from Africa, and so on. The longer married, the more ostentatious the displays. To anyone entering our home, it was clear from the imposed minimalist style that I was a newlywed.

At first, Adrian enjoyed married life. He walked to work each morning with a smile on his face and came home again at lunchtime with an appetite, though he had little interest in food. He seemed proud of me too. His truck would often stop outside the house, and out of the back would tumble six or seven "squaddies" all on tea break. I had inherited my mother's flair for hospitality and enjoyed seeing the truck pull up. I loved the banter and playing "mother" to many of the single lads. What I found disturbing and offensive was the manner in which Adrian spoke while in their company. He used much more vulgarity than when we were dating and didn't care whether I heard the dirty jokes or not. It was as though I had faded into the wallpaper, and at times, I wished I could. Some of the lads were embarrassed for me, so I would invent something that needed my immediate attention in another room to avoid the discomfort of sitting among them while the misogynistic comments assaulted my ears and my sensibilities. Later in bed, I brought up my concerns.

"Adrian, I need to talk to you."

"Uh-oh, sounds like trouble. What about?"

"Well, I'm hurt by the way you talked to me today in front of the lads."

"What did I say?" he asked defensively.

"Well, when you said, 'Here she is, Doris the Docker,' I wanted to see the funny side, but I think it's mean to call me that."

"Oh, for Christ's sake, Julie! Get a sense of humor, will you?" his impatience growing.

"I have a sense of humor. I'm just telling you, I'd rather you didn't call me names."

"You're too sensitive. That's your problem. There's a lot worse I could call you."

"I don't think I'm too sensitive. It's just unkind." I was being as assertive as I knew how.

"This is the army. You better toughen up and get used to it."

"I don't want to get used to bad language and sexist comments. That may be how you speak when you are in the barracks, but it's rude to speak like that in front of women."

"What women? You were the only one there!"

"I know, but that counts! My dad was in the army too, and I've never heard him swear or speak to my mother disrespectfully, so I don't think I should have to 'get used to it.'"

"You're such a prude, Julie. Your Catholic upbringing was too sheltered. You need to experience real life more and grow a pair."

"Well, when you told me in front of your friends that I should close my legs because my breath was smelling, I was mortified. It was really embarrassing for me."

"The lads thought it was funny." He snickered.

"Well, it's not funny, and I'm really hurt by it." My argument was weakening as my voice cracked, and I grew closer to tears. I was upset that he wasn't listening. He was focused on defending his behavior rather than being open to what I had to say.

"Oh, don't start blubbing. I'm going to sleep. Some of us work, you know." As he rolled over on his side, with his back to me, I turned towards the wall and cried silently, swallowing the sobs before they could escape and willing every muscle in my body to be still as the tears rolled over my nose and on to the pillow. Over time, I perfected that cry. Not because I see crying as a sign of weakness—I don't—but because I was afraid of making Adrian angry.

In the morning, Adrian wanted to make up. "Come here," he said as he stroked my shoulder until I turned to face him. "I hate fighting," he added quietly as I nestled into his chest.

"I hate it too." I sighed.

"Well, then don't start fights with me, love." His voice was sweetly patronizing. It was clear that he believed the blame was all mine.

"Can you see my point though, Adrian?" I needed reassurance that I had been heard.

"Yes, I see," he conceded. Or so I thought. "You've had a very strict upbringing, so you don't understand the funny side of stuff. It's not your fault—I blame your parents. I'm not mad at you anymore."

"Well, can you please introduce me as Julie, or your wife, or your sweetheart, but just not Doris the Docker?" I pushed back.

"Can you say you're sorry for starting an argument?" he countered.

"I am sorry that we argued." I was playing with semantics. I was sorry we had argued, but I did not feel sorry for bringing up the subject. My answer satisfied him.

We hugged before he left for work, and he was back at lunch-time to satiate his appetite.

At first, I looked forward to Adrian coming home from work. I wanted our marriage to be a great one and did all I knew at the time to keep him happy. My mother had given me some advice, which stayed with me in those early years:, "You are responsible for your husband's happiness. If he's not happy, you must look to your own behavior."

Within a few weeks of marriage, I was at the doctor's office, at Adrian's urging, to find a remedy for painful intercourse. I was embarrassed discussing such a personal topic with anyone, but very relieved to see that my new doctor was female and very gentle. After examining me and finding no medical issue, she asked, "How often are you intimate? How many times a week do you have sex?"

"A week? Well, when my husband is here, about twenty. He comes home at lunchtime too," I explained. I had no idea as to what was considered average or normal. All I knew was that sex was immediate, rushed, and uncomfortable, most of the time. For me, sex was at its best when it was the culminating act of love after a day of warmth and connectedness. I could not disassociate it from love, and although I wanted to please my husband, if I had not received tenderness during the day, I couldn't simply switch on the romance at will.

"Well, you're a newlywed," said the doctor, as though that was part of the problem. "So things should settle down soon. In the meantime, I'll write you a prescription for Librium to be taken an hour before intercourse to relax you. Okay?"

"Okay, thank you for your help," I said, taking the prescription from her hand and heading off to fill it at the chemist's, looking forward to a more satisfying and pleasurable intimacy with Adrian.

Three Librium a day was not good for me, making me drowsy and lethargic. It didn't improve our love life either. But I took the month's course of pills anyway, not returning for a refill.

I was determined to make Adrian the happiest husband in England. By his definition, a good wife is one who is perpetually cheerful, always at home when he calls, daily cleans the house, washes the clothes, cooks tasty meals, buys the groceries, irons ruler-straight creases into his uniform, polishes a brilliant shine on his boots, makes copious cups of tea on demand, laughs at his jokes, knows how to cook an egg properly, and *always* says yes to sex.

I found out very quickly that making Adrian happy was exhausting and thankless work. I persevered. If he complained about the gammon, chips, and mushy peas that I served for dinner, then I switched to spaghetti bolognese. If he asked for a cup of tea, I no longer replied, "Let me just finish this, and I'll make you one." I stopped whatever I was doing and put on the kettle immediately. If he didn't like to see evidence of my industry in the laundry pile yet to be sorted, I made sure laundry was done while he was at work. If he came home unexpectedly to find I was out, I made all future appointments for early in the morning to coincide with his arrival at work. Whenever he wanted to have sex, I obliged, though I did pray, "Dear Lord, this can't be how sex is meant to be. Please let me experience the true joy of sex before I die."

Yet in spite of all my efforts, I could not make him happy. Now, of course, I know that we are responsible for our own happiness, that no one can be all for another; but as a young and eager wife, I was committed to providing Adrian with a good homelife, foolishly thinking that my efforts would be enough.

Soon after arriving in Colchester, I realized that marriage, though it had changed everything in my life, had not interfered with Adrian's social routine and lifestyle at all. He had many single pals with whom he spent his Friday and Saturday nights drinking on the *Strip*, as it was called, where squaddies could be found spilling in and out of pubs, sometimes with girls in various stages of inebriation and undress, on their arms. He still frequented the same pubs and hung out with the same women that he had met in the couple of years before marrying me. Pubs such as the Hole in the Wall, the Robin Hood, the Angel, the Beehive, the Swan, the White Horse, the Grapes, and more lined the streets from Goojerat Barracks into town and back, doors open, sirens' songs inviting, waiting to scoop up the paychecks of the single squaddies and the husbands.

I felt very lonely on these nights, sitting at home with the TV for company and wondering what state Adrian would be in when he got home. Sometimes he was maudlin, presenting me with a rose stolen from a neighbor's garden as he swore his undying love for me. At other times, he was merry and home before the pubs shut. Those nights, I was relieved and showed my gratitude. But there were other nights when the drink got the better of him, and he came home bleeding after a brawl with a soldier in the Queen's regiment, or after splitting his knuckles open after shattering the wing mirror of a parked car when he mistook his own reflection for an adversary scowling back, or when he was just plain drunk, broke and without a cigarette. Those were the nights I dreaded. I had two choices: I could pretend to be asleep when I heard the key in the lock and avoid further argument, or I could wait up and offer him coffee in the hopes of pacifying him. Neither way succeeded. Scenario one would go something like this:

"Oh, so you can't even stay up and wait for your old man, huh? Some wife you are!" he declared belligerently.

"Oh, sorry, love. I was just so tired." It was a feeble response.

"Too tired to wait for your husband to get home. Thanks a lot for nothin'!"

"Sorry, Adrian, I didn't know when you'd be back." I hoped that he would stumble off to the bathroom before collapsing into bed. Sometimes he mistook the closet for the bathroom, ensuring I would be busy scrubbing floorboards and rewashing laundry the next day.

Scenario two—waiting up—went like this:

"Oh, waiting to catch me out, are you? Think you can wait up and have a go at me, is that it?"

"No, Adrian, I was waiting to see if you wanted a cup of tea or coffee."

"Oh, 'cause you think I'm drunk and need sobering up, is that it?"

"No, love. I wanted to make sure you're okay."

"You're not my mother, ya know. You don't need to keep your beady eyes on me."

"I know that, I just—"

"Ah, piss off, why don't you? Just piss off!"

These seemingly weak responses on my part were an act of survival in that moment. I knew from experience that challenging him when he was drunk was disastrous. By the next morning, he would claim to have no memory of the previous night's events. Then as I recounted our conversations, he showered me with fervent apologies and convincing promises that it would never happen again. For a long time, I believed him and forgave.

I was more an idealist than a realist in those early years together. My optimism and faith in the intrinsic value of each one of us propelled me forward in my quest to help Adrian see that he was loved. I was not an idiot, though some might judge me so. I did not passively accept mistreatment and disrespect, and I certainly did not enjoy it. I had a deep faith and held out immeasurable hope that one day we would both revel in each other entirely and free from fear. The words of 1 Corinthians 13, read at our wedding Mass, were always close in thought: Love is patient, love is kind…love keeps no record of wrongs…love perseveres." So with these inspirational words giving me strength, I treated every apology that Adrian made as sincere and eagerly began rebuilding our marriage. I willed it to work.

Our life together was like a threatening storm hovering menacingly overhead, with intermittent glimpses of radiant sunshine fostering delight in the prospect of what could be. I clung to the promise of the sunshine and regularly reminded myself of my vows. I assumed the task of providing shelter from the storm for both of us, being ever vigilant. I paid close attention to Adrian's moods, doing all that I could to reduce his stress and eliminate any triggers that might arouse his rage. It was a dance of hope and survival. In the beginning, we were content, looking forward to a long life together. Sometimes it seemed like the sun would shine for days. But as swiftly as the delicate feathers of my dreams drifted upward towards the light, they were annihilated by the oil slick of dark reality.

The first incident that was part of my awakening happened just three months into our marriage. Adrian had been advised by the paymaster to open a joint bank account so that his wages could be paid in automatically, giving me access to our money when he was away on duty. So when he showed up at the pay office for his cash as usual, there was nothing for him, leaving him empty-handed and annoyed. Since we both needed to provide the bank with signatures before any funds could be withdrawn, he dashed home to get me before it shut. "You're home early," I said as he pushed past me in the doorway.

"We've got to go to the bank. Get your coat," he called urgently from the bathroom.

"Why?"

"Just get your coat! Hurry up. It shuts at three!" he directed, adding, "I've no money." I did as I was told and followed him out the door. He set a swift walking pace that I had difficulty maintaining. "Walk faster!" he barked as we dodged the shoppers on the sidewalk.

"I'm hurrying," I replied, irritated that he couldn't see how breathless I was from my effort to keep up.

He turned and scowled at me in a fury. "Come on! You stupid cow!" he spat, his words stinging. Passersby who heard the insult glanced over their shoulders more out of curiosity than concern, some possibly sharing a joke about another couple having a "domestic"; others were oblivious to the name-calling as I came to an abrupt halt. I folded my arms and stood like a statue in the center of the path as people maneuvered their way around me, my eyes fixed on Adrian, demanding an apology.

"Don't ever call me that again," I warned.

"Come on! Don't be stupid," he urged.

"I'm not budging until you apologize." I was insisting on respect.

"What?" He was confused by my response.

"*Say you are sorry,*" I reiterated, enunciating each word clearly, "or I'm not moving."

"I'm sorry!" He grunted. "Now come on!" It was begrudged, but it was an apology. We got to the bank, gave proof of our signatures, withdrew some money, and bought cigarettes. We then walked home at a more sedate pace in silence.

As Adrian opened the front door and stepped inside, I followed, relieved to be home. Turning around after closing the door, I heard a dull thud and realized it was my head being slammed against the wood by Adrian, who, grabbing my hair with one hand while clutching my throat with the other, his knee in my stomach, pressed my back against the door. I gasped in shock, unable to process what was happening or why.

"Don't you *ever* humiliate me in public again," he hissed, cracking my head on the door a second time to emphasize the word *ever*. Then he sauntered away, leaving me stunned and speechless, confounded by the violence. As I crept into the bedroom, I knew that a different woman had stood up for her dignity in the high street less than an hour ago. It would be twelve years before that woman returned. The front door banged shut, alerting me that Adrian, now with cigarettes and cash, was off to join his pals in the pub. When he left, the tears came as I absorbed the lessons that, even without a drink, my husband could be violent and that I should never challenge him in public again.

I thought about leaving him right there and then—packing my bags and just going. But to where? I asked myself. To whom? With what? And so soon into our marriage. It would make a mockery of my vows. For better or worse, remember? 'Til death do us part, remember? I have to work harder. *It's the only answer*, I thought as I prayed, "Please, God, help me become a better wife."

Adrian apologized the next day, and we discussed in length the changes that must be made if we were to both be happy. One concession he agreed to was a date night once a month. We were missing the emotional intimacy so critical to a healthy relationship. Time enough when we had children to mourn its loss, but not yet. Adrian seemed as excited as me at the thought of rekindling the romance and treated me to a date-night outfit—a charcoal-gray pencil skirt with a deep slit up the side and, to go with it, a snugly fitting white shirt. My petite frame carried it off well, and I was elated at the prospect of going out with him soon. In the meantime, I cooked hearty meals on Fridays and Saturdays, intending to line his stomach well before he went drinking. I kissed him goodbye and held my breath, hoping he would come home merry, not mad. Weeks of relative calm would pass, interrupted by a few days of work away, which offered some respite, but I never relaxed—I was ever vigilant.

We were both very social and extroverted and loved hosting informal get-togethers for both married couples and single men during the weeknights. Many of the single chaps were very young and missing home, so having a friendly place to go other than the pub on their night off was welcome. If we were not offering hospitality, we were receiving someone else's. It was a comfort to know there were so many in the same situation, needing to make friends. The one night we did not host, though, was date night. My little triumph.

Our first date night arrived. I was excited to have a reason to dress up and put on some makeup. With a final splash of Charlie perfume Adrian had brought back from his last tour abroad, I descended the stairs. "You look great!" he said approvingly, his broad smile cheering me. I loved to see that smile.

"Thank you. You're not so bad yourself," I replied cheerfully. The night had started well.

We meandered from pub to pub, bumping into squaddies who had been chugging mugs of tea in our living room earlier in the week. I enjoyed seeing the familiar faces as someone called out to us, or waved across a bar, or sidled over, beer in hand, to say hello. It seemed that "Hey, Shorty!" was the refrain in the pubs and on the streets as regular drinking buddies, men and women, caught sight of him. He would stop to chat with them and inevitably buy a round over which to linger while I waited to be introduced. Though I prayed he would not repeat the embarrassing description of me used on a previous occasion, when on meeting some lads for the first time, he said, "This is my missus. The one with no tits." Some of the young soldiers had laughed nervously as I stood stunned and red-faced, watching them glance at my breasts momentarily to check if he was telling the truth before they too blushed when their eyes met mine. One of them later shared with me that having seen my reaction, he no longer believed the rumors that I was "an upper-class bird who liked a bit of rough."

It was clear that Adrian was a well-liked and popular figure in the town. He pointed out a few people whose names I recognized from his causal conversations with the lads. Now I would know whom he was talking about, at least. "There's Juanita. We call her that 'cause she's only got one tooth in the front of her mouth. Get it? One eater." He thought it was funny.

Glad as I was to be out with my husband, I was also disappointed that our time was shared with so many revelers. I discovered that his idea of date night was allowing me to tag along while he was preoccupied with his friends. Nevertheless, I was grateful to be out with him rather than staying home alone where I would be waiting and wondering.

Our monthly date nights ended when I found out I was pregnant. We were both elated. Now we would be a family, not just a couple. Adrian was keen to be called daddy. It was heartening to witness how interested he became in my pregnancy and in the idea of fatherhood. We did all the things that first-time parents do. We browsed shop windows to evaluate the best value in strollers, cribs, and all baby paraphernalia. We gawped at my growing belly as Adrian rested his head and listened to baby's heartbeat. We sang lullabies like "I See the Moon," which my parents had sung to me as a child, to the little person growing inside of me, and we studied the myriad baby names from *Aaron* to *Zebediah* in hopes of finding one we both agreed on. "How about *Lemuel*? Lemuel Long—it has a certain ring to it," Adrian kidded.

"I'll pass. What about Archibald Long? I like that, or Gladys?" I suggested, keeping the lighthearted mood going.

"What about William? Willie for short. Willie Long." We both laughed aloud at that one.

"Hmm, no thank you! Can you imagine the poor child who has to live with that name?"

"Yeah, on official documents where last name is first, he'd be Long Willie! Nothing to be ashamed of," he joked. It was such silliness that brought us closer. We couldn't agree on names so arrived at a compromise. I would choose the boys' names, and Adrian would choose the girls'. We were making progress.

The nine months sped by quickly. Well, eight months passed quickly; the ninth dragged on interminably. I was worrying about going beyond my due date. Adrian had been told to be ready to go to Cyprus with the UN forces for six months a few weeks after the baby was born. He was also going to be away during the pregnancy on exercises to prepare for the posting. I was anxious about him missing the birth and dreaded the looming six-month separation. I hoped and prayed he could be with me as we welcomed our first child into our family.

This had been the most peaceful and contented time in our marriage so far. We were sharing in the excitement of imminent parenthood, our hopes and dreams were aligning, and Adrian was spending less time in the pub.

The idea of childbirth frightened me. I would take encouragement from new mothers at the NAAFI doing their grocery shopping and think to myself, "Well, she looks okay. If she can give birth and be walking straight and smiling afterward, so can I." There were always new mothers, often in the same stage of pregnancy. It was easy to identify which regiment a woman's husband belonged to by checking out the size of her belly. If there had been a significant separation, on the soldier's return, the couple made a baby. It wasn't unusual for a pregnant woman to be asked if her husband was in a particular regiment before being asked, "When is your baby due?"

When Adrian was called away in the last four weeks of my pregnancy, Den, who by this time had split from Sybil, invited me to spend a couple of weeks with him and his new partner, Jenny. They thoroughly spoiled me, insisting I take it easy and relax. "You'll need all your energy soon enough," advised Jenny when I asked if she needed help in the kitchen. We had lots of time to chat and get to know each other better. It was such a gift.

"So is Adrian treating you well?" Den enquired.

"We're getting along really well at the moment. He can't wait to be a daddy," I gushed.

"It's a big responsibility, but with two of you, putting your child's needs first, it can work." He was being encouraging. He then went on to tell me of the first time Adrian had caught me in his sights at Glebe House. "I told him to leave you alone. Now look at you!" He smiled, pointing at my baby bump.

I looked down at my tummy and smiled.

"Has he dismantled the fridge yet?" Den asked.

"The fridge?" I was puzzled.

"Well, the fridge, the washing machine, the lawn mower. Are they all still in one piece? He was always taking things apart and try-ing to put them back together again."

"Oh no, the fridge is in one piece—but he has painted the tele-vision green to match the walls if that counts, and the furniture." We both laughed at Adrian's impulsive need to tinker.

There was a new peace about Den. Nothing distracted him from simply being in the moment. I felt safe. He told me about Adrian's childhood and the trouble he got into at school and with the police. I had not heard any of these stories before. I don't know if he thought he was elaborating on tales I had already been told or was aware of my ignorance, but he continued, telling me how Adrian played truant from school, set fires, stole bicycles, and broke into an estate agent's, stealing cash from the safe before treating his pals to fish and chips. He told me how Cambourne, Redruth, was such a small place; that if a person sneezed at one end of the street, someone from the other end dashed up with a tissue.

Adrian was known by everyone, in part, because of his endearing charm and lively personality, but also, it seems, for his delinquency. He even waved cheekily at the local policeman while riding a stolen bike. He was so well known for his recklessness that the police got into the habit of calling on his home first whenever there was trouble. The situation was made more fraught due to the fact that for twelve years, Sybil cared for her aging mother while raising six children. For Den and Sybil, managing Adrian was exasperating. The army, Den told me, seemed like the place they believed he would learn some well-needed discipline. And after a three-month spell in jail, Adrian had limited prospects. His younger brother David was already in the military and thriving, making a career of it, so Adrian joined him in the light infantry. Tensions arose when David was promoted, and Adrian was obliged to take orders from him. Arguments often ensued when they were both on leave, Adrian accusing his brother of being too bossy and forgetting his place now that they were off duty. It had been a smart decision to transfer to the RCT.

I shared my concerns about Adrian's drinking habits with his dad and alluded to the violence that sometimes followed. I didn't go into the specific details as it would serve no purpose but to hurt this good man whom I considered a protector and an ally. He revealed that alcohol had contributed to the unhappiness in his marriage too. It was a family problem.

Why had Adrian neglected to tell me that he had spent time in jail? Surely that is something that should be disclosed before getting married. It made me wonder what other significant information he might have withheld. I was bursting with questions for him.

I returned home to an empty house as Adrian still had a couple of weeks of military exercises before heading abroad for six months. Like all pregnant women, I did not want to go past my due date, but not just because of the discomfort. There was a tiny window of time when the baby could arrive while Adrian was present, so I set that as my goal. I began doing housework more vigorously than usual. I took the stairs up two at a time and jumped off the bottom three steps when coming down. I danced Irish jigs to disco music on the radio and waited. And waited.

The twinges in my back and tummy announced that labor had started. Or so I thought. That's the trouble with giving birth for the first time. Your only information has come from books and mothers who, I thought, exaggerated. Experience, as I discovered over time, is the best teacher. I certainly felt enough pain to ask a neighbor to take me to the military hospital where the duty nurse examined me. "You're not quite there yet," she assessed.

"How will I know when I *am* there?" If anyone could answer that question, she could.

"Oh, you'll know—believe me, you'll know."

I'd heard mothers use that expression often, but not until I felt the equivalent of molten glass spilling onto my belly as an iron fist twisted my internal organs into an excruciating knot of searing pain did I understand why. "Oh, you'll know," was the only appropriate response.

"I suggest you go home, Julie," she said kindly. "Have your husband keep an eye on you and come back if things get any worse."

"He's away on exercise," I explained.

"Well, in that case, we'll admit you and monitor your progress here." She seemed concerned that I was on my own.

My neighbor promised to alert the squadron leader in the hopes Adrian would be given permission to come home in time for the delivery. I said a quiet prayer that I wouldn't have to go through this alone.

I felt like a fraud taking up a bed, especially as there had been no further twinges since I was admitted. But now that I was here feeling relaxed and confident in the care of experts, I prayed for the pain of real contractions to come soon, maybe in a day or two to give Adrian time to get here and hold my hand. At 8:30 p.m. the night-duty nurse, curt and efficient, introduced herself and, after examining me, announced that the baby would be here before she went home at eight-thirty in the morning. "We'll make sure of it!" she added defin-itively before transferring me to the labor room.

"Get some sleep," the nurse advised. "You're going to need all the energy you can muster." But elusive sleep slipped out the door with her as she left me in the dark, alone.

Every couple of hours, the nurse returned to check on my progress, growing visibly more impatient each time. I began to feel guilty that she was working so hard, and I was just lying there. At midnight, she put me on a glucose drip to "speed things along," even though the baby wasn't due for almost another week. At 6:00 a.m., her sense of urgency seemed misplaced, but she had made up her mind that this baby would be delivered on her shift. So she broke my waters with a forceps, leaving the impression of the instru-ment on the baby's skull.

I berated myself for trying to force things along at home with my selfish antics. This was developing into a frighteningly unpleas-ant and lonely experience. Why had I been so impatient? Why hadn't I trusted Mother Nature to do her thing? Where was Adrian? Where was my mother? Where was *anybody* who cared for me?

The contractions intensified, and I finally understood what was meant by "Oh, you'll know."

I begged for something to extinguish the excruciating spasms of pain and received an injection of pethidine, which, along with reduc-ing the pain, gave me terrifying hallucinations before inducing sleep. The medical staff in attendance were now floating near the ceiling, bobbing about like giant balloons in the Macy's Thanksgiving Day parade, auditioning for the role of Peter Pan, urging me to "Push!" But all I yearned for was sleep. A hard slap to my face jolted me back to consciousness and the pain.

"You need an episiotomy, or you'll tear," the doctor informed me as the nurse jabbed another injection into my thigh. I felt the snip of the scissors as he exclaimed, "My God! You've got skin like the hind of a rhinoceros!"

That did it! With every atom in my being, I called on the only friend I had in that moment as I gave a final determined push.

"Jeeesusss!" I screamed.

And Jesus delivered. Brian Peter Long, seven pounds, eight ounces, was born at 8:40 a.m., ten minutes after Nurse Grumpy had gone home.

Adrian arrived the next day. He had left a husband and returned a father. His presence banished the horrors of the night before and replaced my loneliness with joy. As we gazed through the glass of the nursery window at *our* boy, I was overcome with gratitude for the miraculous gift of this tiny infant who had the capacity, vulnerable and fragile as he was, to elicit such tenderness in us for each other. We were a family. It was sufficient. The weighty responsibility of parenthood was a consideration for another day.

Knowing that we had only a couple of weeks to bond as a family before we were wrenched apart by his posting to Cyprus, every moment together presented an opportunity for deeper intimacy. Family life became a daisy chain of cherished memories, created by our living deliberately and consciously, held together by our choice to love. We were aware of the clock ticking and determined to cram all the loving we could into each day. There were new grandparents to visit, a baptism to arrange, and a baby to introduce to the world. And it all had to be done between feeds.

This was not the time to bombard Adrian with questions about his adolescence. Those questions seemed insignificant now anyway. Our focus had changed. There was now a precious child, totally dependent on us, calling us to be better people.

Standing on my mother's stoop, our baby cradled in my arms, Adrian and I hugged awkwardly. My parents and siblings, having already said goodbye, stood in silent attendance, waiting to offer comfort.

"I'll write every day, I promise," Adrian assured me. "Take care of Brian."

"I will. I'll write every day too. Be safe."

"I will. You too." The final exchange of remarks could only stall the inevitable unwelcome departure. Was there one last thing to ask him, to hold him here just a few more minutes?

"Do you have your passport?" I asked.

"Yup!"

"And your toothbrush?"

"My toothbrush?"

"Well, I'm just checking to make sure you haven't forgotten anything," I said feebly as I brushed invisible flecks of dust from his shoulders.

"I haven't forgotten anything. Don't worry."

"Don't forget us."

"How could I forget the most important people in my life?" he said, kissing baby Brian's forehead and then mine. We held on to each other, both of us reluctant to let go, but the time had come. "I've got to go, sweetheart. I'll miss my train."

"Just one more thing," I whispered. "I love you."

"I love you too. Be good," he whispered back before picking up his gear and getting into the car. The family gathered about me as the vehicle disappeared from sight, my youngest sister, Lulu, waving at it enthusiastically. "Bye, Adrian. Bye-bye." Almost immediately, I was smothered by a flurry of cheery comments intended to distract me and ease my distress.

"He'll be back before you know it."

"Time will pass quickly, you'll see."

"At least you've got the baby for company. That's something."

"I'll help you with the baby."

"I'll give you lots of hugs."

The words, though well intentioned, were just background noise. I heard them but was not listening. I had journeyed inward for solace where my soul sent me tears.

So it was back to the letter writing for six months, and back to my parents' home for company and support as I adjusted to the demands of motherhood without my husband. The separation was tinged with sadness because of the missed milestones and the wrenching apart of our family at such a critical time in its formation.

I felt fortunate to be back with my family, especially my siblings, who doted on baby Brian and competed with one another for a chance to cuddle him, take him for a walk around the neighborhood, or play with him. They were not lining up to change his diapers, however; that unpleasant duty was my reserve.

Once again, waiting for the postman became my pastime as letters were our only communication link. Now there would be photos of our growing baby boy to include.

Having experienced how strong our relationship could be when motivated by pure, unselfish love, I wanted to ensure it was nurtured. Our love, like the soil, was living and dynamic—in need of careful attention to enable and support healthy growth. Just as soil needs water to sustain life, we too required a life-giving element to sustain our love. Distance and forced separation compounded our efforts. So like the absent and diligent gardener who doesn't leave things to chance but instead programs her water sprinkler, we had a decision to make. We weren't leaving anything to chance either. We both needed regular showering of affection and affirmation, so our letters and simple poems became our water sprinklers.

Winter 1977
"Absent Father" by Julie Long

*You think that I'm not missing you? Well, let me put
    you right.
I've never felt so lonesome as I do these wintry nights.
When you rang me up that evening, it was bliss to
    hear your voice,
But I'd rather have you with me, if I only had the
    choice.
I know it will be half a year that we're to be apart,
But when the month of May arrives, then joy will
    fill my heart.
So please believe me, Darling, when I say I'm missing you,
And also that there's no one else could love you as I
    do.*

*Dear Daddy you're so far away, I wish that you were
    here.*

But Mummy's told me often that you're coming home next year.
I'm looking all around me now and sometimes smiling too.
It will be nice to have you home then I can smile at you.
Sometimes at night when Mummy cries, she comes and cuddles me.
And tells me that she's missing you, but you're not here to see.
I hope that when you do come home you're coming home to stay.
Because we need you, Daddy. We get sad when you're away.
I'm just a little baby now, but soon I'll be quite grown
So please don't go away again and leave us on our own.
You're so important to us, Dad. We love you more and more.
I'll be so happy, so will Mum, when you walk through that door.
It's time to get my nappy changed, so now I'll have to go.
But please remember, Daddy, that we really love you so.

Chapter 5

On Adrian's return from Cyprus, we returned to our home to begin again. Adrian couldn't wait to show off his little boy and eagerly took walks with us, stopping to chat with other new parents in much the same way dog owners admire, compare, and discuss their pets. Predictably, within a few months, women at the grocery store were asking, "Is your husband with the RCT?" as I, along with so many other squadron wives, was pregnant.

Date nights were a distant memory, a part of my past, though Adrian's nights out with the lads were as constant as the British weather. No life event was significant enough to interrupt that manly routine. With social drinking such a part of the military culture, and the six months in Cyprus where most free time was spent in the bar, we suffered a setback as Adrian slipped closer to dependency on alcohol. I was worried for him and for our family.

When I broached my concerns, I was accused of spoiling his fun, of being too uptight and too demanding. His response was to go for a drink to get away from what he perceived as my incessant nagging and to avoid lashing out violently. The erosive qualities in alcohol were damaging more than his liver, causing a destructive cycle that spiraled downward into a crippling misery. The only way to avoid rousing his temper was to be quiet, so I continued to do my duty as a wife in all respects, to love and protect my children, and to shut up.

I discovered that denying a problem does not erase it. Eventually, I had to face the monster head-on and fight as though my life depended on it. Because it did. I decided to take on the Grendel of alcoholism after Adrian came home drunk in the middle of a Friday afternoon—his entire uniform saturated.

"What on earth have you been doing?" I cried as he stumbled, soaking wet, into the hall.

"I've been for a wade in the boating lake—and I'm wet!" he said, plopping into the armchair. There was no point in asking him to get up. I'd have to dry out the cushions later.

"Why aren't you at work?"

"We got the afternoon off," he slurred, his head, too heavy to hold up, dropping to his chest. "I'm going to bed," he declared.

I helped him up from his seat and followed behind as he struggled to mount the stairs. Then I waited as he removed the sodden uniform and boots.

Once back downstairs, I thought about our life together and how far we had strayed from my vision of marital harmony. I glanced over at Brian playing in his playpen, oblivious to my worries. I was twenty-one and pregnant with our second child, feeling hopeless and alone.

I jumped up from the couch when I heard the front door open and looked out the window, where, to my horror, I saw Adrian crouching on the front lawn in his blue dressing gown pooing on the grass in full view of passersby. I closed my eyes, hoping when I opened them again, it would have been a disturbing mirage. But he was still there, crouching. Part of me wanted to dash out and rescue him, and another part of me wanted to hide. Instead, I froze.

He came back in and went back up to bed. I knew we would have to talk about his behavior, but arguing when he was drunk was not only frustrating and futile, it was dangerous. The next morning, over a cup of coffee, I tackled the subject. "Adrian, you were in a terrible state yesterday. You've got to get some help with your drinking. Please," I pleaded.

"Oh, here we go again—the same old record. Give it a rest, will you?" The agitation was clear in his voice.

"I can't give it a rest. You were out of control yesterday. We can't go on like this."

"So I went for a paddle. Big deal!"

"And the rest," I said, trying to contain my exasperation.

"What are you on about?" He didn't seem to remember.

"No dog did that!" I barked, pointing out the window at the pile of excrement.

He joined me out of curiosity where it took him a few seconds to see what I was pointing at and to understand what I was telling him. Then he let out a hearty laugh. My annoyance escalated as I considered how different we were. What mortified me, he found amusing. What I believed was eroding our marriage, he saw as a necessity. What I wanted more than anything —a happy life together—he claimed to also want. His attitude and behavior baffled me.

"Adrian! It's not funny!" I cried out, my patience exhausted. "Why do you treat everything as a joke?"

"Why do you make such a big deal about everything?" he replied, turning the question back on me. I remembered that the baby was in the room, so I monitored my tone and, in a calmer voice, said, "Our family *is* a big deal. We're having another baby, and I don't want us fighting every time you've been drinking. I don't understand why you can't see that it's the problem."

"That's right, blame me. It's all my fault. The only pleasure I have in life, and you want to take it away."

"Your only pleasure? What about us?" I asked, referring to our family.

"Us? Us? What a joke! What pleasure do you give me, huh? Screwing you is like screwing a pound of liver." I was dumbfounded by his cruelty. He had chosen to insult rather than focus on the problem. I refused to join in the tirade of abuse, but my silence fueled his increasing rage. "Huh, you can't answer can, you? 'Cause you know it's the truth."

The tears welled, but I forced them back. I knew better than to cry in front of him. Instead, I picked up Brian and went into the back garden, feeling dejected and useless. Adrian, as was his way, used the argument as an excuse to leave and did not return until Sunday night.

I pretended to be asleep when he finally got home, though the fact was that I had been so desperately anxious when he didn't return on Saturday that I had called a priest for advice long after the pubs had closed. The young priest, a stranger to me, whose name I plucked from the yellow pages, came immediately to our house and listened attentively as I described the miserable state of our marriage.

"What do I do, Father?" I implored. "I vowed to love for better for worse, till death do us part."

"This isn't what God wants marriage to be." His tone was sympathetic. "He wants you to be happy. He wants all of us to be happy. You don't have to endure this," he insisted gently. It was as though he was advocating my leaving Adrian but was hesitant to say it plainly. "Though, as an unmarried person, I am no expert. Maybe I can put you in touch with a Catholic marriage guidance counsellor. Would that be helpful?"

"Yes. Yes. Thank you." I was grateful for his attentiveness and concern.

"Do you want me to stay with you until your husband comes home?" he offered.

"Oh, God no! Sorry, Father. My husband would misunderstand your presence. It would make things much worse." I didn't need to explain any further. He understood.

"Well, I'll be going then. Are you sure you'll be all right?"

"Yes. Yes. Thank you, Father. I'm truly grateful for your kindness."

"Oh, I wish I could do more. I pray that you can get some helpful advice from the counsellor." As he stepped onto the porch, he handed me a slip of paper on which he had jotted down the number of the Catholic Marriage Guidance office. To him, it was a telephone number; to me, it was hope.

I prayed that Adrian's bad mood had dissipated. It hadn't.

"Hey, I know you're awake. Get your lazy ass up and go make me a cup of tea," he ordered. I got out of bed and went down to the kitchen in silence, doing as I was told. He followed.

"Don't you want to know where I've been?" he goaded.

"I guess you'll tell me if you want to," I said, trying to conceal my fear. He was so unpredictable when angry that I had to manage my responses second by second to avoid launching him into a violent assault.

"That's where you're wrong," he said in a calculating tone as he set his mug on the table and stood up to face me. My mind raced frantically, trying to anticipate what he was going to do as he held my gaze, his eerie calmness unnerving me.

"I'll give you a hint," he said mockingly. "Her name begins with *S*."

"Why are you being so cruel?" I asked, desperate to reduce the tension.

"I'm not being cruel. I'm being honest. Isn't that what you want? Openness and honesty?"

"Not like this. Please don't do this."

"Guess!" he demanded, ignoring my plea and poking me in the shoulder. "Guess!"

"No." I winced as I said it, summoning my courage, also knowing that a refusal to respond would be punished.

"Don't you dare say no to me!" he spat as his arm swung back to give momentum to the slap to my face.

"Please, Adrian, don't wake the baby," I begged, holding my cheek.

"Well, don't make me mad then. It's simple. Do as you're told," he replied, his patronizing tone reducing me to a four-year-old.

"Her name begins with *S*. Who is she?" I felt trapped and frightened. I wanted the ordeal to end.

"Sheila?" I offered quietly. Another stinging slap.

"Nope. Try again."

"Sally?" Another slap.

"Not doing very well, are you?" he commented. I didn't know anyone in Colchester called Sheila or Sally so was just recalling the *S* section of the naming baby book, willing this torture over.

"Sarah?" I instinctively drew my hands up to my face in a protective move as I dropped my head, but it didn't prevent the blow from landing.

"Adrian, please, no more," I begged.

"I'll stop when you guess the name—so you better get a move on, hadn't you?" His voice was cold and controlled.

"Sandra?"

"Bingo! Finally. My arm was getting tired." He sneered. "Yup! I stayed the night with Sandra. Now *she's* good in bed."

"It's not true, is it?" I wanted it to be a sick drunken joke, some twisted need he had to pick a fight in order to release pent-up tension where, unfortunately, I became the punching bag.

He took a gulp of tea before answering. "It's true. She's not the first either," he bragged.

"You've had sex with other women since we've been married?" It was too devastating to imagine.

"Yes, I have," he replied, daring me to react.

"I'm pregnant!" I screamed. "You could have given me VD! This baby could be born blind and deaf!" The horror of the child I was carrying suffering because of his selfish behavior was unbearable.

"Oh, calm down, will you? You don't have to worry. I always wait four days after sleeping with someone else before having sex with you."

"What?" I was dumbfounded.

"If I've caught something, then the symptoms show up in four days." He sounded almost considerate.

"Why, Adrian? Why? If you aren't happy with me, why don't you leave? Why torture us both like this?"

"Why would I want to leave when I have someone to do the donkey work for me?"

"I thought you loved me. I thought you wanted a happy life with me. That's what I want," I said pathetically. "You weren't like this before we were married. What's happened?"

"Nothing's happened. This is who I am," he said matter-of-factly.

"You've changed. You were different before. You were kind. I don't understand why you can't still be that way now."

"Well, you don't chase the bus once you've caught it."

"I don't understand," I repeated. My mind was still processing the news of his infidelity.

"Would you have married me if you knew what I was really like?" he asked, almost rhetorically.

"No! I wouldn't. Of course not."

"Well then, there's your answer." He took another swig of tea and went to bed. It was as though he had just tidied up for the night. Nothing to it. I was speechless and didn't move from the room till morning, wondering how this mess would be resolved.

The next day, while he was at work, I gathered up all my loose coins and called his father from the telephone kiosk. He was appalled at what I told him, even though it was severely edited, assuring me of his support. He agreed with me that the alcohol was an obstacle to our happiness, as it had been to his. I felt reassured. Den believed without question what I had shared. Just knowing that he appreciated the seriousness of my plight gave me strength. I then called the Catholic marriage guidance counsellor and made an appointment.

At my request, the counsellor from Marriage Guidance arrived when Adrian was at work. I was eager to hear what advice she would give. I wanted always to do the right thing by following church teaching, and in my mind, this wise lady had the authority to direct me. Since speaking with the priest, I had been mulling over his message that God wanted us all to be happy. The priest's assessment of our marriage and his affirmation of me had provided the courage to consider another way of living. One that did not include Adrian. Now I expected the good lady to confirm that, yes, indeed, this life was intolerable, and I should get out. I was looking for permission from my church to leave my husband. If I had the blessing of a priest and encouragement from a Catholic counsellor, then my parents, whom I had protected from the truth about the abuse, would accept more easily that the marriage had ended, and I would be spared the harsh judgement reserved for those selfish women who abandon their wifely duties.

What I got instead from this officious, rule-following product of an oppressive male-dominated church was a lecture on my duties as a Catholic wife and mother, echoing my mother's message that my husband's happiness is my responsibility. There was no mention of the wife's happiness. That, apparently, has to be sacrificed at the altar of oppressive patriarchy.

"Your husband sounds very unhappy. He needs to know that you love him. Have you thought about sitting on his lap when he is in one of his moods, putting your arms around his neck and saying, 'I love you'?" This was her solution? I was incredulous. She had not listened. She had ambushed me with her own agenda to make sure that I understood that it was imperative to preserve the sanctity of marriage. She understood nothing of our struggle to do just that for the past few years.

"Besides," she went on, "who would want you with two kids?"

These two comments summed up her interpretation of the teaching of the church on marriage. It's the woman's duty to guarantee her husband's happiness even at the cost of her own, and being trapped in an abusive marriage is preferable to the scandal of divorce.

Chapter 6

Our home became as quiet and cold as a cemetery in winter, inhabited by the ghost of the girl I buried a long time ago but who refused to rest in peace and who haunted me every time I looked into a mirror. I gave Adrian no reason for recrimination and steered well away from criticizing him.

One afternoon, he returned home from work in a wild rage, slinging his beret onto the chair while cursing one of his workmates. "That bastard! I'm going to sort him out," he fumed.

"Who? What's happened?" I asked. He gave the name of a soldier I didn't know and continued with his rant.

"I'll kill him. I swear it, I'll kill him!" I was still clueless as to what had happened. "It was him. It must have been him. He's had it in for me for ages."

"Adrian, what's happened?" I pressed.

"That bastard reported me to my CO for drinking on duty, and now I've been ordered to go for treatment or be kicked out of the army. That fucker is dead."

I knew in that instant that it was not a workmate but Den, who must have reported him. I knew too that Adrian was very capable of grievously injuring the falsely accused lad before checking his assumptions. I couldn't let that happen. "Adrian, it wasn't him. It was me." I braced myself for an assault, but he was stunned by my remark.

"What do you mean it was you?"

"Well, when you came in drunk and angry a few weeks ago, I called your dad because I was worried about you—about us—and told him I blamed your drinking for our problems. He must have called your commanding officer."

He was quietly absorbing my explanation, looking defeated and deflated. "Well, who knows, maybe it'll do some good," he said resignedly. We were getting another chance.

As an act of loyalty and support, I volunteered to go with Adrian to his counselling appointments at Woolwich Hospital. It was another tenuous sliver of hope to cling onto if our marriage was to survive. We joined a circle of men and women of all military ranks who shared a common addiction. Stories of how their dependence on alcohol had disrupted lives were told as layer upon layer of pain and hurt peeled away, revealing lost and vulnerable souls desperate to reclaim happiness some other way. I admired their courage and honesty as they exposed their deepest fears, regrets, and longings. I saw it as a blessed experience and was encouraged that this indeed could be our saving grace.

It was Adrian's turn to address the group. I held his hand as a sign of my loyalty and squeezed it gently. He began by explaining that his dependence on alcohol had stemmed from his social nature and being in a culture of drinking both inside and outside of the army. His audience nodded encouragingly. They could relate.

"Have you ever been violent with your wife when drinking, Adrian?" asked the facilitator.

"Oh no! I'd never hit my wife, or any woman. Would I, love?" He turned to me and squeezed my fingers in warning as the group looked to me for a reply. My heart was yelling, *Liar, liar!* But as I could not give credence to his answer with my own, I chose to remain mute, hoping that my silence screamed the truth.

"Why did you lie?" I challenged when we got home.

"They don't need to know all our business," he replied dismissively.

"Well, you've got to tell the truth if you sincerely want help."

"Look, the army will kick me out if I don't go. So I'm going, okay?" He wasn't interested in any recovery program. He was in denial, and I was worn out carrying him.

"Well, you're not the only one who's going," I declared bravely. "I'm going too. You obviously have no desire to make things better, so I'm leaving." I didn't have a plan. I didn't know where I was going, pregnant and with a toddler, but I couldn't maintain this fiasco of emotional and spiritual suicide any longer. I was exhausted trying to understand him and convince him that he was loved. A love he was perpetually testing.

"You won't leave me. You're Catholic. You told me yourself you don't believe in divorce." He was reminding me of my vows.

"I can't live like this anymore, Adrian. It's not living." I wasn't angry, just jaded.

"Nah, you're not leaving," he replied confidently.

He didn't know that the encounter with the marriage counsellor, though not what I had anticipated or hoped for, had engendered a burgeoning epiphany. As a result, an inner rebellion had begun as my soul challenged and replaced the distorted messages presented by the church with unassailable whispers of truth. Finally, I understood that I could no longer look to external authorities for answers but must trust the Divine within me.

Adrian's brother David and his wife, Julie, offered me shelter for a few weeks until I could make other arrangements. They provided a sanctuary safe from name-calling, violence, and fear, and they listened.

Adrian couldn't bear the separation. He was bereft. He inundated us with phone calls, all a variation on the same message, imploring me to return. "I'm sorry, Julie. I've seen the mistakes I've made. I know I've hurt you, and I'm so sorry. Please, please come home. Things will be different. Just tell me what you want. But come home," he cried. He was relentless in his pleading and in his promises. But I kept a steely resolve to move on without him.

I researched the services available for victims of domestic violence and found them sorely inadequate. I couldn't make a permanent home with Julie and David, for whose kindness I would be ever grateful. I also had no money, being financially dependent on Adrian, so felt guilty about being a drain on them. Neither could I return to my parents' already full house, especially with two small children in tow. My options were shrinking. So with nowhere to go, I returned to Adrian, but with a renewed sense of my own worth and a list of conditions that he must accept. Name-calling and violent outbursts had to cease, counselling for alcohol addiction had to resume, and date night had to be reinstated. He agreed to it all.

Life was good again. The shock of my leaving seemed to have helped Adrian value family life in a way he couldn't before. Brian now had a baby brother, Michael, and my faith and optimism were restored. Adrian completed the counselling sessions and convinced himself that he could manage his drinking, just so long as it was all in moderation. Date nights returned, and we both focused more on each other's happiness.

Then in 1981, Adrian requested a three-year posting to Lisburn, Northern Ireland, where his job was to run the squadron bar. How on earth could this happen? Did no one look at his records before assigning this job? Did they not know the risks? I was shocked and dismayed. Adrian, however, was delighted with his new responsibility while I spent even more time praying.

Adrian had wanted to reunite with his friend Ian "Geordie" Strachan, with whom we had both developed a strong connection. Ian and his wife, Sue, had become my advocates and cheering section when dealing with Adrian's unpredictable aggression. We threw an engagement party for them at our home in Colchester, and Adrian was the best man at their wedding. Now, in Sue, I had a friend and confidante just as she had in me. We were as close as sisters. So even though I recoiled when I heard that Adrian would be running the bar, I was relieved to know that Corporal and Mrs. Strachan were going to be there to welcome and support us, especially as I was expecting our third child.

Chapter 7

Every change in our routine provided an opportunity for a fresh start. Promises were renewed as the excitement of a new place, new people, and new experiences beckoned enticingly in our future. A posting to Northern Ireland, though, was fraught with danger. When we arrived, Bobby Sands, an Irish nationalist, was protesting British rule in Ireland by going on hunger strike in the Maze prison. After sixty-six days, he died, considered a martyr by many. The tension in the province was palpable. British soldiers were viewed as an invading force by the Catholics who had suffered oppression for hundreds of years. Everyone was judged on their religious affiliation, pitting Protestant against Catholic in a vicious cycle of sectarian violence. Bombings, shootings, killings, and kneecappings were a daily occurrence. For me, as an Irish Catholic married to an English Protestant soldier in Northern Ireland, life was precarious. Catholic girls who had dared to date British soldiers had been tarred and feathered as a warning to others who may be considering such a traitorous act. I had not only dated a British soldier; I had married one.

We were instructed to keep secret the fact that we were with the army. "If anyone asks, your husband drives a bus for Ulsterbus," cautioned the commanding officer. Families living within the boundaries of the barracks were protected by armed soldiers patrolling and guarding the entrances and the perimeter, allowing no entry without a military-issue ID. Once inside Thiepval Barracks, where most families lived, it was like being back in England. Restrictions were relaxed; it was considered a relatively safe zone. For those of us who didn't live inside the barracks because of a shortage of housing and an increased military presence in the country, the rules were strictly enforced. We lived in local rented housing along with the civilian population, which was mostly Protestant. We could not display any military paraphernalia inside our homes, we could not hang the uniform out on the line to dry, we could not leave the house without checking for car bombs on our vehicles, and soldiers could not leave or return to the house in their uniforms. They also grew their hair long so that they would be harder to identify when wearing civilian clothes.

While watching the news on the TV at night, the commentator would report that a bomb had exploded in a street I had shopped in earlier that day, or that soldiers drinking in a local pub, the Robin's Nest, had been lured by local girls to a private apartment where they were ambushed and killed, or that the IRA (Irish Republican Army) or the UVF (Ulster Volunteer Force) had been involved in bloody acts of sectarian violence. Though I was anxious about the real and deadly threats to our safety from outside, the potential for violence inside our home was far more frightening.

So we moved into our beautiful civilian house in Harmony Hill. I took the name of the place as a sign that we would do well here. Our immediate neighbors were also in different branches of the army, though it took me a while to figure that out because of the need for secrecy. My natural tendency to chat to everyone I meet from the checkout person to the bus driver had to be curtailed for fear of inadvertently revealing our military ties and putting my own and others' lives in peril.

"We're back together again!" I announced as I hugged first Sue and then Ian, who had come over to help us move in to our new house.

"So glad you're here with us. Life is improving by the minute," said Sue. "I love your house! So much nicer than the barrack quarters."

"Thanks for coming over. I'm so happy to have you so close. You've no idea," I said with a mix of joy and relief.

"Put the kettle on then. Let's celebrate properly with a good cuppa," Ian ordered, mimicking a sergeant major.

"Yes, sir!" I said, saluting him.

Sue and Ian knew Adrian's dependence on drink spoiled our relationship, and they could manage him in a way I could not. When we went out as a foursome, my safety was guaranteed, and I was able to relax in their company and have fun. As the Strachans lived in the barracks, we often called in on them before heading to the club or to a dance put on by the army. For one such occasion, I had bought a new dress, an Asian-inspired sleeveless white dress with a mandarin collar and black bamboo design. Sue admired my dress, though I was a little disappointed in the fit. Around the hips was snug, but the material around the bust area was noticeably droopy. I spotted the cotton balls on the dresser and asked Sue if I could use them, then stuffed as many would fit into my bra to fill out the dress more. Turning sideways to check my profile in the mirror, I was impressed with the result. When we got to the dance, I noticed what every girl dreads: another woman in the same dress, and she was glowering at me. She must have lived in the barrack housing as she left and came back a few minutes later in a different outfit. The small victory cheered me up.

Before long, Sue and I got up to dance to Gloria Gaynor singing "I Will Survive." That's the benefit of having female friends; they'll dance with you when your husband won't. Everyone, it seemed, was in the same gloriously happy state. Some nodded in my direction and smiled. Others brought their hands to their mouths to stifle a laugh while others waved both hands in the air. It was seconds later, when glancing at the floor, that I realized why I'd received such attention. There, keeping our handbags company and mocking me, were the escaping cotton balls.

On nights like these, in the company of good friends, I felt lighter. It was a taste of fleeting contentment that I was yearning to have permanently in my life. Whenever the four of us were together, Adrian's aggression subsided, so between us, Sue and I created numerous occasions that required all of us to be present. When Ian and Sue came to our house, Ian would whisper to me, "Whatever Shorty asks you to do, me and Sue will do it. You just stay put. Okay, pet? We'll see how long it takes him to notice." It was a gentle poking of him that they could get away with. Their attempt to show him that he could be a better man. So when Adrian, lying full length on the couch, said, "Hey, Julie, put the kettle on." Ian winked at me and headed for the kitchen. When he returned and handed the tea to Adrian, another request followed, "Close the curtain. The sun's in my eyes." Sue then popped up and pulled the curtains together. "Fetch me an ashtray." Ian left his chair and handed the heavy blue glass ashtray to Adrian, who took it without thanks. "Turn the telly to BBC. *Sportsnight*'s on." Sue sauntered over to the television to switch channels.

"What's going on?" he eventually asked.

"Shorty, mate, what did your last servant die of?" Ian chided. "No wonder Julie's the size of a beanpole with all the running around you've got her doin'."

"Ah, that's what a wife's for. To take care of her husband," Adrian responded, half-kidding.

"Excuse me!" interjected Sue. "A husband is supposed to take care of his wife too, you know!"

"Wey, aye, man! Sue's right. Julie's not your skivvy. Besides, you could use the exercise, lying there on your backside like Lord Muck." And so the lighthearted banter continued for a while, exposing the bleak truth that my husband viewed me as little more than a maid.

With good people like Ian and Sue around, I felt safe. So when Adrian told me that a couple, newly arrived, were going to be staying with us for a few weeks while waiting for army accommodation to become available, I was excited. I had just given birth to Sean, my energetic little redhead, so now we had three boys under the age of four. Rather than be daunted by the prospect of hosting guests, I knew that I would instead be welcoming a friend who would jump into the fray and help me with the increasing demands of motherhood. Army wives form unique bonds and understand the need to make friends quickly. Moving around so much doesn't afford the luxury of taking time to decide if someone is compatible or not, so we choose to become friends first and get to know one another over time.

Janet and Andrew settled in immediately. They were relaxed, friendly, and fun-loving. I envied their relationship and how openly

they showed affection to each other while engaging in saucy banter and laughing together. Always laughing—such a welcome and
life-affirming sound. Adrian too enjoyed their presence, sharing a
similar raunchy sense of humor that still left me feeling uncomfortable. Both of them went with him each evening when he opened
the bar while I stayed home with the boys. I enjoyed the relative
peace, knowing that Adrian had to remain sober while at work and
confident that with guests in the house, he was less likely to lose his
temper with me on his return.

When Janet and Andrew moved into their own home, we
became regular visitors along with other military couples. In
Northern Ireland, we had to make our own entertainment as it was
too risky to venture into the town at night. We were grateful for the
parties that sprung up in different houses each weekend, where we
could gather and relieve the stress of living in a dangerous place. I
had to get used to Adrian's new routine of heading to their home on
a Saturday night for an after-hours nightcap, or three, and crashing
on their couch rather than coming home. He justified it by saying
they lived closer to the barracks where he had to be on Sunday afternoon to open the bar.

It was on his days off, when his friend Taff took over the bar,
that I became most anxious. Instead of dispensing drinks, Adrian
was one of the customers having "earned" a drink while I was confined to the house and the care of our boys. His increasing volatility
when drunk was becoming more difficult to manage, and my fear
of injury at his hands was constant. Violent outbursts also became
more common since I had returned from his brother David's home,
causing me to be even more diligent in monitoring and responding
to his moods. I believed his repeated threat, "I'll break your fucking
neck if you leave me again, do you hear?" He had proven that he was
capable of seriously harming me when out with friends in a Lisburn
pub classified as "safe" by the army.

The night began reasonably well, with a group of us meeting at
the pub and disco. Adrian was in his usual lively and engaging mood,
ready to entertain everyone else, ignore me, and get drunk. I was
grateful to be in a group where I could chat and dance while moni-

toring his alcohol intake. Four pints of beer was his limit. Any more, and he was dangerously unpredictable. As was typical, the group split along gender lines: the men heading towards the bar while the women, and their handbags, spilled onto the dance floor, where, from to time, I glanced over to the bar, paying attention to Adrian's demeanor and gauging his level of intoxication, often unaware of the shots of whiskey surreptitiously consumed between pints of Newcastle Brown and bitter.

Later, when the music slowed, emboldened by being in the company of wives whose husbands feigned reluctance as they were coaxed onto the floor, I bravely asked Adrian, "Would you like to dance?"

"Nope. I'm too knackered."

"Oh, please, Adrian. Just one dance."

"Look, I don't feel like dancing, okay?" He wasn't to be persuaded. So we sat side by side, he staring into his beer while I stared at the couples swaying to the music, leaning on each other in comfortable and familiar embraces. I let out a deep sigh as I watched one wife reach behind her back to remove her husband's hands from her bottom and reposition them around her waist. He, smiling into her eyes, resumed the cheeky hold, daring her to repeat her move, and so the game went on till she surrendered by grabbing his bottom too. "Look at those two," I said, turning to discover I was talking to myself as Adrian had wandered from the table. Hurt was now obscuring the growing resentment as I thought, *Not only will he not dance with me, he won't even sit with me.* The world, it seems, was happy on the dance floor with me on the outside looking in.

I scanned the room to see where he might be; and there, to the strains of Spandau Ballet's "True," was Adrian dancing with Janet—her arms around his neck, his wrapped around her waist, his hips pressed against hers, knees finding spaces to fill as they moved in rhythm to the music.

"Hey, Julie. Let's have a dance," said Andrew, taking hold of my hand.

"No thanks." I shook my hand free and headed onto the dance floor.

"Shorty's right. You are armor-plated," he called after me, irked by my rejection. I weaved between the swaying couples until I was standing next to Janet, who looked surprised when I interrupted them. I had abandoned caution, taking a risk in challenging Adrian so impulsively and publicly, but it was too late now to retreat. "Adrian, you said you were too tired to dance with me. But you're not too tired to dance with someone else, are you?" I had thrown down the gauntlet in a direct challenge. My heart was racing as he glared at me. Janet removed her arms from around his neck even though Adrian's arms still held her in place. "Stay put," he directed her.

"No, it's okay. I'm thirsty anyway." She released herself and headed back to Andrew at the table, as Adrian and I faced each other. "We're going home! Come on," he said, roughly yanking my arm and moving to the edge of the dance floor.

"I've got to get my handbag," I said, stalling, as I returned to the table while he headed towards the exit.

"Where's Shorty?" asked Taff.

"He's waiting for me. We're going home," I explained. "I'll chat with you tomorrow. Good night."

"Good night. Take it easy."

I rushed to the stairs, not wanting to aggravate Adrian any further. I glanced around but couldn't see him so assumed he had already headed out. I dashed down the stairs, and as I stepped out into the rain, his fist crashed into my face. He had positioned himself for an ambush, standing with his back flush against the wall, until I stepped out unprepared for the shock of the blow. I was facing a two-mile walk home with a man in a rage, but my instinct for survival directed me immediately back upstairs to the safety of the group.

"Changed your mind, eh? Having too much fun with us, weren't you?" said Taff as I sank into the seat next to him, clutching my nose. "Oh my God, what happened to you?" he asked, his voice laden with concern. Before I could respond, Adrian had grabbed my arm and was pulling me out of my seat.

"Get your ass up. We're going home, NOW!"

"I'm not going home with you when you're like this, Adrian," I said defiantly. My courage had returned now that I was back with friends. They rallied round us both in a protective shield, the women examining my face for marks of injury while offering support and sympathy; the men, with a united purpose, to calm Adrian down before leaving me alone with him.

"Come on, mate. Let's have a chat," said Taff, steering him towards the bathroom, a comforting arm around his shoulder.

I was regretting my lack of self-control. "It's my fault. I shouldn't have had a go at him when he's drunk."

"It's not your fault. Don't worry. The lads will have words with him." The ladies continued in this vein, offering encouragement. I knew they were trying to be helpful and supportive, but nothing they said could quell my all-consuming sense of dread. A few minutes later, Adrian returned with Taff, his rage subsided.

"You're going to be okay, Julie," Taff explained. "We've had a long chat, and Shorty has promised me…haven't you, mate?"—his arm patting Adrian's shoulder affectionately—"that he's not going to hit you again."

"Thank you, Taff." I was grateful for this intervention. Adrian may break his word to me, but a promise made to a brother soldier would never be broken. I had confidence that I would be spared a beating because of this unquestionable loyalty.

Adrian and I left together, Taff escorting us down the stairs. "Remember your promise to me now, mate, no hitting." I looked back at Taff, who winked kindly and gave me a thumbs-up. It was going to be all right.

Outside in the rain, I opened my umbrella and struggled in my high heels to keep pace with Adrian, who was striding out at a swift clip. I had said enough to him this evening already, so chose to remain silent for our walk home, unless of course, he asked me a question. The only noise I heard was my shoes clicking on the pavement as I worked to keep up.

"What are you doing with that?" Adrian asked, pointing at the umbrella.

"Keeping dry. It's raining." I adopted a conciliatory tone, hoping to pacify him.

"If I'm getting wet, then you're getting wet," he said, snatching the umbrella from me and hurling it over a wall into someone's garden. I didn't protest. I just kept walking, with him following close behind. "Walk faster!" he demanded, pushing me between my shoulder blades.

"I'm trying to, Adrian. It's hard in these shoes." I didn't want him to interpret my slowness as defiance. The shoes and the tight skirt I was wearing were restricting me to short strides. "Go on, skank! Keep moving." He pushed me again, harder this time, causing me to stumble.

"Adrian, you promised Taff that you wouldn't hit me," I reminded him gently.

"I'm not hitting you. A push isn't a hit." His smug reply alerted me to the danger I was in. I decided not to speak anymore unless he required a response and to pick up the pace so that he would have fewer opportunities to touch me. His anger was increasing with each shove, which was accompanied by another insult. "Keep moving, slut!" I wished now that I had ignored his dancing with Janet, that I'd kept my thoughts to myself. All of this upset could have been averted. When was I going to learn? Another shove, another crushing insult, "Move faster, you fat-assed scrubber!" I tried to block out the sound of his voice and focus on moving forward, but with each assault, I was reminded of another from an earlier time. Like the time he removed our wedding photo from the wall and deleted my face from it using a lit cigarette before ripping the photo in two. Or the time he erupted in a rage when I questioned him about the condoms and pornographic magazines he had in his suitcase after a trip to Denmark. I was sure that he wouldn't hit me if I was wearing glasses and holding our baby, but he gently lifted the baby from my arms, placed him in his pram before carefully removing my glasses from my nose and breaking it with his fist. Or when he was taking shots at sparrows in the back garden with an air rifle and wanted a cup of tea. I took too long preparing it, so he shot me in the chest while I stood in the kitchen doorway. "It's your own fault," he told me. "I said I'd shoot you if you didn't hurry up with the tea. You should pay attention. You'll listen next time, won't you?"

Another poke in the back and another even more vile insult. I had to get away from the tirade of abuse. I had to run. Some part of me knew it was futile, but my dignity demanded it. I had to rebel in some way to maintain some semblance of self-respect. In the past, passive-aggressive acts had saved my sanity like sneaking a cigarette from his pack and crumbling it into pieces without him noticing, or adding extra hot spices to his plate before adding the curry, which we were all eating for dinner. Covert rebellion, I believed, was the only safe way. The situation now, however, received a different response.

I yanked up my tight skirt to give me a longer stride and ran. I was sober. Adrian was drunk. *Surely I can outrun him. If I can only get home, I'll be safe*, I thought foolishly. Even drunk, Adrian could outrun me. But I had already started charging down the wet street, focusing on the streetlights ahead, hearing the gasps of my breath as I inhaled and exhaled, my heels scratching the pavement, my heartbeat now a pounding drumbeat in my ears as the heavier quickening footsteps of my husband grew louder and closer. Adrian's arm stretched forward, grabbing me by the shoulder, and spun me around. "Oh no, you don't!" he yelled, clutching the front of my jacket and shoving me backward into a ditch, the buttons wrenched from the jacket still in his grasp.

Looking up, I spotted a man in jogging gear approaching as Adrian bent forward, his hands on his hips, catching his breath. "Please, please, help me!" I called out, once again relying on others to provide protection. The runner, perhaps surprised to hear a woman's voice rising up from the ground, turned his head towards me, looked into my pleading eyes, and increased his speed as he passed by the spot where I was lying. My call for help incensed Adrian, so as I scrambled to extricate myself from the muddy ditch, he set off running towards home, leaving me to fend for myself.

I arrived home a while later to find all doors locked. I was wet, dirty, tired, and defeated. I tapped lightly on the glass of the front door but got no response. Adrian was teaching me another lesson. I crept around to the back of the house to where the babysitter, Ronnie, was sleeping. Picking up a handful of anthracite by the coal bunker, I began pelting his window while calling out his name, careful not to disturb the neighbors, but to no avail. I spent a long, cold, lonely night outside with only the stars and my thoughts for company.

I felt like I had been dealt the fate of Sisyphus, who was punished by Zeus for placing Thanatos (death) temporarily in chains, destined for all eternity to push an enormous boulder up a hill only to watch it roll to the bottom where he had to start the thankless yet necessary struggle all over again and again and again. Adrian was so insecure, always putting my love and loyalty to the test. I didn't know how to impress upon him that he was loved. His treatment of me was wearing me down. True love, we are taught, is absolutely selfless, asking nothing of the beloved in return. Maybe that is why God is love. God alone is capable of perfect, unconditional love. I, in spite of all my efforts to emulate God's love, was sorely inadequate and in need of divine intervention. Maybe if Adrian was totally dependent on me for everything, he would finally see that he is loved. I would care for him tenderly and faithfully annihilating the question and the need for it once and for all. So I prayed a most fervent prayer, standing in the rain and looking up to the heavens, "Dear Lord, help me to help Adrian see that he is loved. If you could just cripple him enough so that he's confined to a wheelchair, he will see how much I care for him." In my mind, Adrian's destructive behavior was a desperate cry for help. I had only ever wanted to love. It was why we are all created. If only he could see that I wanted us to be happy together and was prepared to do anything to that end, including taking care of him when he was incapacitated, then maybe, just maybe, he could find peace. So my prayer that God put him in a wheelchair was borne out of a desire for him to know real love and, in the process, end the hurt and cruelty meted out on me. In that moment, it seemed a reasonable request.

The next morning, when Adrian opened the back door to let me in to the house, the children were watching cartoons on the TV. He made no comment about the previous night but instead asked, "Will you find my shoes? I don't know where they are."

"Where did you take them off?" I asked, trying to be helpful.

"If I knew that, I wouldn't need help finding them, would I?" He was still in an agitated state. I set about looking for the shoes I had recently bought him for his birthday and located them quickly

in the hall by the front door. "Found them!" I called out, holding
them up for him to see.

"Not those ones—my old comfy shoes," he insisted before muttering, "Never mind. I know where they are."

"Where?"

"In the fire. I threw them in there when I got home last night."

"Why did you do that?"

"I thought they were new ones you bought me." His voice was
quieter now. He had wanted to punish me and knew that destroying
the gift I had given him would hurt my feelings. There was some
irony in the fact that he only owned two pairs of shoes, and by setting
fire to the old ones by mistake, he would now have to wear the pair
I got him.

"Oh dear," was all I could think of to say.

I had a flashback to our first Christmas together when Adrian,
broke and without a cigarette, decided to spend Christmas Day sulking in bed. I tried to cheer him up by giving him the presents I had
bought for him. He was in a sullen mood, asking, "Is it useful?"
before unwrapping each gift. When it came to the *whatchamacallit*
ornament I had found, with two little figures standing each side of a
grandfather clock, the inscription on the bottom reading, "Each second of each hour of each day I love you," I considered the question
and handed it to him, saying, "Well, not useful, exactly." He got up
out of bed, which I interpreted as a good sign, relieved that he had
decided to join me for our Christmas dinner, which I had so eagerly
prepared. But instead of sitting at the table, he went over to the bin
and dropped the gift, without even unwrapping it, into the garbage.
He knew how to hurt me.

Now, still holding the shoes, I asked, "Would you like a cup of
tea?"

"Yeah," he answered listlessly.

I busied myself preparing the tea as he stood behind me in the
kitchen, his arms around my waist, his head leaning on my shoulder.
"I'm sorry, love."

"I know," was all I could muster, and all he needed to hear in
that moment. He felt forgiven. Whatever horrendous cycle we were

trapped in had come full circle. Now to begin again. I was living it but didn't have time to analyze it. I just did what I could to maintain peace, however fragile.

Apologies were often followed up with a burst of positivity and activity from Adrian in his attempt to demonstrate his desire to change. For a short while, he revealed his brighter, attentive, and unselfish side. This was the man I had fallen in love with. He played with the children, building dens in the woods with them, took them to the park, and prepared our family meals. These cherished times together were also a part of our reality. I just prayed for them to become the norm rather than the exception. At the end of these happier days, in which we had genuinely enjoyed being together, we had our most intimate conversations, the children asleep and we in bed chatting till the wee hours.

"If truth be told, I'm jealous of you, Julie," Adrian confided during one such conversation. "You get to go to confession and get your sins forgiven. Where do I go?"

"Oh, Adrian. If you are sincerely sorry, then your sins are forgiven too. Jesus died for all of us, not just the Catholics." I wanted to comfort him, not knowing he was about to test me on my beliefs.

"Well, that's easy for you to say. It's harder for me to believe it." The sadness he felt conveyed in his tone. "I am sorry, though, Julie, honestly. I know I've hurt you in the past, but I'm going to be better. I'm not hanging out with Janet and Andrew anymore, for one thing. Having them in our house was a big mistake."

"Yes, I know. You spent too much time with them afterwards too."

"Yes, it wasn't just time, though…," he was hesitating, maybe waiting for my invitation to continue.

"What else was it, Adrian?" I asked, dreading his answer, my stomach churning with anticipation.

He took a deep breath. "Well…look, I'm really sorry, okay? Please don't be mad at me. This is tough for me."

"I'm not angry at you. Just tell me what you have to tell me." I was being as kind and loving as I could but also feeling manipulated at the same time. I felt as though he was taking advantage of this temporary respite from the tension in our marriage to assuage his guilt and relying on my forgiving nature.

"Well, Andrew and I had an arrangement," he went on.

"What sort of arrangement?"

"We swapped wives," he said, his voice dropping to a whisper in the darkness.

"What? I don't understand. What did you do?" I was trying to persuade myself that I had misheard.

"Well, Andrew said I could sleep with Janet, and I said he could sleep with you. They do it all the time with other couples," he added, somehow legitimizing the practice.

"You *know* I'd never agree to that, Adrian. What were you thinking?" I was shocked at his confession. I was not a commodity, and regardless of how he treated me, I upheld my own moral code, always rejecting Andrew's and others' advances, ignorant of the sordid arrangement.

"I know. I said I'm sorry."

"So did you?"

"Did I what?"

"Did you sleep with Janet?" I was becoming exasperated.

"Yes, but I won't do it anymore, I promise." He sounded penitent.

As I lay on my back staring at the ceiling, I was trying to come to terms with this new revelation. An unwelcome image of my husband and Janet having sex had now intruded my mind.

"She's not even pretty!" I blurted.

"Well, you don't look at the mantelpiece when you're poking the fire," he said casually, by way of explanation.

"Adrian! This is not the time for that! What else? Just tell me, for goodness sake!"

"Well, Andrew was pissed off that you wouldn't cooperate, and he felt cheated."

"*He* felt cheated! How do you think I feel right now?"

"Look, Julie, I'm trying to be open with you. I want this behind me. Please don't make it more difficult than it already is. You deserve the whole truth."

"Go on." I sighed, forcing down the feelings of betrayal and hurt.

"Well, when Janet and I were having sex on their living-room floor the last time, Andy was watching, like he usually did, but this time he joined in. When I felt a rough hand groping my balls, I was out of there like a bat out of hell. I didn't even put on my trousers. I just wanted to get out of there. It was getting too weird."

"Oh, so it was because you were feeling uncomfortable that it all ended. Not because you were thinking about me and how this might hurt me?"

"No! I wanted to stop anyway. I love you, Julie, only you, honestly. I am *so, so* sorry for having hurt you like this."

"I am *extremely* hurt, Adrian. I thought we had moved past this sort of behavior." I was shocked and overwhelmed as the details of the infidelity swam around tauntingly in my head. I felt exploited as I listened, but in the spirit of reconciliation and in my attempt to show compassion, I wanted to start over.

"Can you forgive me?" he asked with what I believed was heartfelt sincerity.

"I forgive you," I said, realizing how tough it was becoming to continue to be forgiving. I witnessed in these rare private moments a vulnerable, hurt, and lost soul who struggled to find peace within himself but who didn't know how to achieve it. I didn't know how to help him, or myself either.

I learned to recognize the rhythm of our lives together. Life would be settled for a while, free from incident or drama, with another of my prayers answered, "Please, God, give me boring." Then with building tension, the only warning, whatever pain needed to find release, usually from a sense of guilt for breaking marriage vows, Adrian would start a fight, often over something mundane like my chatting over the fence with a neighbor instead of finishing the laundry, or overcooking the eggs, or taking too long to make a cup of tea—this failure, on my part, giving him permission to explode. After the release of fury, the apology, the confession, my forgiveness, the destructive cycle began again. I prayed each time for the cycle to be broken. I so wanted our marriage to be calm. But as time passed, the violence escalated, the peaceful interludes grew shorter, and I grew increasingly weary. How many is seventy times seven anyway?

"So you'll be home at two, and we'll take the boys to the park, right?" I checked, making sure Adrian remembered his promise to the children.

"Yup, 2:00 p.m.! I'll be here," he confirmed. "See you then. See you later, boys," he called out as he went off to join his pals for a lunchtime drink. Life had been incident-free for a while even though a kernel of fear had taken up residence within me. When Adrian kept his promises, I was delighted. When he didn't, I was disappointed, hurt, and angry. But I always clung to hope.

Three o'clock arrived. The boys, all in their identical outfits, were sitting on the couch like the three wise monkeys, patiently waiting. Fortunately, they didn't understand time yet, but I knew that if Adrian wasn't home in another half an hour, he wasn't going to be in any fit state to take the children out anyway.

Thirty minutes later, I announced cheerily, "Ready, boys? Let's go to the park."

"Is Daddy coming?" asked Michael.

"No, Daddy can't make it. But we'll have lots of fun anyway, won't we?" My tone was upbeat, disguising how miserable I felt. Out we set for the two-mile trek to the park, Brian holding on to the handle of the stroller as Michael and Sean squeezed into the seat designed to hold one child. We sang songs and played "I spy" to pass the time, though my mind was elsewhere, wondering what condition Adrian would be in when we got home, if he would even be there at all.

He was stretched out on the couch when we returned a few hours later, so I gave the boys their dinner and put them to bed. It didn't matter that it was still light out or that it was too early for bedtime, I had to protect the children. I had hung a dark woolen blanket over their window to persuade them that it was later than it actually was. I got away with it when they were small, but when they got older, I had to explain that the early bedtime was for their own good and pray that they believed me.

When I got back to the living room, Adrian was smoking a cigarette.

"What happened, Adrian?" I asked while in my mind predicting his answer. He had lost track of time, and then he was too drunk to come with us anyway so may as well stay and have another drink.

"I lost track of time, sorry, sorry," he slurred. "It was too late then anyway. I'll take them next weekend." He took long drags on the cigarette between sentences as he struggled to open his eyes, managing only to raise his eyebrows.

It's pointless to engage him in conversation, I thought, so I sat in the armchair and watched as his hand dropped, the cigarette still burning between his fingers, to rest on his jeans. A year before, I would have crept over to him and carefully removed the lit cigarette from his grip in an act of protectiveness. But now I was so angry with him for breaking his word to the boys that I just sat and stared as the smoke rose from the singed denim till it burned through the fabric, scorching his thigh. He slept through it. A flash of rage surged through me as I considered picking up the heavy ashtray and cracking his skull with it. I know that the blow would not only have to be on target but also powerful enough to render him unconscious. I ran the scenario through my mind. I saw myself quietly lifting the dense blue glass ashtray from the coffee table, then creeping over to the end of the couch where his head was resting, and clutching the ashtray with both hands, raising it high above my head, and slamming it down swiftly on his forehead. But my aim was off. The force of the blow was absorbed by the cushion on which Adrian was resting, with only the edge of the ashtray nicking his temple. Startled awake, he leaped up from the couch, snatched the ashtray from me, and in his fury, crashed it into my face, killing me with one swipe. I hastily abandoned the idea of revenge and instead watched the red glow of his cigarette burn through his jeans and the skin underneath smolder.

Appalled by the thoughts of violence that had just invaded my mind and even more horrified that, for a brief moment, I had considered acting on them, I determined that never again would I entertain such dangerous impulses, praying earnestly for a serene and compassionate heart.

Chapter 8

Adrian had one year left to serve in the army before transitioning to "civvy street." "The army is tough on families," he said. "We'll be much better off out of it, you'll see. A fresh start, that's what we need—away from all the destructive influences." He was skilled at projecting blame. I agreed. We were both ready for a change of direction. We were sent to the garrison town of Tidworth, Hampshire, for the last twelve months of military service prior to starting a new chapter of life as a civilian family. Twelve months in a dull, dreary place with few amenities that many in our transient community considered a "punishment posting." The one redeeming aspect of the location was that we were now only about an hour and a half's drive from my parents.

The army offered to assist us in securing a home and employment for Adrian. We had no savings, so buying a house was impossible; but fortunately, there were plenty of places in the United Kingdom with council housing, a form of social housing provided by local government agencies. We began our search for a home and were disappointed to discover long waiting lists for accommodation in many of the towns close to family where we had hoped to settle. Eventually, we received information about the Development Board for Rural Wales, a relatively new organization which was actively marketing the region around Newtown in Powys, hoping to reverse the trend of depopulation. The board had taken measures for economic and social development through house building, job creation, development of industrial sites and factory construction—spreading its net over the whole of Great Britain. We had no links to Wales but were persuaded by the glossy leaflets that we should at least explore the possibility of moving there. Adrian, with his heavy goods driving license, would also find work easily.

We knew that wherever we ended up would be our forever home. We also understood that it was unlikely, given our social and economic status, that we would ever be able to afford own our own house. Newtown, a small market town nestled in a valley surrounded by verdant hills, seemed ideal. We were surprised to be given our pick of six houses in different parts of the town, from which we chose a house on the newest estate, Vaynor, on the banks of the River Severn. It was a delightful meandering walk into the small market town, following the course of the river away from the noise of the traffic.

We both felt hopeful as we settled into a different lifestyle outside of the army and one we planned on being more stable. Adrian was working for a moving company, the children were enrolled in the St. Mary's Catholic School for a free education, and I had joined the parish. I was grateful to be welcomed by the small church community, especially the women, and was soon elected the president of the Union of Catholic Mothers, affording me a night out once a month as my presence was required to run the meetings. Adrian found it more difficult than me to adjust. He needed the camaraderie of friends too, and whereas I found it in my church community, he cultivated it in the pubs.

Our routine was simple. I stayed at home and looked after the children and the house while Adrian worked, brought home the paycheck, and gave me a housekeeping allowance, and then met up with his friends in the pub, where I was not invited. He made new friends, many of whom I never met; and I made new friends, all of whom knew Adrian from either the children's school or Holy Spirit Catholic Church.

Other than Sunday Mass, the mothers' meetings were my social life. Once in a while, Adrian and I would go out for a Chinese or Indian meal, but that was rare. I also connected with some of the mothers who walked to and from the school each day, glad of their companionship. Soon it became our routine to meet for coffee on Tuesdays after morning Mass. Tuesday was market day, when the town was abuzz with activity, the various stalls selling everything from hoover bags to jellied eels lining the sides of High Street, Broad Street, and Market Hall, as people from the town and the country, united by one purpose, went in search of bargains. The cheeky calls of the stall holders provided the soundtrack as they vied for the attention of everyone passing by. "All right, darlin'? Get your fruits and veggies here. Look at that ripe pair of melons—the best you'll find."

"Fresh fish! Fresh fish! Come on, lovely. Lotsa protein in fish. Gotta keep your man fed well. Needs protein for stamina to keep up with you, beautiful! How's about a nice piece of cod for supper? No? You're breakin' my heart, girl. Breakin' my heart."

The cafes and pubs were crammed with people for whom market day was their one chance to catch up on one another's news and the latest gossip. Evans Café on Broad Street became my other church, providing nourishment in the form of the stickiest, plumpest, tastiest Chelsea buns and comforting cups of warm frothy coffee as we ladies shared our stories and buoyed one another up with laughter.

Before long, I was pregnant again, heralding yet another new beginning, but tragically the baby died at fourteen weeks. It had been my first miscarriage. We were both devastated, never before even considering the possibility of losing a child.

December 1985
"To My Baby, Unborn" by Julie Long

From the moment of conception you were there.

Though I was not aware you were there.
When I knew of your existence, I offered no resistance,
But joyously declared, "How I love you."

From that moment onwards it was you.
Every thought, every word was of you.
Deeper feelings than affection, for the babe I was expecting,
Showered down with the words, "How I love you."

As the flower that never blossoms is still a flower,
So were you, my frailest Darling, still my child.
And though never will I hold you or look into your
eyes,
I'll embrace your memory.
How I love you.

When I finally arrive at Heaven's gate
And my invitation to enter in, I'll await.
As our Father comes to meet me, you'll be with Him
there to greet me,
Re-echoing my words, "How I love you."

By the April 17, 1986, due date, however, the sadness of the loss, though not erased, was eased by the knowledge that I was carrying another precious life. We hesitated before announcing the pregnancy out of fear of jinxing ourselves, but we needn't have worried; the child was robust and healthy. We already had three boys and hoped, maybe, that this child would be a girl but, without access to ultrasounds, had to wait until its miraculous entrance into the world to find out.

Adrian was still eager to name one of our children. He chose the name Amy if it was a girl, and I chose Adrian if it was a boy, another testament to my optimism about our relationship. I was so relieved that Adrian, now out of the army, would be with me at the birth. I had opted to refuse any anesthetic except gas and air, during the subsequent labors and deliveries after the frighteningly disturbing experience of Brian's birth. Of course, I always regretted that decision when in the late stages of labor, pleading with the nurses to give me something, anything, to ease the pain. I was told, "Sorry, love, it's too late."

The baby was on its way. By the fourth one, I knew the signs, choosing to stay at home as long as tolerable before heading into the hospital. Labor stretched over two days, and I was told a transfer to another hospital in Shrewsbury was scheduled if baby hadn't arrived by 2:30 p.m. I was tired, fed up, and miserable and didn't want to go to anywhere! So I crossed my ankles stubbornly and told the nurses, "I've changed my mind." They laughed at me.

"It's not funny! I can't do this anymore," I whined. Of course, saying "I can't go on" but then going on anyway, seemed to be my pattern. This was no different. A few minutes later, I was asking the doctor, "Who is it?" having instructed him to reveal the name of the child, not the sex, when it was born. "It's Aaaaay"—oh, why did we both pick a name beginning with the same letter, I thought, as the doctor dragged out the name—"meeee!" A girl! We have a girl! We were thrilled. After so many years of blue, I was looking forward to buying pink.

We agreed that our family was now complete, so Adrian had a vasectomy. I was grateful that he assumed the responsibility. Life was improving.

Then he lost his job. I didn't know if it was just bad luck or if it had something to do with his drinking, but whatever the reason, the fact remained, we were now relying on the dole until another job was found.

Adrian now had less money and more time, a dangerous combination. He reduced the housekeeping amount he gave me each week, switched from packets of cigarettes to rolling tobacco, and still went to the pub.

On such a meager income, I became creative with everything from meal planning to acquiring school uniforms. We each owned only one pair of shoes, which were replaced only when holes appeared in the soles. Then after putting on the new shoes while in the shop, I placed the worn ones in the empty shoebox and handed them to the cashier to discard. I trained the children to find money in the street and then turned it into a game so that we could buy bread. We discovered that people are careless with coins, especially at bus stops, fiddling through the change in their purses or pockets as the bus approaches, leaving behind any pennies that drop to the ground as they board the bus. At the checkout in shops too, people fumble with loose change and, not wanting to hold up the queue or appear too miserly, for the sake of a penny, ignore the renegade coins that have slipped through their fingers.

So with the pantry empty and the only thing in the fridge a half-full bottle of ketchup, the boys would be sent out for twenty minutes with the challenge to bring back the most money. They never disappointed. With the handful of coins they recovered, I would walk over to the neighborhood shop and, after counting the slices in the loaves on the shelf, decide which gave most value for money. If the boys had a bumper haul, we also bought margarine. I became good pals with the milkman, who also delivered yoghurt and who allowed me to skip a week of payments once in a while, settling the debt when I could. At school, the children, now entitled to free lunches, were encouraged to ask for seconds so that their tummies would be filled there, in case our cupboard was bare. I loitered around the fruit and veggie stall at the markets on Tuesdays, waiting for the prices to be reduced for a quick sale. One sensitive trader anticipated my visits and always had a variety of produce "spare" at the end of the day for a token sum. I volunteered at church festivals and jumble sales where I got to rummage through the donated secondhand clothes before the doors opened to the public. I bought raffle tickets when a food hamper was the prize. And since maintaining a veneer of normalcy and routine was so important, I still met the ladies in Evans Café for our weekly frothy coffee and Chelsea buns, and Adrian still went to the pub.

Our first year there, I bought five tickets at the school Christmas bazaar, wisely putting the children's names on them. Michael won a hamper crammed full of sweet seasonal treats and excitedly stepped forward to pick up his prize to cheers and loud applause. Then Sean's ticket was called. Beaming broadly, he marched up to receive the second food hamper that was almost as big as he was, containing an array of cheeses, crackers, and our Christmas dinner—an enormous ham. Adults shot expectant glances in my direction while holding their applause. Surely, I wasn't going to claim *both* prizes? The proper and expected thing to do was to hand one of the prizes back and let someone else have a chance, but my name was not on the tickets. They were not my hampers to refuse.

I was so relieved that Christmas dinner had been secured but anxious that Santa's visit had not. There was insufficient money to pay our bills and feed us, so I was desperate to figure out how to provide presents for the boys. Amy was too little to understand or care, so I didn't have to worry about her as she entertained herself playing happily with Tupperware containers and wooden spoons. The boys, however, were swept up in all the pre-Christmas hype, excitedly drooling over the latest Star Wars toys enticingly displayed in the shop windows. They believed the lyrics of the songs that promote good behavior in children so guaranteeing Santa's descent down the chimney. I realized what a terrible message that is and what a burden it is on parents who love their children but cannot prove it in a consumerist society that equates material success with goodness and poverty with badness. My children were obedient, kind, generous, and poor. I was determined to remind them of their innate goodness by ensuring that their eyes lit up with wonder and joy on Christmas morning too.

I went to the library and checked the "For Sale" ads in the paper. I also let friends know that I was looking for bargains and was delighted when one of them then sold me her son's old toys as she made room for his Christmas bounty. I was excited to have something to place under the tree for the children to open, hoping it wouldn't matter that everything was secondhand.

On Christmas Eve, Amy was stricken with a rasping cough. I needed to get her some Snufflebabe, a salve to rub on her chest. I checked my purse and saw that I had just enough money to buy garbage bags and the medicine if I walked into town instead of catching the bus. So I headed off on foot, leaving the children at home with Adrian, very conscious of the time.

While standing in the queue at Woolworth's, the garbage bags and jar of ointment in my hands, I glanced into the shopping carts of other last-minute shoppers at the colorful wrapping paper, boxes of chocolates, stuffed teddy bears, and all sorts of twinkling and glittering goodies. The parish priest, Father Carson, was ahead of me in line. I waved at him and wished him, "Happy Christmas, Father!" When I got outside, he was standing by the exit door, so we chatted for a few minutes before he handed me an envelope.

"Some parishioners, who want to remain anonymous, asked me to give this to a family I think could use it and wish them a happy Christmas. I want you to have it. Happy Christmas."

"Oh my goodness! Thank you, Father. Please thank them. This is so kind." I had no idea what was in the envelope; all I knew was that the compassion of others was being showered on my family.

"I will. God bless." His words reminded me that I was blessed.

I scooted across the street to Evans' Café where I slid into a booth and, holding the envelope under the tabletop, opened it surreptitiously. Inside were six crisp new ten-pound notes. Oh my! What amazing generosity! Affirming love coursed through me, touching every part of my heart and soul, filling me with confidence in the beauty and goodness of life. Someone out there had chosen to be kind. Father Carson hadn't known to which family he would give the money; it had been an act of serendipity that we bumped into each other. How lucky for us. I wanted to share the all-consuming joy. I wanted someone else, a stranger, to feel what I was feeling in that moment. I decided to share the money with a person whom I thought looked in need. I took ten pounds from the envelope and tucked the rest safely in my pocket as I headed to the corner of the street and stood under the town clock. Adrian would be expecting me home soon, having calculated how long it takes to walk both ways. I gauged that I had about half an hour before he would be concerned, and as I could now afford to take the bus home, I had enough time to find someone with whom to share the love.

I knew that the best way to judge if someone is poor is to check their shoes. So I gazed down at the feet of passersby, impressed and a little frustrated at how many well-heeled folk were out and about on Christmas Eve. Then I spotted him. A bearded scruffily dressed man in his thirties, his knitted red hat pulled down over his long matted hair, his grubby coat secured with string and on his feet a pair of black rubber wellies. I moved towards him, smiling, "Excuse me, I've just had some good fortune, and I'd like to share it with you." I presented him with the ten-pound note.

"What?" he said, looking at me suspiciously.

"I've had some good luck, and I want you to share in it," I explained.

His eyes were scrutinizing mine as I spoke. I smiled when he took the money from me, but the smile was eclipsed when he held the note up to the light and asked, "Is it real?"

"Yes, yes, it's real. I just received it myself," I assured him.

"Is this a prank? It's not funny, you know." He sounded annoyed.

"Oh gosh, no. I wouldn't play a joke like that. I just want to share my good fortune," I insisted.

He handed back the money. "No thanks, it could be fake." I watched as he walked away and felt sad that he didn't trust me. Being kind to strangers was proving harder than I expected. But I persevered. The rain had started to fall as I stepped in front of another shabbily shod younger man and repeated the script, "Excuse me, I've just had some good fortune, and I'd like to share it with you."

A loud, startling "Aaaagghh!" was his response as he backed away from me in terror. Why was this being so difficult? I was just trying to be kind. I hated that I had frightened him. This wasn't what I had planned at all. I guess people aren't used to women on street corners handing out cash. I decided that a change of location might be needed. I moved away from the corner and stood outside Boots, the chemist. I also changed my approach, knowing that time was moving quickly, and I had to get home soon. I spied an old lady coming towards me carrying two light plastic grocery bags with very little in them. By now I was desperate to get rid of the money and get home. "Please, you've got to help me," I pleaded, rushing towards her.

"Oh dear, what's the matter, pet?" She was concerned.

"I've been given some money, and all I want is for someone to share the joy, and no one will take it. I've asked two people already and they both refused it. Will you please take it?" I said, plaintively, offering her the now soggy note.

"Oh, that's very kind, dear, but I couldn't take your money," she said, declining politely.

"Don't tell me you can't use another ten pounds at Christmas," I coaxed. "How much is in your purse?" I was being as assertive as I could.

"Well...," she drew out a little change purse, and as she opened it, I leaned in to see a couple of lonely pennies. I shoved the ten-pound note in to keep them company before she could protest.

"Now you can treat yourself to something nice for Christmas," I announced victoriously.

I had finally achieved my goal. I had shared the joy. I looked up, expecting to witness her beaming face, but instead she was crying. "No, no! Don't cry! Please, don't cry. I didn't want to make you cry." I had underestimated how tough this self-imposed assignment would be. I had raised the suspicion of one man, terrified another, and now bullied an old lady into surrender—all while trying to be loving.

"This is the nicest thing anyone has ever done for me," she sobbed. "I've got grown children who don't care about me, who don't visit me, my husband's in a wheelchair...," I stood listening as she shared some of her painful story, crying with her in the rain. I had found the right person, for whom ten pounds would buy a few extras but who needed more than money to know that there is kindness in the world.

I hurried to the shoe shop with the remaining cash and bought five pairs of shoes. This time, I wanted to keep the boxes, which I cheerfully and proudly balanced over each arm as I headed to the bus stop.

"Where the hell have you been?" bellowed Adrian as I skipped happily into the living room. His anger bouncing off me left me unscathed. The afternoon had been a spiritually uplifting experience that lingered, filling me with indescribable bliss. I knew now that there was a divinely created place within that was protected from harm and that dispelled fear. Nothing Adrian, or anyone, could say or do to me would ever damage that sacred space. It was empowering to have experienced love in such a tangible and life-affirming way.

"I've been shopping! Happy Christmas, everybody!" I dropped the shoe boxes on the floor and handed Adrian his pair as the children, squealing with happiness, tumbled over each other to find the pair that belonged to them. "Let me tell you a Christmas story," I invited, once they had put on their new shoes, a story that would be repeated year after year. "A story about kindness and love."

Chapter 9

Heading into 1987, our financial circumstances were dire. Fortunately, our rent was paid for us through the welfare system, so at least we had shelter, and we also received the government-issued weekly family allowance that provides a few extra pounds for each child. We switched from paying our electricity bill quarterly to having a coin-operated meter installed. We did the same with the television, feeding the Telebank with fifty-pence pieces for a few hours of TV and becoming very selective in our viewing.

For almost a year, Adrian had drifted from one temporary job to another, sometimes driving taxis or picking potatoes or doing odd jobs for friends and neighbors for cash that went into his pocket. At one point, he even applied to the prison service, but to no avail. Being out of work for so long created an additional strain on our marriage. His need to control intensified, affecting not only how I spent the money but also how I spent my time. He became jealous of any time I was away from him, needing to know exactly where I was going, with whom I was talking, and how long an errand would take. He even timed the journey into town and assigned me a time limit for any trips I made. I could no longer stop and chat casually with friends when our paths crossed and had to dash in and out of the shops quickly before rushing home, always conscious of the clock ticking. On one occasion, I arrived home breathless after rushing to complete the shopping, to once again be ambushed by him as he waited behind the front door to thump me because I had exceeded the time limit. He could still surprise me.

To supplement our meager income, I took on a couple of house-cleaning jobs where Amy, who was still a baby, could come with me.

When I visited Mrs. Leonard, who had multiple sclerosis, they kept each other company for the hour as I vacuumed and dusted, Amy in her stroller and Mrs. Leonard in her wheelchair.

I also took in ironing to do when the children were in bed, which came earlier and earlier for the children as I tried to protect them by limiting their exposure to Adrian's volatility. Most of the time, the boys weren't tired enough for sleep, so would talk and play together quietly in their room. That was fine until Adrian, in one of his erratic moods, threatened to harm them. "You better go up there and shut those kids up before I go up and knock their blocks off!" he warned.

"Okay, I'll have a word with them," I said, switching off the iron. "They'll settle down."

"Better be more than a bloody word, or else I'll go up to them and sort them out, and there'll be hell to pay."

Knowing what violence he is capable of, I dashed into the kitchen and got the wooden spoon from the drawer, remembering my mother brandishing one just like it when I was a child. I had sworn that corporal punishment would have no place in my home, yet I also knew that if my children didn't believe I would smack them, they would be in much graver danger from their father.

"What's going on here? Get into bed!" I shouted in my sternest voice as I opened the door, making sure it was loud enough for Adrian to hear me, as three little bodies leaped from the floor with fright, scrambled into their beds, and cowered under their covers.

"You're supposed to be sleeping!" I continued, bringing the wooden spoon down heavily on each bed, just close enough to their feet to make them draw them up, but not close enough to actually touch them. My heart was reaching out to them as they apologized, "Sorry, Mum, sorry."

"Never mind you're sorry. Now GO TO SLEEP!" One last yell and one last smack on each bed with the wooden spoon to satisfy Adrian and ensure they wouldn't make any further noise.

"Listen, boys," I said in a whisper, "you've got to be quiet, please. I don't want your dad to be angry with you. Please do as I say. This is for your own good." They didn't answer me. They were being good boys and staying quiet. I hated myself for becoming the shrew that caused them to suffer, but I didn't know how to protect them any other way in that moment. I returned to the neighbor's ironing and prayed for peace in my home.

Even with the few extra pounds I earned each week, we often ran short of money. "Have you any cash?" Adrian asked one day as he rifled through my purse and pockets, looking for the price of a packet of cigarettes.

"What's this?" he asked, holding the scrunched-up Cadbury's chocolate wrapper he had just pulled from my jacket pocket.

"I had a bar of chocolate," I explained.

"That's right, steal from our children so you can stuff your face." He was angry, but not because I had treated myself to some candy.

"Don't be ridiculous! I make sure the kids are fed properly." I was annoyed that he was accusing me of selfishness. But I also knew it was pointless to argue.

"If you were more careful with money instead of spending it on rubbish, we wouldn't be in this mess," he scolded, obviously considering his own spending choices essential. "I need some fags. Go next door and borrow some money. Tell them we'll give it back next week."

"Why don't you go, Adrian? I don't like asking." In fact, I hated asking to borrow money, even though we always paid it back.

"No, you go. Tell them it's for bread. They like you. They'll lend it to you." I felt embarrassed and humiliated as I stood on my neighbor's doorstep, begging, knowing well what would happen if I didn't.

The following week, when Adrian gave me the week's housekeeping money, he had reduced the amount. "Adrian, are you sure this is right?" I queried.

"Yes, it's right."

"Um, I don't think so. It's a bit short." I was hesitant to challenge him, but I needed every penny.

"You obviously had money to spare last week," was his explanation.

"I never have money to spare, Adrian." I was puzzled by his response.

"What do you call the money you spend on coffee with your friend Theresa and the others every week then? And the chocolate I found in your pocket? Well, you can forget that now. No more Evans coffee mornings. Do you hear me? You're not wasting my money on that stuff anymore."

"Adrian, that's not fair," I responded, not expecting him to change his mind but needing to say it regardless.

"Fair? What's fair? Life's not fair. Get used to it." The conversation was over.

He reduced the allowance again a few weeks later after we had bought a cheap carpet remnant in the market that would fit our living room. I was grateful for his generosity, not realizing that he planned on recouping the money the following week. I would have made do with the bare floors if I had known he would deduct the cost from the housekeeping money.

Fortunately, we were supported in part by family, who, now that we were back in England, wanted to see us and were eager to meet baby Amy. These visits always lifted our spirits temporarily. Den and Jenny arrived in March during a snowstorm, staying long enough to have some tea and share the cake they had brought then, slipping me some cash as they left. Den, also a smoker, slipped Adrian some money too, understanding the addiction.

My mother, who had recently passed her driving test at the age of fifty-four, was now keen to celebrate her newfound freedom by paying us regular visits. My dad, who didn't drive, came a couple of times but was mostly left at home to "mind the house." The trip from Pucklechurch to Newtown took close to four hours, but that distance did not daunt my mother as she imagined she was competing the Monaco Grand Prix in her bright-yellow Yugo Zastava. She relished the independence driving afforded, always arriving laden down with sweets for the children and groceries for me, sometimes unannounced.

One Saturday morning, I woke to one of the boys shouting excitedly, "Granny's here! Granny's here!" I jumped out of bed, scrambling to get dressed, panic surging through me.

"Quick, boys, help me tidy up!" I knew that Mam would be doing the white-glove test once she came into the house. She couldn't help herself. "Here, Michael, quickly! Put this in the cupboard in your bedroom," I urged, handing him a black garbage bag full of the clean laundry still waiting to be ironed I had just stuffed into it. She wouldn't understand that ironing someone else's clothes had priority. "Brian, go out and see if you can help Granny with her things." What I really wanted to say was, *Stall Granny while I clean up. Stall her!* I open the windows to dispel the stale smoke, seeing the familiar yellow car parked out front. Then a final plumping of the cushions on the couch as I kicked the stray toys into the corner of the room, hoping that would be enough to pass inspection.

"Hello, Mam! This is a nice surprise. You should have told us you were coming," I said cheerfully, just a little out of breath.

"Aw, Julie, the smell of smoke. It's awful." She put down the groceries on the table and wrapped her arms around the boys, who had rushed at her for a hug. "Hello, boys, are you happy to see me?"

"Yes, Granny. We're always happy to see you," Brian was stating the truth. The children were precious to her, and they knew it from her tight and tender hugs and, of course, the presents.

"I know, I know, I'll open more windows," I said apologetically. "Would you like a cup of tea, Mam? I'll put the kettle on." She was busy handing out sweets to the boys.

"Yes, but not in a mug. Put it in one of those nice cups I bought you," referring to her previous visit when, much to her disdain, I presented her tea in an earthenware mug. "What will people think?" Before she went home that time, she went into the town and brought back a set of bone china tea cups and saucers for future use.

"There's an apple tart in the bag somewhere. We can have a slice of that too, and there's some scones as well, and *real* butter, not that cheap margarine you buy." Apparently, my use of margarine was bordering on sinful.

"Oh, thank you. I love butter. Margarine's just cheaper, that's all." I busied myself making the tea and asked about the journey as Adrian, quietly wrapping his arms around her from behind, surprised her with a friendly squeeze.

"Hello, Mum!" he chirped into her ear.

"Oh, Adrian! You startled me!" She was laughing, her hand over her heart. "How are you? Have you found another job yet?" She loved Adrian and was always wanting the best for him, knowing him to be a bit uncouth, but not knowing him as well as I did. I was happy that they got along, deliberately keeping my parents ignorant of the abuse. I didn't want them harboring resentment for him when I had forgiven him. *It's better that they don't know*, was my reasoning. It had been easier to hide the truth from them when we were in the army.

"Nah, no job yet. Not from lack of trying, though. There's not much work about," Adrian explained.

"Well, don't lose hope. Something's sure to turn up. You have so much to offer. Look at all the work you've done for us in our house. Surely someone needs a handyman with your talents? There's got to be others out there who need your help." She was being true to character, building him up with encouragement. "I'll keep praying for you."

"Yeah, let's hope so. Thanks," he replied, less optimistically.

Mam's prayers were answered. A few months later, Adrian joined many of the other Newtown folk who worked in the Laura Ashley factory in Carno. He would never look for work again.

By this time, we had been living in Newtown for three years and had just been moved from our three-bedroom house to the four-bedroom one right next door, 150 Lon Dolafon. Our family was complete, and I felt comfortable knowing we would live in this town for the rest of our lives. Adrian was still dependent on alcohol and had become increasingly possessive as I forged strong connections with people in the community, getting angry if I was not home to take a phone call from him in the middle of the day. His anxiety over my making new friends extended to him choosing the clothes I wore each day, wanting me to look frumpy and dowdy, unless we were out together. He once came home unexpectedly to discover I was wearing a different blouse than the one he had put out for me that morning. He immediately accused me of having a man in the house, and it wasn't until I pulled the vomit-stained garment from the laundry basket that he accepted that a change of clothes was necessary due to Amy throwing up on my shoulder after a feed. His insecurity also drove him to be jealous of the female friends I had, accusing us of being lesbians. His need to control every single aspect of my life, forcing me to be totally dependent on him, was stifling. I was so grateful for the strong connections I was making outside of the home. It was these friendships that sustained me and bolstered my faith in the innate goodness of life and people.

One of those friends was Derek, an ex-army pal of Adrian's who had also ended up in Newtown after his military service. He arrived on our doorstep late one night in great distress, his shirt ripped and bloodied. Adrian opened the door as I waited on the landing to see who it was before running down the stairs. "Come in. Come in. What's happened, mate? Are you all right?" asked Adrian, ushering Derek into the hallway.

"She went for me with the frying pan. I was just watching *Children of the Corn*, minding my own business," he explained. His marriage had been unstable for some time, he and his wife, twelve years his senior, living separately under the same roof. "She just flipped and flew at me, scratching and clawing. I'd just come home with a Chinese takeaway and was settling in to watch the film. She's crazy. I can't go back there."

"You should have smacked her one, mate," Adrian stated.

But Derek, who had often shared his views on violence against women, even in self-defense, refused to hit back. I was filled with admiration and compassion. "No, I don't hit women," he said simply.

So Derek moved in with us until he could figure out what to do next, the irony not lost on me. Here was my husband offering shelter to a victim of domestic violence, the loyalty and trust formed between men in the forces being proven now. I soon discovered that Derek was a stellar human being, a man of integrity, compassion, and strength who, for a while, took on the post of my guardian angel.

Once again, I felt safe. Derek, though Adrian's friend, had respect for me and strong protective instincts. I thoroughly enjoyed his company the six months he lived in our home before leaving for a new life in Australia on January 16, 1988.

Chapter 10

It was August when I received a phone call from my mother that, though I didn't realize it at the time, was the prelude to a radical divergence in my life.

"Hello, Julie?"

"Hello, Mam, how are you?"

She ignored my question, asking one of her own instead, her voice light and cheery. "Guess who's here?"

I was thinking, what an odd way to begin a phone call, but played along anyway. "Um, I don't know. Granny?"

"Nope!"

"Um, Aunty Mai?"

"Nope!" She was enjoying this little guessing game she'd started. "Try again," she coaxed, a hint of mischief in her tone.

"Oh, I give up, Mam. Who's there?" I could have gone through a list of relatives for another five minutes, but curiosity won out. There was a pause; then a familiar voice from my past greeted me.

"Hello, Julie. How are you?" That distinctive American accent could not be disguised.

"Father Bill? Oh my goodness! Father Bill? What are you doing there?" My heart was racing as I pelted him with questions. "It's been almost twenty years! How are you?"

"Oh, I'm fine. I'm in Wales for a sabbatical and have a few days off, so came to visit your parents. It's great to hear your voice, Julie."

"I'd know your voice anywhere. You sound exactly the same." I couldn't believe that we were talking to each other after such a long time.

"Your mom wants a word. Hope to speak with you again soon. Here she is." I didn't have a chance to say any more as my mother reclaimed the phone.

"So I was thinking that maybe I could bring Father Bill to see you on Thursday for the day," she suggested. "Would that be okay?"

"Yes, yes! Of course. I want to see him." My mind had already jumped ahead to our meeting. I was going to see my friend. A feeling of bliss enveloped me as I breathed out a deep sigh. I could hardly believe it.

"That's what we'll do then. We'll come in the afternoon and stay for dinner. Does that work?"

"You can get here earlier if you like. Yes, that's perfect. Thank you."

"See you on Thursday then. I'll call if plans change."

"Okay. Thursday, it is. See you then. God Bless." I put the phone down and started planning and praying that nothing would interfere with our reunion—not sickness, not a flat tire, not a hurricane, not Adrian. "Please, Lord, let this happen."

I glanced around the living room with its worn and cheap mismatched furniture and felt ashamed. At least it was carpeted. I had three days before Father Bill stepped into my home, and I was desperate to create a good impression. The dining room, with its bare gray tiles and dull walls, reminded me of a prison cell in its grimness, not at all inviting. I would need to be creative to brighten it up.

When my friend Carol popped in for a cup of tea later that day, Derek and I were discussing what could be done to improve the look of the place.

"It's so bleak, Derek. I really want it to look nice on Thursday."

"Well, it's lucky that I'm off today, so I can paint the dining room for you," he offered.

"Oh, can you? Really? That would be fantastic." He was so kind. I was happy that at least there would be a fresh coat of paint to add a bit of cheer. "There may be some old paint in the shed," I said, trying to be helpful.

"No, that won't work. There won't be enough in there anyway."

"Maybe we can paint one wall. I don't have any money for new paint." I was still thinking creatively.

"I'll buy some new. You can take it off my rent," he joked. I didn't know what rental arrangement he had with Adrian, though he often gave me money for food when Adrian wasn't around.

"Aw, thank you. I am so grateful, Derek. You've no idea."

"I've got some Laura Ashley fabric at home—forget-me-not design with little blue flowers on a white background that I could make you some curtains with if you want," Carol suggested, joining in the excitement.

"Oh, Carol. Could you? Thank you." I was being reminded of the goodness of the people in my life. "Will you have enough time?"

"Yes, plenty of time. I'll go and get my tape measure now, and I'll start on them tonight."

"That's settled then. I'll paint the walls blue to match the material, and I'll paint the trim with white gloss," Derek added.

And so my two dear friends got busy, putting aside their own plans while they helped me prepare for my special guest. Now all that was left to do was to tell Adrian of the impending visit. I greeted him with the news when he came home from work.

"We're going to have a visitor on Thursday, Adrian! I'm so excited."

"Who's coming?"

"Well, my mother is coming, and she's bringing Father Bill with her. I'm so happy that you get to meet him finally." Adrian knew of Father Bill because of the picture of him displayed on the wall with all the other family photos. He had also seen a photo of him on my parents' mantelpiece and heard his name mentioned in the list of people who had asked for prayers when we said the family rosary.

"How long are they staying?" he asked.

"Just for dinner. Oh, I can't wait." I was giddy with joy, which I hoped would be contagious but instead caused some consternation.

"Well, calm down. There's no need to get your knickers in a twist," he said gruffly. I knew by the tone of his response that I would have to manage my emotions, be more subdued, if I wanted Adrian to be accepting of my friend.

The next two days were a mixture of frantic activity, joyful anticipation, and brewing tension as I busied myself cleaning the house, shopping for groceries, and monitoring Adrian's moodiness. I was in a quandary about what to cook Father Bill for dinner and, as I was on a tight budget, knew that whatever I prepared had to be both classy and cheap. In my judgement, any meal containing potatoes was peasant food, not fancy enough to offer to someone so important. I eventually decided to use Sue Strachan's spaghetti bolognese recipe, which I had successfully cooked before, confident that it would be enjoyed by everyone. I was sure that my mother would bring an elaborate cake for dessert, but just in case, I bought some ice cream that could be served with tinned mandarin oranges. The menu was set.

The dining room was coming together well too. Derek not only painted the walls blue and the trim white but went on to spruce up the chairs with a coat of gloss to match. When Carol came to hang the curtains, she brought with her new covers she had made for all the chair seats, a tablecloth, a runner for the side board, and mats on which to rest my potted plants—all in the same forget-me-not fabric. I felt that the room, which had undergone such a transformation, should be on the front page of *Homes & Gardens* or some other illustrious magazine.

Adrian grew increasingly petulant because of the flurry of activity and attention given to Father Bill's visit. But I, now impervious to his sulking and happily distracted from the usual routine, was not allowing anything or anyone to impede my joy.

Thursday finally arrived. My emotions were in flux. On the one hand, I was bordering on euphoria to be in the company of my friend again; and on the other, I was anxious, worrying about Adrian's reaction. I didn't understand what I was experiencing, but I did acknowledge this encounter as a gift of grace.

Our house was tucked into a corner, with most of the windows facing the back, so I sent the boys outside to wait and watch for Granny's car coming into the cul-de-sac while I fussed over minutiae inside. I had made the meat sauce in advance and had it on a low simmer on the stove. The dining-room table had been set, the tea tray assembled with Mam's fine china cups, and the pot for the pasta was filled with salted water, ready for when we needed it. I had done all I could to guarantee more time to chat with Father Bill. Adrian was pottering about in the back garden, keeping busy too.

"They're here. They're here!" called the boys, rushing into the hall and back out again just as quickly. I picked Amy up from the floor where she was playing and, balancing her on my hip, stood in the front doorway, waiting. A surge of happiness swept over me as I recalled the last time I had seen Father Bill as a child. Then I watched as a man wearing a baseball cap stepped out of my mother's car. *Oh, he's gotten old,* I thought to myself as he adjusted the cap, revealing his balding and graying head. He was fifty-three.

Smiling, he approached the house, my mother following behind with the boys, who, like energetic puppies, were scampering around her feet.

"Hello, Father Bill! Welcome," I called out as he came closer.

"Hello, Julie. How marvelous to see you again after such a long time. Almost twenty years." He leaned in and kissed my cheek. "This must be Amy. What a doll."

"Come in, please. Come in. I can't tell you how good it is to see you." I beamed.

"It's great to see you too. You look terrific. Four children. Wow! Last time I saw you, you were just a little girl."

"Yes, I've kept busy," I said, beaming, as I guided him into the living room. "Please, have a seat. I'll make some tea."

"I've sat long enough in the car, thanks," he said, moving towards the french windows to look out at the back garden.

By now, the children and Mam had joined us, so while introductions were going on, I went into the kitchen. I could see Adrian through the kitchen window and signaled to him that I was making some tea and that he should come in and say hello.

"Where are they then?" he asked as he came through the back door.

"In the living room. Please be friendly, Adrian. He's a really nice man," I urged.

I brought the tea and biscuits into the room, which was abuzz with chatter as the children made a new friend. Adrian, having introduced himself and dispatched with the formalities, picked up his tea, excused himself, and went back outside to continue working on whatever project he had started that morning, only resurfacing at dinnertime.

The afternoon passed pleasantly and far too quickly. The children, soon bored with the adults and having told Father Bill all the jokes they knew, went outside to play while Mam, Father Bill, and I chatted about his time in Britain, about Mam's recent successful surgery for the removal of a brain tumor, her hopes to retire to Ireland, and about family life in general.

"So Dad couldn't come?" I asked slightly teasingly, knowing that Dad, who had taken early retirement, hardly ever travelled long distances in the car with Mam, whose unique driving style made him extremely nervous.

"No, we're selling a carpet, and he had to stay home in case someone came to look at it," Mam said, explaining his absence. Though I knew the truth that Dad's constant backseat driving greatly irked her, and on this trip, she wanted to enjoy Father Bill's company without the distraction of my father's hand constantly reaching for the steering wheel, alerting her to every pedestrian, cyclist, tractor, and bend in the road.

"Aw, thank you for bringing Father Bill to see us, Mam," I said a while later as she rinsed out the cups in the kitchen sink before we served up dinner. "I'm so happy it worked out."

"He asked if he could see you, and I don't mind the journey," she replied. "Besides, I got to have a nice long chat with him on the way here. He's one man I would leave your father for," she added as an afterthought.

"Mam! Wash your mouth out. He's a priest!" I said, trying to sound horrified but chuckling when she winked at me mischievously.

I knocked on the kitchen window to let Adrian know that dinner was ready. A few minutes later, the rest of us sat around the table in my new blue-and-white paradise, waiting for him to join us.

"Father Bill, will you lead us in grace before meals?" asked Mam.

"My pleasure. Shall we wait for Adrian first?" He asked.

"Let's give him a minute, Father," I said. "He shouldn't be long. Brian, go and see what's keeping your dad." Brian scooted out of his chair and returned a few seconds later.

"He'll be here in a minute. He said to start without him."

"All right then, let's eat before it goes cold. Father?" Mam nudged.

Grace was offered, and I served up the bolognese.

"One of my favorite dishes," said Father Bill, rubbing his hand together in delight as I passed him his plate. I felt pleased that he was looking forward to it so much. I had done something well.

When Adrian joined us, I passed the bowls of pasta and meat sauce down to him.

"What's this shit?" he exclaimed, silencing the lively chatter and directing all eyes to focus on him.

I was mortified. Things had been going so well, and now he was embarrassing me in front of company. "It's spaghetti bolognese—you know, like Sue makes." I was trying to sound helpful, eager to restore the cheerful mood that had permeated the room only seconds before.

He filled his plate with the pasta and sullenly ignored the conversations that had resumed around the table.

"Father Bill, would you like some more?" I offered a short while later, seeing that his plate was almost empty.

"Oh, indeed. It's delicious—thank you." I reached over to pick up the bowl of pasta, but Adrian grabbed it first. I watched in dismay as he scooped its contents onto his plate before handing me the empty bowl.

"Oh dear, it looks like it's all gone," he said, staring at me coldly. "You obviously didn't make enough."

"Oh, that's okay," said Father Bill cheerfully, trying to relieve the tension. "It's important to leave room for dessert."

But it was not okay! If one of my children had behaved so rudely, I would have punished them for having bad manners. I wanted to cry but held back the tears. I was good at that. Instead, I remained silent and busied myself clearing the empty dishes from the table.

The day had been a joyful interlude up until Adrian's outburst. I had wanted my friend to leave my home with only good memories and positive energy, but now all he would recall is my husband's ignorance.

A little while later, as Mam prepared to leave, I chatted on the doorstep with Father Bill, "How long are you going to be in Britain?"

"Well, I have a thirty-day silent retreat to do, but I do get a little break in the middle of that, so I'm planning on coming back to your Mom and Dad's in November for a weekend. Then I go back to the States in December, just before Christmas."

"Thirty days of silence? Oh my goodness, that's got to be tough," I replied.

"It's not too bad. But I do look forward to the break. We can get mail while on retreat, you know. Perhaps you can drop me a line or two?"

I was overjoyed by the invitation. "Oh, definitely. I can't wait to pick up our correspondence again." I was already feeling happier at the prospect of renewing our connection through writing and receiving letters.

"Okay. Are you ready, Father?" my mother asked. "We'd better head out, or it will be midnight before we get home."

"Yes, I'm all set. Bye, kids. It's been great to meet you. Hopefully I'll see you again sometime." The boys gathered around to distribute hugs. It was clear from their energy that they had enjoyed themselves. "Say goodbye to your dad for me."

"Okay, we will. Bye, Father Bill. Bye, Granny. See you soon."

"Bye, Mam. Thanks again for coming. I've had a lovely time," I said, hugging her.

"Bye, love. Thanks for dinner. Bye, boys! Bye, Adrian." The last goodbye was called out in a louder and more scolding tone, more for my benefit than Adrian's, who probably couldn't hear her anyway. "I'll be in the car, Father."

"Be right there, Ena," Father Bill replied as he put both arms around me in a tender embrace and whispered quietly in my ear, "Nobody takes this shit." Then he was gone.

Once they were out of sight, I stood there for a few minutes looking at the empty street, his voice still echoing in my ears, "Nobody takes this shit."

He said *shit*. That good priest said *shit*. I was so distracted by his choice of word that I ignored the content of the message. It was quite a while before I gave myself permission to say *shit* too.

My life took on a new energy as I looked forward to writing and receiving letters once again. I reveled in the fact that there was someone who could create such a serene feeling of calm and peace within me, reminding me of the nature of love. I felt resurrected.

I wanted to see him at least once more before he returned to the United States, so began planning for us to visit my parents in November to coincide with his visit to them. Adrian loved long drives, especially when we were meeting up with our families. We could include a quick visit to some of his siblings while we were there. I decided to be extra frugal between now and November so that I could offer to pay for the petrol, anticipating one of the obstacles Adrian might present.

As it turned out, my parents moved to Ireland before November. Mam's poor health prevented her from continuing her work in the prison, which she had taken on after my dad's retirement; and since they could no longer live in prison housing, they were transferred temporarily into government housing while they made plans to move. My brothers Sean and Stephen had taken on the quest of finding them a house in their homeland of Ireland and discovered a beautiful, quaint isolated cottage surrounded by hills in Garryglass, Tipperary, that needed some attention and which was to become Mam and Dad's favorite place on earth. With a generous loan from a donor who wanted to remain anonymous but was later revealed to be our old parish priest, Father Wilbur Boswell, they were able to buy it outright for just twelve thousand pounds. So Father Bill's planned visit to see them could not happen.

St. Beuno's
Spiritual Exercises Centre,
St. Asaph, Clwyd,
North Wales LL17 OAS
Telephone: Community 0745 583 444
October 4, 1987

Dear Ena and Danny,

We begin our 30 day retreat Thursday eve-
ning so I thought I better write to let you know
everything goes well so far. First a wee bit of bad
news—they advised us on one of the opening talks to
not go to Ireland during the post retreat break. The
main problem is the final break day is on a <u>Sunday</u>
(November 15) when transportation in England
is bad and in Ireland is terrible. As we can't get
started until a bit late on Thursday (Nov. 12)
there would be a chance I couldn't make it to your
house by Thursday evening which means I'd only
have Friday to see you. So unless a miracle happens
(somebody with a car from here going to Ireland) I'll
probably not be able to visit you—ah well—this is a
good excuse to come over to Ireland next summer (or
a summer soon). Julie's town is only 2 ½ hours away
by train so maybe I can visit her for a day.

What is the news on the house—do you have
a definite moving day? I certainly wish you all the
luck with the move—I'm sure God will be with you
all the way. Don't be afraid to write—they do let us
get mail on our break days (about 1 every 8 days).

The remainder of my stay is Scotland was very
enjoyable. I took a 3 day trip (only planned on 2)
to the Highlands. Started out leaving at 4:40 a.m.
from Edinburgh, then missing a 5:40 am train
from Glasgow to Fort William—had to wait until
<u>9:40 AM.</u> This changed plans but worked out for

the best. I stayed in a Catholic Church rectory in Fort William overnight—even met the Bishop of Oban. Had some good meals and a "dram" or two. Climbed half way up Ben Nevis—said the parish Mass at 10:15 next morning, then was driven to Kyle of Lockalsh by a parish priest from there— west by ferry to the Isle of Skye where I got a room and walked for miles along the beautiful coast. I took a train back to Edinburgh the next day, stopping about 3 ½ hours in Inverness—got back to Edinburgh about 10 p.m.

St. Beuno's is still very much as I remembered it—with a few improvements—much better food, rugs, fire doors and new thermo-pane windows. The Valley of the Clwyd is as gorgeous as ever. I've done much walking and climbing (to about the top of Mt. Snowdon—it got so misty up there we couldn't stay on the trail). It was fun and even the mist was impressive. My knee just about gave out prior to the climb but luckily I did bring some injection material from the states. An Irish nun who is a nurse in Dublin is on the retreat and she gave me the shot. Incidentally she is from Tuam (her name is Myra Fahy). She asked me your maiden name, Ena— was it McGrath? She said she lived on one of the major streets out of town. She has a rather strange Irish accent.

In all there are 36 in our retreat group—18 men and 18 women. Five Anglicans are in the group.

Incidentally, tell your priest in Bristol (Fr. Mc) that I did stay with his friend in Fort William (Fr. McNeill—he is a character).

Again—thank you for the super hospitality and just for being good friends—and especially for the continuing prayers. Please keep them up

*and I'll remember you in a special way during the
retreat. If by some miracle I can get to Ireland I
will phone you—otherwise I'll see you when I see
you (God willing).*

Love,
Bill.

When I received a phone call from Father Bill, asking if he
could visit us instead, I was thrilled at the prospect of spending more
time in his company. My only challenge would be earning Adrian's
approval for the visit. I decided to say yes immediately and then
worry later about how to persuade Adrian to allow it.

St. Beuno's
Spiritual Exercises Centre,
St. Asaph, Clwyd,
North Wales LL17 OAS
Telephone: Community 0745 583 444
October 17ᵗʰ, 1987

Dear Julie,
    *This is our first "break" day in our retreat (we
can talk!—get mail and send some) so I thought I'd
get a note off to you. If it's still ok (I mentioned it
on the phone) I'd love to visit you during our inter-
term break (Nov 12–Nov 15)—after 33 days of
praying and silence I would love some conversation
and playing with the kids! I had originally hoped
to go to Ireland to stay with your mum and dad
but transportation there and back (especially back
on a Sunday) seems impossible. Believe it or not I
can actually get a ride (via car) to Newtown and
back (from a nice Anglican lady in our group) who
lives just across the border only about 15 miles from
Newtown. So first—can you put up with me for
3 days? (Thursday noon to Sunday afternoon –and*

do you have room?—a couch will do). Otherwise,
maybe a B and B nearby? Don't worry about the
extra food cost—I'll take care of it—30 pounds
sound ok? I'm almost saving that much on train fare!

If you think (or Adrian thinks) this might be
too much of a burden—or you have other plans
during that time—feel free to say so. If it is ok—
please send directions to your house (I don't think I
can remember the way). We would be coming from
the north on 483 I imagine.

Keep me in your prayers these days (5 hours a
day of praying is a long time). I'll remember all of
you in mine.

Love,
Fr. Bill

P.S. I've forgotten your postal code.

Adrian did not welcome the idea of another visit from Father
Bill, still bothered by how happy I seemed when he was here with
Mam. I knew that three days of Adrian sulking in the back garden
would be disastrous, so I had to come up with a plan to ensure Father
Bill had a pleasant stay. My parents would need someone to help
them settle into their new home. Someone with handyman skills
who could put in cupboards, lay carpet, and paint walls. Someone
like Adrian. It was time to call my mother.

"Hello, Mam, Julie here. I'm just wondering if you could use
Adrian's help moving in to your new house?"

"Oh, Julie, that would be a great help. Your dad's hopeless, as
you know. He started putting up the anaglypta wallpaper inside out,
can you believe it?"

"Poor Dad. Do-it-yourself was never his strong suit, was it?
Well, I'm not promising anything, Mam, but I'll ask Adrian and see
if he can get some time off work."

"Tell him I'll pay for his fare on the train and the ferry, if that
helps." She was understandably keen to be settled in her home,

almost as keen as I was to find somewhere else for Adrian to be when Father Bill came to see us.

I asked Adrian if he would consider making the trip to Ireland to help my parents. He agreed and managed to get a week off beginning November 14, the day before Father Bill would be leaving our house to return to St. Beuno's. I was hopeful that once Adrian and Father Bill had a couple of days together, they would connect in a positive way, and Adrian would see why I valued his friendship.

St. Beuno's
Spiritual Exercises Centre,
St. Asaph, Clwyd,
North Wales LL17 0AS
Telephone: Community 0745 583 444

October 29th, 1987

Dear Julie,

Thank you, for the prompt reply. I will be looking forward to seeing you on Nov. 12th (probably around 10:30 or 11:00 am). Do you want me to bring a pillow by any chance?—Sometimes these are scarce. If by chance you do want me to bring one—drop a line, otherwise I won't.

I'm sure you enjoyed the weekend in Bristol though all the kids on the trains must be a handful. Your mother's party was a super one I'm sure. Sorry I had to miss it.

You asked about the retreat being rather demanding—it is!! I do my best at the 5 hours of prayer—it's really the rest of the time that can go by slowly (nobody talks—even at meals). So you can see why I'm looking forward to 3 days of action and noise. Aside from visiting Newtown and maybe a walk or two there is really nothing special I wanted to do. Some good chats will be superb.

I stopped to pet a horse the other day and I asked him "How 'ya doing?"—(I always talk to the animals—they seldom answer). This one did—he promptly passed gas for 10 long seconds. As I was feeling somewhat the same way, I said "So do I" and went on. Another St. Francis of Assisi!

See you soon—love to Adrian and the children.

Love,

Bill.

Father Bill arrived on Thursday afternoon as planned. The boys welcomed him like an old friend, and I was reminded of his visit to my parents' home when I was a child. They offered to take him down to see the river while I prepared dinner.

"Has he arrived then?" asked Adrian when he came in from work.

"Yes. The boys have taken him down to the river. They should be back soon."

"Oh, poor him! You've got him babysitting already." He sounded sympathetic.

"He wanted to go." I was relieved that we were chatting comfortably, Adrian's mood more relaxed as he looked forward to his week off in Ireland. "Maybe, after work tomorrow evening, you'll take Father Bill out for a drink. Just the two of you. It'll be a chance for you to get to know him better," I suggested.

"Yeah, could do that, I s'pose."

"Great! Dinner won't be long." I was encouraged by his receptive mood.

The rest of the evening went well, with Derek, Adrian, and Father Bill engaging in casual chatter while I assumed the role of attentive hostess by blending into the background and leaving them to their conversation, knowing that I would have my time later.

On Friday, the children and I took Father Bill into the town along the river path, stopping in the ruined churchyard on the way. We had a peaceful, pleasant time, chatting and renewing our friendship. I felt entirely at ease and recovered a deep-rooted serenity that had evaded me for so long. Oh, how I yearned for this peace in my marriage too.

Later, Adrian and Father Bill headed off to the Flying Shuttle pub, only a two-minute walk from our house. I conjured images of the two of them propped up at the bar, pints of beer in hand, shooting the breeze like two old chums, discussing topics that hold no interest for women. It was the perfect scenario in my mind—two men whom I loved also growing to love each other.

I waited up for them to get home so that I could make sure Father Bill was comfortable before I went to bed. They both seemed to be in a good humor, and I was glad to see them getting along so well.

"Did you have a nice time, Adrian?" I asked a few minutes later when we were lying in bed.

"Yeah, it was all right. He seems okay." This was tantamount to him saying, "He could be my best friend."

"Well, thank you for taking him out. Thank you, I *really* appreciate it."

"Well, you can show your appreciation right now," he said as he climbed on top of me to claim his conjugal rights and mark his territory. He knew that Father Bill was in the next room, and he wanted him to hear us, so his grunting and heaving and swearing was deliberately amplified. I repeatedly begged him, in desperate whispers, "Stop. Please, stop!" He wouldn't. He didn't. I wept.

All my hopes and feelings of contentment from earlier in the day had been obliterated in five minutes of his possessive rage.

I felt acutely embarrassed making breakfast for Father Bill the next morning, the excruciating memory of Adrian's abhorrent behavior reverberating like a clanging gong between us. Words were redundant. So as Father Bill sipped on his coffee, I thirstily drank in the healing grace from his gaze, our hearts crying out to each other in sacred silence.

Adrian left for the train station about an hour later, "You're to go nowhere with Father Bill on your own, do you hear me? Derek can go with you," he ordered as he hugged me goodbye.

"That's fine. I don't have anywhere to go anyway," I surrendered. "Safe travels. Say hello to Mam and Dad for me." *Just leave, just leave, just leave me in peace*, I willed.

Then as if a dark and heavy shroud had been lifted, the mood in the house brightened instantly as the promise of a day of togetherness unfolded. A day that I would forever cherish.

"So I'm your appointed chaperone, am I?" Derek said cheekily as we discussed where we might take Bill for his last evening.

"Yes, I hope you don't mind," I said apologetically.

"Well, it's not on, is it?" he teased. "I'll feel like a gooseberry or a spare part or a third wheel or whatever, unless…"

"Unless what?" I was keen to hear his solution.

"Well, unless you ask Theresa to join us, and then I won't feel so awkward."

"What a terrific idea. Let me call her right away and see if she wants to come. I'll sort out a babysitter too while I'm at it."

And so it was that my dear friends Theresa, Derek, Father Bill, and I went out on the town. The time moved so swiftly. I asked Derek, who knew the pubs in the town much better than me, to select the most refined pub for our outing. We ended up in the Elephant and Castle, where a brawl broke out, with one drunken soccer fan attacking another with a broken bottle. We were not doing so well impressing our guest! Then all too soon, last orders was called, but I wasn't ready for the evening to end.

"Derek, is there anywhere else we can go that stays open later?" I pleaded.

"Well, there's always Crystals."

"Oh, good! Let's go there then." I had decided. Anything to stretch out the night. It would mean a couple more hours enjoying each other's company. Derek and Theresa grinned at each other and then at me, amused. They weren't so sure about Crystals: a disco that attracted a strange blend of young lusty lads who, after a night of drinking, were looking to get lucky and "pull a bird" and girls who fought them off because they simply loved to dance.

What was I thinking? Crystals was heaving with young sweaty bodies gyrating to music, the decibel level of which was guaranteed to cause deafness within minutes. Father Bill looked stunned, so we ushered him to a table in the farthest corner of the room and abandoned all thought of continuing a conversation as our voices were swallowed up in the din. There was nothing left to do but dance, so Theresa and I took our places on the floor. Father Bill, meanwhile, graciously endured the ever-increasing *thud, thud, thud* of the music, probably offering it all up for the souls in purgatory. Every time I waved at him, he waved back, smiling. Eventually, much to my dismay, it was time for the last dance, signaling the end of our outing. I plopped down next to Father Bill on the red velvet seat to watch as young couples spilled onto the floor to dance to the only slow dance we had heard all evening: "Lady in Red" by Chris de Burgh.

Father Bill leaned in towards me and, mustering all the breath in his lungs, yelled in my ear, "Would you like to dance, Julie?"

"Yes, please," I yelled back as I took his hand and led him down to join the sweating mass of humanity.

All sense of time, place, occasion, and other people dissolved as we felt the touch of each other's arms. Nothing in the world mattered anymore except this moment of transcendent bliss. Nothing could ever steal this memory from us, no matter what had happened in the past or what was to come in the future, recalling this moment would remind us that love exists and is part of us.

Too soon the music ended, leaving us feeling connected and secure. Derek, unsuccessful in finding us a taxi, led us home along the narrow river path, now in darkness, our only light the moon. As he escorted Theresa home, I was aware that he had probably fibbed about the taxi, allowing Father Bill and I just a while more to talk without a chaperone. I was grateful to him for his sensitivity, which allowed for stories and secrets to be shared in the darkness.

When we arrived home, Amy was crying and needed feeding. I sat on the couch next to Father Bill, my legs tucked under me, ready to soothe Amy, who was still being breastfed.

"Um, I should leave you in peace," he said, offering to give us some privacy. "I'll be off to bed then."

"Oh, no need. Please stay. I'm not embarrassed if you're not."
I knew that that if he left the room now, the next time I saw him
would be to say goodbye, and I was not ready yet to do that.

"Okay, if it really won't bother you?" It was half question and
half statement.

"Oh, it never bothers me. I've breastfed all the children, whenever they needed feeding and wherever I happen to be at the time.
Even in church," I added with a smile.

"In church?"

"Yes, at Michael's baptism. He was screaming the place down,
so I fed him. No one minded."

He reached out his hand and stroked the length of my foot
gently with his index finger. The brief gesture of intimacy poignant
in its simplicity.

Amy's tummy was full, and she was content—but not a bit
sleepy. For once, I was grateful to be kept up as she gave me an excuse
to spend more time with Father Bill. For the next few hours, we chatted easily about life and spirituality, philosophy and love, while she
amused herself by pulling books off the bookcase and then trying to
put them back on the shelf again.

There's something reverent about late-night conversations.
The late hour somehow inviting a deeper honesty and vulnerability
as we both opened our hearts to each other, revealing our broken-
ness in need of healing. I spoke of the challenges of being in a troubled marriage, sharing details entrusted to no one else. He listened
sympathetically.

"I knew from my first visit that this is an unhealthy relationship," Father Bill confided. "It was patently obvious in the way
Adrian spoke to you. You deserve to be treated with love, attention,
and respect, Julie. Everyone does."

"Thank you. I know it in my heart, but it's so difficult to insist
on it." My response sounded feeble.

"When I met you as a little girl, there was a light in you that is
still there but is being gradually extinguished. I would hate for that to
happen. You have so much love to offer the world." He was encouraging me to stand up for myself, his words the oxygen I needed.

So I breathed in deeply, hoping I could gain strength from his life affirming message.

When it was time to sleep, my heart was lighter, stronger, and filled with renewed courage. I felt cherished and loved by this good man, who was so concerned for my happiness.

Sunday was not welcome. Sunday was the day of Father Bill's departure. I was filled with a deep gratitude mingled with a sense of real peace as we all prayed at Mass together. Later, as once again I had to say goodbye, I was overcome with sadness, wondering if I would ever see him again. I maintained a brave exterior, wishing him well, promising to write, and thanking him for his friendship, but inside I was crippled by a sense of loss at his going. As his friend Irene, who had come to pick him up, reversed the car out of the cul-de-sac, she observed, "That woman is in love with you."

I could hold in the tears no longer, collapsing on my stoop as he disappeared from view. My heart was speaking to me. When would I listen?

> *St. Beuno's*
> *Spiritual Exercises Centre,*
> *St. Asaph, Clwyd,*
> *North Wales LL17 OAS*
> *Telephone: Community 0745 583 444*
> *November 16, 1987/*

> *Dearest Julie,*
> *Again, let me thank you so very much for the four marvelous (almost mystical!) days with you and the children. The pub, disco, and walk home along the river, plus our talk while Amy played and fed will <u>always</u> remain among my most treasured memories. I was so proud of just being seen with you I almost burst with joy—I was really getting some envious looks at the dance—and no wonder. You were indeed the most beautiful woman there— with a beauty that is not only external but also from*

within—a rare combination that is seldom, if ever, to be found.

As I said on the phone, leaving you in a state of unhappiness, was one of the hardest things I ever did. I wished I could have bundled you and the kids up and transported you to a world where you could find someone who would <u>treasure</u> you as you deserve to be. But we'll have to leave it in the care of God (who <u>certainly</u> can handle it better than I!). Not only can handle it, but <u>will</u> take care of it.

I'm enclosing 40 pounds (a Xmas present!) for you to do with as <u>you</u> please—maybe a high chair for Amy? It would certainly make you less tired at meals. If you can find a used one cheaper, buy yourself something—you deserve it.

In closing, I guess I'll give you a far-Eastern greeting, "NAMASTE!" which means something like, "I greet the Divinity in you." Believe me, in your eyes and whole being, the Divinity is <u>marvelously</u> present. You were as valuable an experience to me as the 30 day retreat!

Don't forget if you get to that stage where the Divinity is being <u>beaten</u> down in you or the children—LEAVE! FOR GOOD!! If you need advice, help, or money, the priest in your parish will be glad to help—I also can help a bit so feel free to write me. From what you said, you'd actually have pretty good grounds to <u>ANNUL</u> the marriage if you ever chose to take that route.

<u>*A final Christmas prayer*</u>—

Jesus' arms to hold you,
Jesus' feet to lead you,
Jesus' voice to call you,
Jesus' heart to love you,

Jesus' hand to bless you,
Jesus' grace to keep you,
Jesus' mother to comfort you.
Jesus' foster father to <u>protect</u> you,
May <u>all</u> these blessings be granted you!

*I will remember you and pray for you all the days of my life—and I will deeply count on your prayers. Thank you for sharing and allowing me to share with you. Yours will be a unique and truly beautiful relationship for me **<u>forever.</u>***

With deep love and affection,
Bill

150 Lon Dolafon,
Vaynor, Newtown,
Powys, SY16 1QY
Nov 17ᵗʰ 1987

Dear Father Bill,
Thank you for your beautiful letter. I'm sure I got far more from you than I could give. My life has changed since your visit. I have a much clearer picture of how my life should be and it's thanks to you.
I am so grateful to you for caring—you make loving so easy and joyous.
Since I was a little girl I've loved you—now even more. I'm not saying that because of my unhappy marriage—if I was in a superbly happy marriage my feelings for you would be just the same. Do believe me.
You are a wonderful, gentle person and there's always room for you in my heart.

I hope you will turn to me in times of trouble. I'm quite sympathetic you know. I've had a few problems myself! It does help to share especially with someone who really loves you.

Thank you for being such a dear friend to me—you are so special.

God bless you always.

Julie xx

Strolling along sequestered path
Near river rushing, never pausing,
Wending unwavering toward embracing sea
November moon for company.

You and I love's flame rekindled,
Tread lingering footsteps and reminisce,
While night's dark veil draws close about us
Honesty urges unburdening souls,
And secrets yield.

Then melancholy vanquished by music,
More than mere melody,
While somnolently we sit side by side
Minds mingling in harmony.

You touch my foot tenderly with healing hands.
My heart weeps without shedding tears,
Finding solace in kind, kindred spirit,
Urging time be still...,
But time unrelenting races on.

In answer to prayer supplication
My lord chose you to comfort me.
You brought me calm compassion and serenity,
Gentle man, I love you.

Since your departure, music and memories remain.
Now during solitary moments my tears flow free
   again.
Each tear a precious jewel adding sparkle to the foam,
As they join the rushing river on its eager journey
   home.

So, as you cross the ocean and catch a glimmering
   light,
You'll know it was a tear that was shed for you this
   night.
Not tears of sorrow, but of joy, in gratitude for loving
   me.
Prompted by thoughts of you which still remaining,
Never leave me,
Never leave me.

Dear Fr. Bill,
   All my love, Julie

Nov 18, 1987

Dearest Julie,
   I never expected such a prompt reply but I
will treasure both your note and the poem all the
days of my life—and will turn to them often for
consolation.
   My four days with you (especially the memo-
rably evening and morning!) have once again raised
my spirits and trust in a God who chose to create
such a wondrously beautiful person such as you. You
are pure and simply a JOY.
   I have shared a bit of your problems with some of
our group who are psychologists and marriage coun-

selors. Their unanimous opinion was for you to leave
for good as quickly as possible. Knowing you, I know
you'll give him another (and yet another) chance, but
please, *draw the line and stick to it. I worry for you,*
and the children (especially Amy). In any event, feel
confident of God's immense love for you.

I'll try to phone you early Friday (maybe
Thursday) evening to see what the doctor had to say.

Take good care of yourself, Julie, I have loved,
love. And will love you always. My very best to
Brian, Michael, Sean, and Amy. My prayers are
certainly with you.

Bill

P.S. Thank Derek again for simply being such a nice
person. I wish him all the success in the world.

THE QUESTION
And so we two came where the rest have come
To where each dreamed, each drew, the other home
From all distractions to the other's breast,
Where each had found, each was, the wild bird's
    nest.
For that we came, and knew that we must know
THE THING WE KNEW OF BUT WE DID NOT KNOW.

We said there, what if this were now no more
Than a faint shade of what we dreamed before?
If love should here find little joy or more,
And done, it were as if it were not done,
Would we not love still? What if none can know
THE THING WE KNOW OF BUT WE DO NOT KNOW?

For we know nothing but that, long ago,
We learnt to love God whom we cannot know.
I touch your eyelids that one day must close,

145

Your lips as perishable as a rose:
And say that all must fade, before we know
THE THING WE KNOW OF BUT WE DO NOT KNOW.
F. T. PRINCE

> *Somehow Julie this lovely poem reminds me of*
> *us. I will love you forever in a unique and special way.*
>
> *Bill.*

With our correspondence resumed, I was happy. I felt invincible knowing that I was genuinely loved. It was a pure, holy, and grace-filled message brought to me through Father Bill and affirming the love of God for all of us. If I could experience such joy from this friendship, then how much greater is God's love for me? I felt inspired to be even more loving with my friends and my family, wanting to be an example of love, knowing now that love, once shared, only increases; it does not diminish.

I was not expecting to see Father Bill again. It had been almost twenty years since our last encounter, but it didn't matter. I knew now I was loved, and that seemed enough. But when Father Bill called and asked if there was any chance I could get to London before he left to return to Cincinnati in a few weeks, I felt a surge of longing and promised him I would do my best to get there.

It was going to be tough to get away. Adrian actively interfered with my independence and monitored practically every movement I made, so getting permission to spend a weekend in London was going to be impossible. I decided to buck tradition by *not* asking for permission and simply telling him that I was going. Before I did that, though, I had to ensure that every logistical issue regarding childcare had been resolved. I explained to my neighbors and friends, Isla and Rob, whose children were pals with the boys, that I would need a babysitter for a weekend in December. They offered to have the boys at their house, across the street from ours, for the entire time I'd be gone. Theresa generously offered to have Amy. I was so relieved that the children would be taken care of. That was one worry dispelled.

Next, I called my sister Edel, a married policewoman in London, to ask if I could stay with her for a couple of nights. She and her husband, Tom, were happy to host my visit. Lastly, I knew that I would have to wean fourteen-month-old Amy from the breast, which was her main source of nourishment. That needed to be started now as I had less than four weeks to get it accomplished. I was determined that I would see Father Bill one more time. I felt empowered, courageous, and confident as I made secure plans that Adrian could not destroy.

November 20th, 1987

Dear Julie,

Great to talk to you again last night and find out nothing serious reported at doctor.

On the chance that Irene_is driving home tomorrow or day after, Sunday (22nd Nov) and Mon return, I will call you today if things work out (here's hoping you get this on Sat.)

Anyway, we still can have Dec 19–20, I hope. I arrive in London on Friday, Dec 18 at 13.47 Euston Station and leave for airport sometime Monday morning, Dec. 21. I'll be staying at our Farm Street Church in Mayfair (Berkeley Square) and I'll be able to meet you or whatever. You set up plans. I'd love to spend a day in London with you—we could see British Museum, National Gallery, Victoria and Albert, or whatever you would like.

If you could let me know what days you would come and return (make it trains if possible) say about 10 days or 2 weeks ahead, I probably could buy your tickets here and charge them on Visa card—then send them to you. If not, just buy them and I'll give you the money.

*One way or another, looking forward to seeing
you. Say hello to Adrian, and the kids and Derek.*

*Love,
Bill*

Adrian was now home from Ireland. He had been very helpful to my parents, who had appreciated all the improvements he was able to achieve in the few days he spent there. While he was gone, I too had undergone a transformation, now feeling so much more confident in myself. Still, I had some nervousness about mentioning my desire to go to London and had practiced the conversation I would have with him about it over and over while looking at my reflection in the bathroom mirror, hoping for a favorable response.

"Here's the housekeeping for this week," said Adrian, handing me a rolled-up wad of cash after having popped into the pub for a "quick drink" on his way home.

"Oh, thanks," I said, shoving it into my pocket.

"Aren't you going to count it?"

"Um, no, should I?" I asked, slightly concerned.

"Well, you might want to see how much you've got since I've taken out the money I spent on your friend Father Bill at the pub," he goaded.

"Oh, Adrian, I thought you were treating him to a pint. You didn't say you were going to charge me." This conversation was not going well. I was growing more anxious knowing that I wanted to broach the topic of my visit to London, so chose to let the money discussion drop. "Well, fair enough," I replied, wanting to reduce his irritation.

As I handed him a cup of tea a few minutes later, I said, "Oh, by the way, I'm going to London for a couple of days in December. I'll be staying with Edel and Tom." I tried to make it sound like I was just popping next door to feed the cat.

"What do mean 'oh, by the way'? When did you start telling me what will be happening?"

"It's just an expression. I wanted to let you know that I'll be gone for a couple of days and staying at Edel's."

"It's about time your bloody sister came here for a visit instead of you swanning off to see her all the time," he said, irritated.

"I hardly ever go to see her. Besides, I'm not going to see *her*," I had hoped to equivocate, but it wasn't working. I had to be honest. "I'm just staying with her while I say goodbye to Father Bill before he goes back to America for good."

"Well, you can forget that! It *won't* be happening." He was already fuming, his face reddening with rage.

"I am going. I've already arranged everything," I said bravely, though my heart was pounding with anxiety. *Please, please, God, help me*, I prayed silently.

"Oh no, you're not! I'll call Social Services and tell them you've abandoned your kids. They'll take them from you then. See how you like that!" he shouted, slamming his fist on the kitchen counter.

"Adrian, shhh, please. Don't wake the children. You're being unreasonable. I'm only going for the weekend." I was sticking to my plan and speaking as calmly as I could.

"I'm being unreasonable? You cheeky cow! You're *not* going! I'm not looking after the kids. If you go, then I'll report you." He was desperate to keep me here.

"I already have a babysitter. Isla and Rob are going to have them while I'm gone. You don't have to worry."

"I'll burn the house down! See how you like that. It'll be your fault for leaving. You'd let your kids suffer for your selfishness, would you?"

"Adrian, I'm not hurting the children, and I'm not leaving. I'm just going to see my friend off." It was pointless to continue the argument. He was furious and unrelenting in his demand that I cancel my plans.

"Bloody right, you're not leaving. You take one step out that door, and you'll be sorry. Just wait."

I didn't answer, feeling helpless in the face of his wrath. I would have to think of another way to approach him so that he would accept that I was going to London. On that decision, I was not deterred.

For the remainder of the month, before the scheduled trip, I suffered Adrian's apoplectic rages, which only made me more determined to go ahead with it. In the past, he would frighten me into submission, often with threats to the safety of our children. I knew he was capable of erratic violence but also knew that the children were in very safe hands with Isla and Rob. But somehow, now that I'd experienced real love, I was prepared to tolerate and absorb the pain of his fury, both physical and emotional, as he repeatedly beat me whenever I received a phone call from Father Bill; on one occasion, ripping the phone out of the wall when he came home and found me in the middle of a conversation with him. But in spite of it all, my mind was made up. He was not going to prevent me from seeing Father Bill again. The violence was escalating, and I was enduring it for now, unaware that Father Bill had alerted my parents to the abuse in a letter.

November 21st 1987

Dear Ena and Danny,
I'm truly sorry to have missed visiting you but with Adrian going to your home and me going to Julie's—things evened out. I had a fantastic (if tiring!!) time with Julie and the children. I did have one night out at the local pub with Adrian. The most spectacular evening/morning was Sat/Sun. Julie got a babysitter so Derek, she and I walked into town to go to a peaceful pub! A brawl started nearby (glass broken over a head—not really a brawl!) so Derek said let's leave and go across the street. This turned out to be a nice disco which turned VERY LOUD as evening wore on. I had fun watching though I did get one dance in (2nd from last) when they finally played a slow one. Because we couldn't get a taxi at 12:30 AM we walked back home (nice night)—I admire Julie the trip both ways in high heels. When back home, the babysitter's mother and her dog showed up to escort babysitter home—Derek went part way. Anyway, Amy woke up and stayed up

'til almost 5am so I sat up with Julie talking. She talked for over two hours about her marriage— mostly of course, about Adrian. I hope things work out but barring a miracle or Adrian getting some serious professional help (which he won't) I have grave doubts. She probably (certainly!) should have left him long ago. I told her story to some nuns and priests here who are professional psychologists and/ or marriage counsellors. They unanimously agreed with me. In fact, if Julie could prove that Adrian didn't tell her so many vital things about him before the marriage, she could have gotten an annulment (maybe still can for all I know!) He really is quite a bit psychologically off base—especially in his domi- nation tendencies—this combined with a streak of violence plus alcoholism could lead to real disaster. I know the problem for Julie is where to go and how to survive, but if necessary, she could. Let's indeed pray that maybe with a bit more pay, Adrian will improve, but as I said, it will take a miracle. So if she ever does leave again please give her the support she'll need and make it for good. She is a fantastic woman (as she was a fantastic little girl!). There is an Indian greeting "NAMASTE"—meaning "I salute the Divinity in you," I have never met any per- son in my life where the Divinity shone through more clearly than in Julie. As the local priest after Mass that Sunday said about her, "Why any man in England would give his right arm to have her." How she managed to raise such lovely children, I'll never know—or I guess I do know. With Amy keep- ing Julie awake so much, I really do worry about her health. In any event—as I said before, let's pray a lot (as I'm sure you do already).

I heard about your moving problems—bad luck does seem to dog you. I hope you can sue the movers or at least get your money back. I saw the material Julie bought for you—I'm sure it will look pretty in the house.

Less than four weeks to go here. Julie mentioned that she will go up to Edel's that last weekend when I'll be in London so I'm thankful I'll see her one more time. The course has been profitable and is moving fast now that the 30 day retreat is over. We have many Irish in our group—I love to listen to those accents. Like a lullaby.

I'll write again or phone you before I leave.

Much love,
(Thanks again for the wonderful
stay in Bristol)   Bill

Dec 3, 1987

Dear Ena and Danny,

Letters from Ireland take almost as long to get here as ones from the US. With the postal strike, goodness only knows how long this will take getting back to you.

A few more thoughts about Adrian. Julie has mentioned two more "awful" scenes with him <u>after</u> he came back. Both times he had been drinking. After the liquor wears off, he admits his personality change, but the question is will he admit he is an alcoholic—and more importantly <u>do</u> something about it. That would be your 1st miracle! Until he takes that step, it will be a **<u>sad</u>** marriage (for Julie) indeed. He senses Julie is "different" and originally blamed it on her good friends but I guess has figured out by now it was me to blame. I hope I've given her the courage to stand up to him and simply draw the line—otherwise she is going to regress into

*a frightened shell and end up as a battered house-
wife. As he both opens her mail (if he gets it first)
and searches her belongings for other plus listens in
on the extension on phone calls, that will make any
further encouragement from me rather difficult. So
here's leaving it up to you. Maybe he isn't a hopeless case but he is the nearest thing to it I've <u>ever</u>
come across. Your prayers will have to be substantial!
'Tis great Julie can always count on you. Her continued simple goodness is truly awe-inspiring. God
certainly must love her <u>immensely</u> but I'm also sure
wants her to stand up for her God-given <u>rights</u> as a
Child of God—enlightened by the Spirit! He never
intended <u>anybody</u> to be a slave!*

*Our course is swiftly drawing to a close. All
we have are two more single break days so I won't
be able to visit you <u>this time</u> around, but <u>hope-
fully</u>, next year or the year after?? I'll have to hope
the dollar goes in a different direction. It has gone
from 1.62 to 1.85 (to the pound) <u>since I arrived.</u>
Things are <u>very</u> expensive to buy here. We are now
on a mini-retreat—I direct someone for 3 days, then
someone else directs me. All with supervision—It's
good training.*

*It sounds as if your Church needs you. I can't
figure out why Catholics tend to sit in the back of
the Church. Seems to happen everywhere!*

*I've finally come down with a bad chest cold
but it is improving. On the 1ˢᵗ night I got sick, three
people showed up at my door offering a substantial
shot of whiskey. They are a caring group.*

*I head back to the States knowing I will miss
a great deal of the peace and quiet here plus wondering if indeed I shall ever see you again. But we'll
hope for the best and leave everything in God's capable hands. I shall still count on your prayers—as I*

said, I'm sure they have brought me through many a crisis. Both of you and your wonderful family have a permanent place in my heart and I shall never, ever forget you and the difference you have truly made in my life. My prayers will be always with you 'til the day I die.

Love always,
Bill

Chapter 11

"Oh, girls, what am I going to do?" I asked Theresa and Eileen over coffee.

"Are you still planning on your weekend in London?" asked Eileen.

"Oh yes, that's still happening, but I don't know how to win Adrian over. He's adamant that I'm not going."

"Well, I think you should stop talking about it to him until the day before and then just tell him you'll see him in a couple of days."

"That's a good idea," agreed Eileen. "Be really low key about it."

"Thanks, Theresa, you always give the best advice," I said, grateful for their friendship and support. It sounded so straightforward and simple: *just stop talking about it*. I prayed it would all work out.

"So what clothes are you taking?" Eileen asked, always so stylish herself.

"Well, whatever he lets me take. I don't have a coat, so I hope the weather stays dry."

"You don't have a coat?" exclaimed Eileen in mock horror. "Well, that won't do! I tell you what. I'll come to the train station on Saturday morning and bring you my maroon velvet jacket. It will dress up any outfit." She was pleased with her contribution to my adventure as she saw it.

"Oh, that's so kind of you. Are you sure?"

"Of course, I'm sure. I have to come into town anyway. You can't show up in London without a jacket in December."

"Do you have your train tickets yet?" asked Theresa.

"Yes, Father Bill sent them to me. I've hidden them in that book you gave me, *Hinds' Feet on High Places*. I had to keep an eye out for the postman as Adrian's been intercepting my letters, and I was afraid he'd destroy them."

"He opens your letters?" said Eileen, shocked.

"Yes, he's always done it."

"Look, if you want Father Bill to write to you at my address from now on, you can give it to him. I'll keep the letters for you," offered Theresa.

"Oh, can he? Thank you, I will." I hated being secretive but, with Adrian's aversion to my friendship with Father Bill, felt that this was the only way to maintain our correspondence.

I took Theresa's advice and avoided the topic of my trip until Thursday evening as I started packing clothes for the children while they played in their bedroom.

"Does Isla know we're coming?" asked Brian, worried that it might not happen.

"Of course she knows., I asked her a long time ago."

"She might have forgotten. You should remind her so we can still go." He was looking forward to a sleepover with his friend Stuart.

"I talked to her today, so no need to worry. She is looking forward to having you all there on Friday."

"We'll be good, won't we, Sean?" added Michael.

"Yes, we'll be *very* good!" Sean replied, stressing the *very* as he jumped on the bed.

"I know you will. You're always good boys when you visit other people's houses. Just remember your manners and put your dirty dishes in the sink when you're done."

"What's this?" Adrian queried as he stepped into the room.

"We're getting ready to go to Stuart's house!" Sean volunteered excitedly.

"Ouch, Dad! What was that for?" Brian cried out as Adrian smacked him across the back of his head.

"'Cause you're annoying me. That's what it's for."

"Adrian, that was unnecessary," I chided, coming to Brian's defense. "He wasn't doing anything at all."

"Well, it can count for the next time he does something that I don't see, can't it?"

"Okay, boys. Thanks for your help. Off you go, downstairs. You can turn on the television if you like." I didn't want them to witness a temper tantrum from Adrian, if one was looming. They didn't wait to be asked twice.

"So you still think you're going, do you?"

"Yes, I'm all set. You won't have to worry about anything," I said, trying to sound upbeat.

"Well, I'm not giving you any money. So you better have that figured out too," he added sullenly.

"I won't need money. Edel will feed me. I'll be fine."

"You're not taking any clothes either. You can manage with what you're wearing."

"All right, I can manage." I was not protesting *any* of his conditions. At least he had begrudgingly accepted my going.

"And don't expect me to come and pick you up at the train station on Monday either. You can walk home," he said, angrily kicking a toy truck on the floor into the corner of the room. I remained calm on the surface, but my soul was celebrating with victory somersaults.

I rose early on Friday morning, leaving plenty of time for the two-mile walk into town for the 8:30 a.m. train to London. I put on the black long-sleeved knee-length dress that Adrian had set out for me, its only adornment a row of tiny false gold buttons from neck to waist.

"I'll need a sweater too, Adrian. It's pretty cold out."

He opened the drawer, pulled out the folded black sweater with a primary colored block pattern on the front, and threw it on the bed.

"Thanks," I said quietly as I dropped some clean underwear and my toothbrush into my handbag. On my way out the front door, I grabbed my bright-yellow woolen scarf from the coat hook and stuffed it into my handbag too. I now had two layers to keep me warm.

"I'll see you on Monday evening," I called from the hall as I left. There was no reply.

Eileen was waiting at Newtown train station with the velvet jacket, as promised.

"Now have a good time. I can't wait to hear *all* about it when you get back." She beamed, handing me the Harrods bag she had put it in. "I had it in a Marks and Sparks bag first, but this one seems more fitting," she added, showing what thought had gone into her gesture.

"Thank you so much, Eileen. I can hardly believe that it's happening," I said gratefully, still half-expecting Adrian to pop up and stop me from getting on the train.

"I won't be able to rest until the train leaves with me on it."

"Well, you enjoy yourself, and don't worry about Adrian," she added encouragingly as the train pulled up for the four-hour journey to London and Father Bill.

"Thanks again, Eileen," I said, stepping onto the train that was taking me towards the light. I settled into a seat and waved happily to her out of the window as the train slowly pulled out of the station. I was drifting away, at least for a while, from fear and pain—towards hope and happiness, however fleeting.

After only a few minutes, I felt a certain lightness in myself, as though with every mile travelled, another layer of heaviness was being lifted from my heart, like the stone being rolled away from the tomb after Jesus's resurrection. As I stared out the window at the changing landscape, I relaxed into the tranquil sensation of floating in an ever-increasing sphere of love, as though my soul, now liberated, was expanding into the atmosphere and infusing every molecule that surrounded me with exquisite and infinite joy.

I stepped onto the platform at Euston Station, still in a state of euphoria, and headed towards the exit where Father Bill was waiting, his arms outstretched in welcome.

"You made it! I was worried that something might have happened to stop you coming," he said, his arms encircling me in a safe embrace.

"Nothing was going to stop me. Thank you, thank you," I said, letting out a sigh of immeasurable relief as I heard the comforting rhythm of his heart beating through his coat.

"You look terrific! I love the yellow scarf. Like a collar of sun-shine lighting up your face."

"Thank you. I like color. It brightens up the black," I said, look-ing up into his kind blue eyes, glad that I had put on the scarf before leaving the train.

"Well, I thought that we'd drop off your luggage in the left luggage office first and then explore the city," he began, both of his hands now resting on my shoulders. "Where are your bags?"

"This is all I was allowed to bring," I explained, holding up my handbag. "I can borrow clothes from Edel if I need any."

"Well, that makes life easy. I could learn a thing or two from you about packing light," he joked. "Let's head over to Farm Street in Berkeley Square, where I'm staying, and then we'll discuss what you'd like to do. What time did you tell Edel you'd be there?"

"Oh, no particular time, whatever works for you. I just told her I'd arrive sometime this evening."

"That's great. We'll do some sightseeing and then eat dinner. There's some magnificent galleries and museums here. How does that sound?"

"That sounds marvelous. Though, I'd be just as happy sitting on a park bench all afternoon in the rain with you," I said as he put his arm around my shoulder and drew me close.

I was being consulted. I was being asked what *I* would like to do. My needs were being considered. This new experience would take some getting used to.

"You wait here a minute. I'll be right back," Father Bill said, leaving me in a small reception area adjoining Farm Street Church, where he was staying. A Christmas party hosted by the Jesuits for the elderly was just ending, and I watched, smiling, as the revelers, some still wearing their colorful crepe-paper crowns and all old enough to be my grandparents, passed me on their way out. Many smiled and called out a cheery, "Happy Christmas!" as they caught sight of me. One gentleman approached me and said, "You are beautiful! Do you know that? Beautiful!"

"Oh, thank you." I was not accustomed to compliments, so hearing this stranger tell me this lifted my heart.

"I'm an artist, you know," he went on. "Come and see me tomorrow, and I'll do your portrait. A Christmas gift."

"Oh, gosh! Thank you."

"Come to the Regents Palace Hotel in Piccadilly Circus and ask for Baron Benjamin. Will you remember that? Baron Benjamin. Opposite the statue of Eros."

"I will remember. Thank you so much. Happy Christmas, Baron Benjamin." He took my hand in his and, putting both hands around mine, smiled into my eyes and said it again, "Beautiful."

"Sorry I took so long," said Father Bill on his return.

"Oh, no problem. I've been very entertained. One old man even told me I was beautiful and wants to paint my portrait!"

"Well, there's no disputing that fact. You are strikingly beautiful," he said, reaching up and touching my cheek gently with the back of his hand. "Though I'd be careful around artists who invite you up to their studios," he teased.

"Before we go off on our adventure, I have something for you, a small gift. Let's go in here," he said, leading me into a small dimly lit room set aside for confessions.

"It's not much, but a little something for you to remember me by," he said, handing me a cassette tape of Tchaikovsky's violin concerto and a small gold cross and chain.

"Oh, it's lovely, thank you. You shouldn't have." I lifted the delicate chain from its dainty box and held the golden cross between my finger and thumb, feeling its smoothness.

"May I put it on you now?" he asked.

"Yes, you may. Thank you, Father Bill." I was quiet as he took the chain from me and deftly secured the clasp around my neck. Now I had something precious to wear close to my heart that would keep Father Bill near me always. I wondered what my mother would say about my accepting *this* piece of jewelry.

"I feel badly as I don't have any gift for you," I said, embarrassed by my oversight.

"Your visit is my gift. I can't imagine a better one," he assured me.

"It's a gift for me too." We both smiled at each other, understanding how special this time would be.

"Julie, I have a favor to ask you," he said, changing the subject.

"What can I do for you?" I could maybe repay him in some way, I thought.

"From now on, please call me Bill. We've been friends for nearly twenty years now. Let's dispense with the title and just use my Christian name. Please."

"I will try. But you've always been Father Bill to me. I will try—Bill. Oh! It sounds funny, just saying, Bill. Bill, Bill, Bill, Bill. I'll get there."

"Thank you," he said, hugging me and smiling. "That music, by the way, is a beautiful piece. Do you know it?"

"No, I don't think so, *Bill*." I grinned as I emphasized his name. "Though I do recognize melodies sometimes but can never remember what they're called."

"Well, I hope you'll like it as much as I do."

"I know I will. It will remind me of this moment every time I play it."

"It will be the same for me too, *Julie*." We both laughed in unison as he imitated my emphasis on his name. With each minute in the company of this kind human being, I grew even more comfortable.

"Now where we will go first?" he asked. "There's St. Paul's Cathedral, the Tate Gallery, the Victoria and Albert Museum, the National Gallery."

"Oh, I've no clue. You choose. I've only been to London a couple of times and never as a tourist. I wouldn't know where to start. What would you like to do?"

"Ah, no. This is *your* weekend. I want you to do whatever will make *you* happy. So you choose."

I was being given choices. It was something not afforded me in marriage, where even my clothes were picked out for me. I was stymied.

"Oh, please don't ask me to choose. I really don't know what I want to do. Anything with you will make me happy."

"Well, do you like art? Or maybe you prefer history or cathedrals? We can see them all if you want. Just pick where we begin," he said patiently.

"I do like art. Turner is my favorite artist, but I also like history and churches too."

"Well, would you like to start at the new Turner Wing in the Tate Gallery and go from there?" he suggested.

"Would *you* like to see the Turner paintings?" I asked, unable to make a decision.

"Julie, we have all weekend. I'm happy to wait till you decide what you'd like to see. Take your time."

"Aagh! Okay, let's go see the Turner paintings. Are you sure that's okay with you?"

"Great idea. Let's do it!"

We spent the sunny afternoon wandering through galleries of incredible art, strolling along the Thames, visiting churches, and breathing in their peace. We admired the accessible nativity scene of the holy family in St. Paul's Cathedral, with Mary playfully tickling the toes of the baby Jesus while Joseph slept in the corner of the stable. We stopped to wonder at Rodin's *The Kiss*, to bathe in the golden light of Turner's exquisite masterpieces and to gasp at the stark rawness of the double nude painting by Sir Sidney Spencer of *The Artist and His Second Wife*.

My heart was light. I felt a new freshness towards everything. My senses heightened as I soaked up the beauty of each moment, capturing and storing the unique memories we were creating together, like invisible treasures in a Fabergé egg, to be hatched later and brought to life when I needed consolation. In this wondrous brief respite from my usually jaded existence, I had been transported, body and soul, to some ethereal place where time was suspended so that I could glimpse something of the divine mystery of creation and my indissoluble connectedness to it. I understood that in my limited human capacity, my mind could never grasp the magnitude of the mystery, yet I also understood that my soul was encountering grace, freely given, by an all-loving and surprising God.

"Hello, you two," greeted Edel, little baby Ross in her arms. "Come in."

"Hi, Edel. This must be a Manning thing, being greeted by mother and baby," joked Bill, stepping into the hall.

"Thank goodness you're here, Julie. Adrian has been calling the phone off the hook, checking on you," said Edel, relieved.

"Oh, sorry, Edel. He must have thought I was coming straight here from the train. How many times has he called?" I asked, leaning in to kiss Ross on the cheek.

"Oh, only about once an hour since lunchtime," she said, a touch of sarcasm in her voice. "I told him I'd get you to ring him once you got here, but he keeps calling."

As if on cue, the phone rang again. "You can get it. It's probably for you," she directed, pointing to the kitchen. I rushed to answer it, the familiar feeling of panic and dread rising in me, superseding all calm as I picked up the receiver.

"Hello? Adrian?"

"You got there then. What took you so long?" he sounded on edge.

"Yes, I just walked in the door. Edel told me you rang earlier. We did a bit of sightseeing before coming here. We saw a really nice nativity set in St. Paul's Cathedral." I was hoping that providing details that he would consider dull might reduce his anxiety. But he wasn't paying attention to what I had to say.

"Are you in for the night now, or are you off galivanting again?"

"No. I mean yes. I'm in for the night. You've no need to worry. I'm very safe with Edel and Tom, my two police protectors." Referencing their profession was a lame attempt at humor. "Do you want to talk to them?"

"No, I spoke to Edel earlier when *you* should have been there."

I paused for a second before continuing, "Okay. Well, if there's nothing else, I'll say cheerio then." I waited for a response, but instead there was silence. "I'll see you on Monday then. Good night." I waited a couple more seconds before hanging up and letting out a deep sigh.

"He's not a happy camper, is he?" said Edel as I returned to the living room, where she and Tom had been chatting with Bill.

"No, he didn't want me to come."

"Well, you're here now, and there's not much he can do about it, so you may as well relax and enjoy yourself," she said definitively.

"Oh, I am. I have been," I replied, glancing over and smiling at Bill.

"Cup of tea? Or something stronger?" she offered.

"Tea would be great, thanks."

"Father Bill?"

"Oh, tea's is fine for me too. Thanks, Edel. I can't stay long—got to get the tube back to Mayfair."

"When are you flying home?" Tom asked.

"Monday morning—about eleven."

"Well, feel free to spend the night here Sunday," called Edel from the kitchen. "It will be easier to get to the airport from here."

"That's very kind of you. Thanks. I'll do that."

"Oh, that's good. I'll be able to go to the airport with you straight from here," I interjected.

"So where did you go today? What did you see?" Edel asked as she handed out the mugs of tea.

"Well, we started off at Farm Street church where an old man there told me I was beautiful and said he wants to paint my portrait tomorrow. Do you think we could at least go in and see him, Bill?"

"Sure. We can pop in there."

"What? An old man wants to paint your portrait?" Edel said in disbelief.

"Yes, his name is Baron Benjamin, and he's an artist," I added, increasing his credibility.

"An old drunk, more like," she said, laughing, Tom and Bill joining in.

"No, he wasn't drunk. He said he works at the Regent's Palace Hotel." I wanted to protect my memory of the meeting by defending him. I was hurt by her comments, which minimized and dismissed the special encounter. Edel probably had no idea that what she said had hurt me. Adrian had told me repeatedly that I was too sensitive, and this proved it. Still, I felt diminished by the conversation. I decided that I would not ask Bill to take me to see Baron Benjamin the next day. What if he had lied to me? What if he was just a drunken old man? Only later did I discover that he was indeed an artist, known for his portraits of visiting royalty. So I wrote him an apology for not showing up and told him how special he had made me feel during the most important weekend of my life.

For the next two days, I met Bill at Green Park station for more sightseeing, though it was the time in his company that I was enjoying as much as, if not more than, the delights of the city. We meandered through Green Park, dotted with its green-and-white striped deck chairs for hire, past Buckingham Palace, and through the stunning St. James's Park studded with glorious flower gardens, inviting meadow-like spaces, and cheeky pelicans.

Our conversation took on a more subdued tone as we acknowledged that this was probably our last time together. We discussed the nature of our relationship, which challenged social norms and yet felt so good and pure.

"Whatever happens, Julie, be assured of my love," said Bill as we leaned on the wall and gazed across the Thames.

"Thank you. I will hold on to that when life is difficult. This has been the best weekend of my life, Bill. You have no idea. You have helped me see how beautiful life can be and how we should treat one another. I will be eternally grateful for that."

"You have helped me too, in immeasurable ways. You are a gift, Julie," he added, reaching for my hand. The intimacy of the gesture and his touch made my heart leap. We held hands for the remainder of the day. I felt safe, secure, and cherished.

"We need to get you a coat!" said Bill as a chilly breeze came in off the river. "It's December, and you're only wearing a sweater."

"Oh, there's no need. I don't need a coat. Thank you, though."

"Are you sure you're not an angel? Angels don't need coats."

"Oh, I feel the cold like any mortal," I assured him, smiling at the image he conjured of me as an angel.

"Well, let's head over to Oxford Street and see what we can find," he suggested.

"It's really not necessary, Bill. I'm quite warm. The sun is out, and I feel fine." I was worried about Adrian seeing me in a coat bought by Bill. I was afraid that it would enrage him to the point of violence. I could be discreet with the music tape and the golden cross and chain, but a new coat would be too hard to hide.

"Well, winter won't always be as kind as it's been today, and if my arms can't wrap around you to keep you warm, then at least I can hug you with a coat."

"Well, thank you." I didn't want to seem ungrateful as we set off for the shops.

"What do you think of this one?" said Bill, holding up a stunning red military-style coat with a black collar and cuffs.

"It's gorgeous, Bill, but it's too nice for my life in Newtown." It was gorgeous too, but I needed to be Jackie Onassis to carry off that look.

"It's your color, my 'Lady in Red,'" he added enticingly. "You looked terrific in that red dress you wore to Crystals."

"Oh, thanks. Red's my favorite color. It's just such a beautiful coat and would be ruined in no time by baby vomit, sticky fingers, you name it." This was going to be tough. I was so appreciative and yet sounding like a spoiled teenager, rejecting all of his suggestions.

"How about this one?" I said, picking up a shapeless beige padded oversized, three-quarter-length zip-up jacket with deep pockets that screamed *ugly*. "This is perfect! It's washable too."

"Are you sure?" he said, questioning my taste, his grimace revealing his dislike.

"Oh, absolutely sure." I could tell Adrian, if he asked, that it was one of Edel's cast-offs.

"Okay. Well, you'd look beautiful in a sack," he said as we headed for the checkout.

Yes, this is by far the closest thing to a sack I've seen, I thought to myself. *But it will keep me warm, and Bill will always be close.*

On Sunday afternoon, we stopped by Farm Street to pick up Bill's luggage. Just seeing the suitcase, the harbinger of loneliness, filled me with a sweeping sadness. I was being reminded that our time was limited and coming to an end.

"When will we see each other again, do you think?" I asked him as we approached Edel's house.

"Well, who knows what God has planned. Let's hope it's not another twenty years. In any event, please know that distance will not alter my love for you." He was trying to be reassuring, though I had no doubts about his sincerity or his love.

Edel and Tom were excellent hosts, providing refreshments and arranging for a game of Trivial Pursuit to pass the time, adding some welcome levity to the evening. But as night drew in, the conversation turned to my marriage.

"What do you think, Edel?" asked Bill.

"Well, I think she should leave him. I've seen what he's like."

"It's harder to do than you think, Edel. I've tried to figure out what to do for the best," I said, by way of explanation.

"Well, I've seen firsthand what he is like too," added Bill. "And it's not safe for you, Julie. I worry about you and the kids." He was sharing his concern for me with my younger sister and her husband, perhaps rallying support for me for some future date.

"Yes, there's no question, the man needs help. Though I don't hold out much hope of him changing," said Bill sadly. "But right now, I'm more worried about Julie."

"Aren't there any women's shelters in Newtown, Julie?" asked Edel. She was being supportive and helpful but, at twenty-three, didn't really know the extent of the abuse or its implications for my safety. No one could possibly know, except someone in the exact same situation.

"I don't know, Edel. I imagine there are," I said lamely.

"Well, you should probably find out. You might need it," she said with an air of authority.

"Yes, you're right. I should."

"What did you make of Adrian, Father?" asked Tom.

"Well, it's clear that he's troubled and aggressive, more so after a drink. He took me to the pub before he went to your mom and dad's house and pointed out all the big-breasted women in the place—in not-too-flattering terms. He might have been testing my reaction. I also saw how he treated Julie when I was there. Just very disrespectful in general towards women."

"Well, I don't know what to do. He goes through phases. Right now he's very upset 'cause I'm here, so goodness knows what he'll be like when I go home."

"Well, what if you don't go home?" said Edel.

"I've got to go home, Edel."

"Not necessarily. Hear me out. What if you stay here, and Tom goes and gets the kids tomorrow and brings them back here. You'll have the Christmas holidays while they're off school to figure something out?"

"Hang on a minute. Don't I get a say in this?" Tom said, sounding concerned.

"Oh, I must go home, Edel. Adrian would say I've abandoned the children otherwise. And he's not going to hand them over to anyone, especially Tom, knowing I'm here with you."

"Well, think about it. You're not safe with him, and neither are the children. You're going to have to leave him someday. Why not now?" she continued, making a relevant point.

"I have to go home," I reiterated.

The conversation had switched from discussing the condition of my marriage to discussing how to get me out of it—and the sooner, the better. I listened, overwhelmed, as different ideas were presented by Edel, Tom, and Bill, all borne out of love for me and a desire to keep me safe. Bill's visit had been the catalyst I needed, yet I still felt helpless. I wanted the topic changed but felt outnumbered, so I sat listening as three good people did what they could to do to arrive at a solution to my problem.

"So it's decided then. That's what we'll do," said Edel. "You'll go home as planned on the train, and Tom will drive from here to Newtown overnight and pick you and the kids up and bring you back here for Christmas. You can wait till Adrian's gone to work and then sneak out. Tom will wait in the car."

"You're all talking about me as though I'm invisible," I said, my voice quivering. "I feel like a child, with the grown-ups making decisions for me." I wanted to cry, but that would only confirm the opinion that I couldn't manage my life.

"We're just trying to help you, Julie," Edel said kindly. "You know that we just want you to be safe."

"I know, I know. And I am grateful for your concern, but I'm frightened that this will all go wrong somehow. It's an awful long drive too for Tom."

"I don't mind coming to get you," said Tom. "I'm off work right now for a few days, so it's no trouble. Besides, what better place to be than in a house with not one but two police to guard you?"

"We'll make it a lovely Christmas for the boys, don't worry," comforted Edel, who was a natural organizer like my mother and already planning our next few days. "It will be nice for baby Ross too. His first Christmas shared with his cousins."

It had been settled. I was leaving Adrian and coming to a very safe home while I figured out what to do next. I began to share in the vision they had created of a new path opening up for me. It wouldn't be easy, but I was being encouraged to fan the flames of hope that would keep the relentless monster of anxiety at bay.

"Well, now that's sorted, I'm off to bed!" said Edel with a sigh. "You're in with me, Julie, and you and Tom are in the spare room, Father Bill. Hope you don't mind sleeping in a bunk bed."

"Thanks, Edel. Bunk bed sounds great."

"I'll be off to bed too. Got a long drive tomorrow. Good night," said Tom, taking his cue from Edel and leaving us alone.

"Good night, Tom, and thank you," we both said together.

"Here's a nightie you can borrow, Julie," called Edel a few moments later as a flowery cotton garment wafted down from the landing.

"Thank you," I called back, smiling at the sight. I was not getting ready for bed yet and certainly not putting that nightdress on downstairs.

Bill and I sat in silence on the couch, skimming over the memories of the past two days, wishing that we could hold time hostage and stay in this dimly lit moment forever. Two people bound together by love but separated by distance and circumstance.

"Oh, Julie. I am so proud of you. Stay strong, okay?" Bill said as he leaned back in the seat, inviting me to rest my head against his chest.

"I will. I promise. I wish you didn't have to leave. I wish we could just stay like this forever."

"I do too. If only things were different," he said, quietly stroking my hair.

"Yes, if only. I *hate* if-onlys! We should talk about what is," I said, staring blankly at his shirt buttons and feeling the rhythmic beating of his heart.

"Well, what *is* true is that I love you and want so desperately for you to be happy." His voice was gentle and tender.

"What is true is that you are leaving in the morning to go back to your life in America, and I am leaving my husband to go where?" My voice revealed my sadness and fear.

"I know. It'll be tough, but you are so ready for this now. Don't give up," he said, encouraging me with his pep talk. "God loves you so much. I am sure he has great things in store for you."

"I hope so. Thank you. I am so grateful for your love in my life. Nothing will ever change that. Nothing."

"If only I was twenty-five years younger…" He sighed.

"There you go again with the 'if only.' I don't care about age, Bill! It's the love that matters. Okay, if we're playing that game, I have an if-only for you—if only you lived on this continent instead of that one."

"If only you weren't married," he countered.

"Well, I might not be married much longer," I reminded him. "If only *you* weren't a priest!" That was our last if-only, my words drifting up to meet the silence that descended.

"Seriously, though, Julie, if things had turned out differently for both of us, do you think you would have married me?"

"I don't want to think about what might have been, Bill. It makes me too sad. It's like saying 'if only' in a different way."

"But do you think we would have had a chance at a life together?" he persisted.

"I don't know. What I do know, Bill, is that I love you. I have loved you since I was eleven. I didn't understand it but knew it was real. Maybe we were meant to be in each other's lives, to encourage and support, even from a distance, just so we could experience pure love."

"Yes, we have certainly experienced love." He sighed, his hand gently tilting my chin towards his face, his soft lips gently and tenderly meeting mine for the first time. Everything else dissolved around us as we immersed ourselves—hearts, souls, and bodies—into the exquisitely blissful realm of passion that emanates from true love. Our souls had found each other, out of the millions of people on the earth, we had been drawn together, mystically and mysteriously and found our way home. Every atom in me craved more than just this kiss, which had awakened within me a yearning for total physical intimacy that we both knew we must resist.

"Oh, Julie," he said, letting out a sigh, "I had to kiss you at least once. It may be the only time I can." The poignancy was clear in his voice.

"I don't want you to go," I said, sitting up and looking into his eyes. "I know you must."

"We'll always have this memory. If we never see each other again, we'll always have the memory of our kiss to comfort us."

"I love you. The words seem so inadequate. There are no words, Bill, for what I feel for you. Please believe me. With all my heart and soul, I love you."

"I love you too, Julie. For all eternity."

We clung to each other in the stillness, knowing that tomorrow we would be saying goodbye without any promises to see each other again. Pledging that our love, eternal and transcendent, not bound by time or distance, would accompany us through life, we said good-night.

As I lay in bed with my sleeping sister, I revisited the past two days in my mind, reliving each tender moment and lingering over the kiss, wondering, *Is this what love feels like? Is this the desire and longing, so natural and good, that draws and holds couples together? Is this what has been absent from my marriage? Is this what a doctor tried to duplicate when I was a newlywed with a prescription for Librium?* I felt that God had answered another of my prayers, though not in the way I had requested. Our kiss was enough to show me how we should respond to a beloved. Bill had treated me with respect always, his attentiveness and gentleness nurturing the love that existed long before we even met. The kiss, a gift of reciprocity, asking nothing in return.

At the airport the next morning, we went into the chapel and prayed together. Holding hands in the pew, we asked God to bless our love and to work within each of us to bring more love to the world. We cried silent tears at the thought of separation, consoling each other with promises to write and promises of prayers.

"Well, this is it. Time to say farewell," said Bill as I straightened the red tie sitting askew around his neck, looking for any reason to touch him one more time.

"Safe journey," I wished him, not knowing how to say goodbye.

"Be careful, Julie. Know that God is with you. I will be with you in spirit."

"I'll be with you too, always. God bless."

"God bless you."

One last gaze deep into each other's eyes as our two souls connected and spoke of love beyond the scope of language. Then two became one.

Chapter 12

As I journeyed back to Newtown, already missing Bill—his touch, his smell, his voice—I knew that my life would never be the same because I was a different person than the one who had travelled on these tracks just two days earlier. I contemplated what I now knew that I didn't know before his visit. I had learned that by experiencing great suffering, we develop an acute appreciation for joy; that being surrounded by ugliness, we are in awe of beauty; and in confronting death, we develop a passion for life.

I cried on the train back home, replaying over and over the blessed moments Bill and I had shared while thoughts of what I had to do tomorrow vied for my attention. *At least my swollen face and puffy eyes will have time to settle once I walk home*, I thought. *Then I will have to tell Adrian what I plan to do.*

As the train pulled into the station, I gasped when I spotted Adrian waiting on the platform. He had told me that I would have to walk home. My face was red and blotchy from crying, and I hadn't expected to see him yet.

"What are you blubbing for?" he asked right away. No "welcome home" or "did you have a nice time?" Just an accusatory question.

"I miss my friend," I answered truthfully.

"Bet you didn't fuckin' miss me, did you?" he growled.

I didn't answer him as I got into the car. *Keep it up, Adrian*, I thought. *Keep being unkind. It will make my leaving easier.*

Edel, Tom, and Bill had suggested that I sneak away without telling Adrian. That I wait till he had gone to work and then gather the children and get in the car with Tom, who would be waiting at 6.30 a.m. down the street from the house. I hesitated to do that because I felt that he deserved to be told, and it was safer for me to tell him the truth than to be discovered sneaking about. I had run a few possible conversations and scenarios around in my head on the train but knew that I would really have to gauge by his mood when the moment was right to tell him that I was leaving and taking the children with me.

The children were excited to see me and share all the stories of their weekend. I knew that they too deserved to be told what was happening, but I also knew it would have to wait until after I had told Adrian. I had so much to think about and so much to do with only a few hours to get organized. I put the children to bed, deciding to tell them in the morning.

I postponed telling Adrian until I had gathered all the important documents I would need to take with us: birth certificates, vaccination records, marriage certificate, social security information, family allowance book, etc. I was afraid that if I told him first, then he might go on a rampage and destroy what I needed to take. But how was I going to be so busy without raising his suspicion? It was also only three days till Christmas, so I had to pack up what few presents Santa would be delivering too and hide them from the children in garbage bags that would be stuffed into the trunk of Tom's car. With each passing minute, I was growing more anxious.

I waited until Derek came in and told him what I was planning to do. "I need your help, Derek. When I tell Adrian that I'm leaving, he may go ballistic."

"Oh, girl, you're taking a chance. He's not going to like it," he said, stating the obvious.

"I know. That's why I want you nearby, to help keep him calm," I explained.

"You've got my support," he assured me. "I bought you a food hamper for Christmas. It's in my room. You can take it with you."

"Thank you, thank you. I'll give it to Edel, if you don't mind," I said, grateful for his friendship and support.

I braced myself, preparing to face Adrian. Since we came home from the station, he had been watching television, not paying much attention to what I was doing.

"Adrian, I need to talk to you. It's very important," I said once the television program ended.

"What?"

"I am not—I've not been happy for a very long time, so I'm leaving you," I blurted out. There didn't seem to be any way to say it to lessen the impact. It would still come as a shock.

"You're what?"

"I'm leaving you," I repeated.

"Leaving me?" he said, puzzled.

"I've had lots of time to think and realize that whatever we're doing isn't working. We're both miserable most of the time. So I'm going. Tom will be here in the morning to pick me and the kids up and take us to London till we sort something out." I wanted to impress on him that it was going to happen, that it was already happening.

"You're serious, aren't you? That bloody priest put you up to it, didn't he?" he said, standing up and walking towards me menacingly.

"Nobody put me up to it. I've been thinking about it for a long time. I'm so tired of fighting." We were standing face-to-face now, his eyes glaring at me.

"I won't let you go," he said defiantly. "You're not going anywhere."

"Adrian, I'm sorry, but it's got to be this way."

"No. It's not 'got to be this way.' You're staying here, where you belong, with your husband," he said forcefully.

I shook my head, at a loss for words that he wasn't prepared to hear anyway.

"I *demand* that you love me," he bellowed, his fist slamming on the table and making me jump.

"Adrian, I have always given you my love freely. If you demand it from me, you will never know whether I did something out of love or out of fear."

"You're not going. Please don't go, Julie. I'm sorry, I didn't mean to frighten you. I'm asking you nicely to stay." He had changed his approach, pleading now instead of shouting.

"I'm sorry, Adrian, my mind's made up. There's nothing you can say or do to keep me here."

Derek, having heard Adrian's fist slamming on the table, came in to the room.

"All right, Shorty, mate?"

"She's threatening to leave me, Derek. What am I going to do?"

"Yeah, I'm sorry, mate, but you'll be okay," he said, trying to console.

"I *won't* be okay. I'll never be okay if she goes," Adrian said, lighting a cigarette, his hands shaking.

I felt cruel, torturing him like this. He looked so fragile and weak, and yet I knew that I couldn't stay in our marriage, which I probably should have left years before. Tom was already on the way, but it would be hours before he got here.

"Adrian, you've got work in the morning. You should get some sleep," I suggested.

"You think I can sleep after what you've sprung on me?" He was right. Sleep would elude us both. I didn't want to cause pain, but pain was an inevitable consequence of my decision. I felt sorry for him as he sat there looking lost and bewildered, smoking cigarette after cigarette. How I wished it had not come to this.

The hours passed, with fewer words spoken between us. Just the occasional repeated plea, "Don't go. Please don't go." I stopped answering it, my verbal rejection of him only compounding his suffering. He may have sensed my resolve as his pleas faded with the dawn.

When Tom arrived, I went out to him and explained that Adrian was aware of my plans. He came in to the house to have a cup of tea, get the Christmas toys, and pack up the car while I woke up the children. I took a deep breath, knowing that the next few minutes would be distressing.

"Boys, boys, wake up. Uncle Tom is here. We're going to his house for Christmas," I said quietly. They were still drowsy as I helped them get dressed, not sure what was happening but cooperating as I ushered them downstairs. "Give Daddy a big hug," I told each one.

"Isn't Daddy coming?" asked Sean, concerned.

"No, Daddy is staying here, with Derek," I explained. "Now go and give him a kiss."

Adrian, seeming resigned to the fact that we were leaving, was crying in the kitchen as the boys hugged him.

I secured Amy in Ross's car seat and urged the boys to squash up close to each other for the five-and-a-half-hour drive to London. Then I went back in to say goodbye for the last time to the man who had been the only man in my life for almost fourteen years.

"Please, Julie, don't go. It's not too late. You can change your mind. Things will be different. I beg you, please stay," he cried, the tears streaming down his face.

"I can't, Adrian. This is how it must be. I'm so sorry," I said, feeling a wave of compassion for him as he got down on his knees and clasped both hands together in supplication. "Please, I beg you."

Crying now too, I repeated, "I'm sorry, Adrian," as he put his arms around my ankles to hold me in place. I looked down at this abject man lying on his stomach on the kitchen floor, desperately clinging to my feet, begging me to stay. I wanted to lift him up and tell him he was loved. Instead, I shook my leg vigorously to loosen his grip and left him inconsolable, feeling torn between sympathy for him and a compelling need to be free.

"Ready?" Tom asked as I climbed into the car.

"Yes, as I'll ever be," I said, feeling miserable about the way things were unfolding. I wanted time to process it all, but the children needed answers.

"Why are we going to Tom's house?"

"We're going there for Christmas to see Aunty Edel and Ross," I said as reassuringly as I could.

"Why was Daddy crying?"

"Well, because he wants to be with us, and he can't."

"Why can't he?"

"Because he can't."

"But why?"

"Because he's got to go to work." I didn't know how to explain to them that after years of subjugation, I was finally making the choice to break free.

"Are we leaving Daddy for good?" asked Brian, who at ten was the eldest.

"Yes, Brian. We're leaving for good," I said, still coming to terms with that reality myself.

"What about Santa?" said Michael in a panic. "He won't know where we are!"

"Don't worry. I've written to him already. He knows that you'll be staying with Edel and will bring your presents when he brings Ross his. Okay?"

"Okay."

"Now be quiet and try and go to sleep. It's a long, long drive. Uncle Tom needs to concentrate."

I too needed to think through what my next steps would be. Edel and Tom had generously offered their home as a safe haven for a week or two, but what then? I had left with a Christmas hamper from Derek, a few pounds in my purse, and my family allowance book, which would all soon be depleted.

By the time we reached London, Tom, exhausted by his eleven hours of driving, was having second thoughts about being around us for the next couple of weeks. He and Edel were practically newlyweds with a new baby, excited about their first Christmas as a new family. Now they had to share it with five other guests. Within minutes of our arrival, they were engaged in a heated argument brought on by our presence.

"I can't do this," Tom told Edel. "I'm going to stay with Wilbur till they're gone."

"You can't do that! What about our Christmas?" Edel said, alarmed at his decision to leave, albeit temporarily.

"I'm sorry, Edel. I just can't do it," he said.

"Tom! That's not fair. You can't just walk out! What if I had decided to walk out and leave you to manage? How would you like that?" Edel's voice raised in protest.

"I'm so sorry. This is all my fault," I interjected. "Please, Tom, don't go on our account. I'll do what I can to make sure the children don't disturb you."

"It's not your fault, Julie. It's just too much pandemonium for me to handle, that's all."

"I'll make arrangements to go somewhere else as soon as I can. Please stay, for Edel and Ross's sake." I was a nuisance, already intruding on their marriage and causing problems.

"You don't have to do that, Julie. This isn't your fault," said Edel, trying to manage the situation. "You'll ruin our Christmas if you do this, Tom," she warned, the tears welling in her eyes.

"Please, Tom," I cried. "Please, for the sake of the children, don't spoil Christmas."

"Look, I can't stay here. I'm going!" Tom had made up his mind to go. I too made up my mind to move on the day after Christmas. The question was, to where?

Adrian's first call came within an hour of our arrival in London, just a few minutes after Tom had left in a storm of upset. Adrian pleaded and cried for our return, once again promising that life would be different, that he would do anything I wanted if only I came home. His next call was half an hour after that, a repeated litany of promises that he would reform. And then another call, and another. My answers were the same each time: "I'm sorry, Adrian, but this is the way it has to be."

Edel was understandably distraught at Tom's departure and would have taken the phone off the hook if she weren't hoping for a call from him saying he was coming home. So we consoled each other and distracted ourselves with the needs of the children, holding our breath and waiting for the phone to ring—one of us hoping to receive a call, the other not.

I called my brothers Sean and Stephen in Pucklechurch, who were renting the house our parents had once lived in and asked if we could stay with them for a few weeks while I sorted out my life. They agreed that I could come on Boxing Day, the day after Christmas, and stay as long as I needed. I was not so confident anymore about how long I would be welcome anywhere.

Another call from Adrian, and this time, emotionally exhausted by the ordeal and having the trip to my brothers already arranged, I surrendered. "All right, I'll come home, but not for a few weeks. I need to clear my head, Adrian, and we need to make sure we get it right once and for all."

I felt stupid, weak, and despondent. In a few hours, I had caused stress on someone else's marriage, uprooted and distressed my children, disrupted three households, and all for what? I felt a failure as a mother, a wife, and a woman.

The phone rang again., "It's got to be for you this time," I said to Edel.

"No, it's for you," she said, handing me the phone.

"Hello, Julie, Bill here, just checking to make sure you got there okay."

"Oh, thank you for calling." My heart, once again, was lifted as I relayed the events of the past thirty-six hours since our farewell at the airport. So much had changed in the last few days, and so much had remained the same.

54 Saville Crescent,
Ashford Common
Middlesex
Dec. 22. 1987

Dear Bill,

It is only minutes since we spoke on the phone, how lovely to hear your voice. It is hard to believe that you are so far away—, I'll just pretend you are back in Mayfair.

Thank you, thank you, thank you for such a wonderful weekend. I have been going over conversations and events to ensure I never forget any little thing that happened.

Saying goodbye was the most difficult thing I had to do. I cried and cried afterward. Since then you haven't left my thoughts for a moment.

Your phone call this evening set my heart beating so quickly, just as it had throughout the weekend. Thank you for calling.

I wanted to touch you.

As I explained on the phone, I have agreed to return to Adrian in about three weeks, for one last attempt at redeeming our marriage. I have to give him one last chance to make amends. That will be it—I am too tired to keep going on in the same fashion—this is his very last chance.

You showed me how I should be treated. I will expect similar considerations from Adrian from now on. Perhaps he can manage it, we shall have to wait and see.

You must keep me up to date with your affairs, too, it will help me to stay close to you.

Do you know what a special person you are? I have never felt so close to anyone in my life. Please trust me enough to confide in me. I have opened my heart and soul to you—I feel a part of you, please be open with me. I do want to be involved in your life from now on.

One weekend every twenty years isn't enough! Oh I wish you were here now.

Thank you for loving me, God bless you,
Write to me soon.

With special love,
Julie xx

54 Saville Crescent,
Ashford Common
Middlesex
Christmas Eve. '87

Dear Bill,

I am sitting listening to Mozart, Edel has taken the boys to the park so the house is relatively quiet—Amy is with me.

I want you to know that I am thinking of you and I miss you.

Edel and Tom have had a row because of my presence here—he has been staying at his friends since Tuesday and didn't intend coming here for Christmas Day—I babysat last night so Edel could go out with him, they have sorted it all out and he will come back Christmas morning.

My children and I are going to Mass Christmas morning so Edel, Tom and Ross can open their presents while we are out of the way.

I feel so intrusive.

Adrian has rung each day, begging me to go home—he is spending Christmas with his brother and family. I am not going back immediately I shall stay in Bristol for a few weeks first.

I feel so muddled—why aren't you here to help me sort things out? I'm so sorry, I'm being selfish. It's just that everything's so right and simple when you are with me—do you understand?

I must learn to stand on my own two feet and stop leaning on you. I love you so much it hurts, I am constantly distracted by thoughts of you—if only—.

We watched a video with the children yesterday—the opening tune was "When You Wish Upon a Star." Yes—Pinocchio. Of course all I could think of was you whistling that tune as we walked along the river in the dark.

There are so many things to remind me of you and our time together. I was so happy then, happier than I have ever been.

I hope you are happy—you must be with so many ladies in pursuit of you—what is it about you I wonder? It must be your gentleness and consideration and your great capacity for loving.

*Be happy—I want that much for you—I just
wish I could be a closer part of your life—you mean
so much to me—you'll never know.*
    Take care of yourself.
    God Bless you—please pray for me.
                               With much love,
                                    Julie xx

Jesuit Community
Xavier University
3800 Victory Pkwy
Cincinnati, 45207
Dec 24th 1987

Dear Julie,
    *It was beautiful speaking to you again but
sad to hear you're stuck in a dilemma. Granted the
options, I guess you <u>had</u> to make the compromise
decision—I hope Adrian realizes what he has to do
to make your marriage work and I will pray with
all my heart that it will. (I did offer that mass for
you as soon as I hung up and God somehow made
it so clear that He loves you beyond all telling!).
The only thing we can do is trust, I guess. But if
things don't change make sure you do start docu-
menting things, including calling police and consulting social workers. It's not pleasant but it's the
only way. Maybe your parish priest can help you out
on this—he should know the people involved. The
main thing is to remember your basic dignity as a
<u>woman</u>—as a child of God! You should never have
to live in fear.*
    *Thank you again for the <u>beautiful</u> days we
spent together—both in Newtown and London. I
have **<u>never</u>** in my whole life enjoyed the company of*

*anyone as much as I did with you. You are indeed
a treasure beyond belief and I sincerely hope your
husband begins to realize it.*

*I have been thinking of our outstanding
moments—the walk back along the river after the
disco. The sitting up with Amy, in London, the dinner in the French Restaurant, the Turner gallery, the
walk by the Thames, Piccadilly, the mummies, the
tube rides, the Trivial Pursuit game, the long discussion, the poor girl trying to get up on the unicycle
at Covent Garden, the <u>peaceful</u> moments at Edel's.
These and <u>every</u> minute will be forever etched in my
memory.*

*Thank you for your friendship <u>and love</u>. I will
go on loving you forever - remembering you <u>every
day</u> in my Masses and prayers. Enclosed is only picture I could find right now. Hang tough, Julie—
you're great!*

You have brought me closer to God and people.

With all my love,

Bill

On Christmas morning, as requested, I took the children
to Mass so that Edel and Tom, who had returned as promised,
could have their private family Christmas with Ross as he opened
his presents. It was a thoughtful request, probably trying to save
me embarrassment as much as create their own tradition and also
compromise for Tom. I had so few presents for the boys and Amy
that watching as Ross waded through all his gifts might have left
them feeling neglected. Nevertheless, I felt even more intrusive,
knowing that we had to be out of the way while they resumed their
family life.

When we got back, the children were eager to celebrate by
ripping open their gifts with the customary *oohs* and *Ahhs* ringing
out happily in the air. Edel had even knitted sweaters for them,
not imagining that they would be worn in her house on Christmas

Day. "They'll grow into them," she stated cheerfully once she saw them on.

It was a happy day, filled with love, laughter, and generosity, and a telephone call from Adrian, who was looking forward to our coming home. Just not quite yet.

The next day, Tom took us to Pucklechurch to stay with my brothers Stephen and Sean, where we planned to stay for the next three weeks. I was eager to have the time to really figure out what I needed to say to Adrian and also the opportunity to enjoy the company of my brothers. I was also relieved to be away from the tension that usually permeated my home—for a little while, at least.

Sean and Stephen were happy to see us, making us welcome and then carrying on with their own lives of work and play. As young single men managing on their own, I think they may have anticipated a few hearty home-cooked meals. I kept the house clean, cooked for us with what limited provisions were there, and prayed hard for the courage to create the new vision I had for my life. My dreary days brightened when a letter arrived from Bill, or he surprised me with a phone call.

Jesuit Community
Xavier University
3800 Victory Pkwy
Cincinnati, 45207
Dec 29, 1987

Dearest Julie,

Just a note to tell you how much I enjoyed talking to you this morning. It did seem as if you were next door—how I wished you were. It's funny how attuned we are to each other—even (or especially) with dreams. I had already thought about that idea you expressed—that it wasn't the retreat at St. Beuno's that called me over to Wales for, but so we could clarify each other's lives with our mutual love. I sincerely hope I see you again but <u>we had more in those brief days than some people get in a lifetime</u>. You are a wonder beyond belief—believe it.

The few things you mentioned about Adrian were encouraging, but the drinking (giving it up) will be the bottom line. I wouldn't bet on him but God indeed can work miracles and for your sake I will pray that He does. My God, how I want you to be happy!

I was telling someone about the Turner wing at the Tate Gallery. He asked me about it and I almost told him all I saw was the beautiful woman I was with! How else could I misplace whole corridors of Rodin? The walk along the river seems like a beautiful dream.

One absolute thing I know about you, Julie, is that I am a better person because of you. I am freer, stronger, and happier (and I hope you are too). Your friendship and love, which I can't now see, touch, or taste, makes all the difference in my life.

My best to Stephen, Sean, and the children.
                                    Love always,
                                         Bill xx

P.S. Will write again when I get your letter.

Jesuit Community
Xavier University
3800 Victory Pkwy
Cincinnati, 45207
Dec 31, 1987
New Year's Eve
7.30pm

My dearest Julie,
    Sitting in my room on <u>*New Year's Eve*</u> *thinking of you. Since it is 7:40 pm here I figure you have gone to bed even if you did stay up for Midnight. Anyway, I wish so much you were here. I'm listening to the Zamfir tape and "The Rose" has* <u>*just*</u> *come on and I'm melting with love. I got some slides back today and there is a good one of you and Amy which I have enlarged and put on my desk. There is a_ <u>pretty</u> good one of the two of us (taken by one of the boys)—we're at an angle but what the heck. I'll have copies made of it and send you one. Also a good one of the three boys both on a chair and in the window of the ruined church.*
    I'm still pouring over memories and our half hour in the chapel at Gatwick comes to mind, plus the Masses both in Newtown and with Edel. The chapel at Gatwick was special—sort of a pledge to love each other in our unique way forever. We have a prayer service tonight at 9:00pm—in Thanksgiving for the year. You will be my primary reason to give

thanks. Your love for me has revitalized my life (as I never tire of telling you) and I sincerely hope mine has done the same for you. I'm getting good at feeling your spirit here with me—and that can <u>never</u> be taken away.

I've said a number of the chapel's Masses— good to see the parishioners again. They seem to have missed me. I've gone to a few movies but they weren't too good. I've tried one racquet ball game—my knee held up—I actually beat a pretty good player. They've installed a Nautilus weight program (big machine) in our sports center. I worked out on them today,—seems to exercise every muscle in your body. I'm tired but I feel good.

I've got a huge teddy bear (which somebody gave me) sitting in my rocking chair. How I wish you were there instead of it and we could celebrate the New Year together.

*Well, as we head into 1988 I pray to God that you will find happiness and **peace**. I guess we both must remain confident that God is directing our lives and certainly was responsible for my going to Wales and meeting you. Though far apart, I will always be with you in spirit (in the stars, along your river, in music, in prayer, and in laughter and love of life). Have a <u>super New Year</u>—be strong and courageous and bathed in the love of God.*

Love always,
Bill
Xxx

New Year's Eve was spent with my brother Donald and some of his friends. I was glad of the company as I realized how much I had grown as a person in the past few months. The year 1988 was going to be my best year yet. I felt stronger, braver, and happier than before. Adrian called me daily, so we were beginning to discuss what needed to change in order for our marriage to work. All of my life, I had striven to do the right thing in all areas. Whenever a problem arose, I would stop and consider, "What would Jesus do?" Then I did it. In all my dealings with Adrian, I had tried to behave in a godly way even when I would have preferred to break a frying pan on his head. It had been such a struggle, but now, because of Bill, I had the courage to fight for a better life.

"Have you heard from Father Bill?" Adrian asked during one of our phone conversations.

"Yes, he has called me, and we're writing to each other again. I've told him that he can write to me in Newtown too when I get back."

"So you're keeping in touch then."

"Yes, Adrian. We've been friends for a long time. I can't explain it, but we do love each other. We've loved each other for a long time, even before I met you. It's difficult to explain, but it's real." I was trying to establish the conditions for my return, and being able to write and receive letters without fear of violence was critical to my peace.

"Well, I guess he's practically a member of your family," he added.

"Yes, and he's a good man, and a priest." I offered this last comment as an added assurance that he was no threat to our relationship.

"Well, I did blame him for our breakup, but I guess it's not his fault."

"No, Adrian, we were headed in that direction already. Neither of us was happy, were we?"

"No, you're right. I've stopped drinking, by the way. I know the evil drink was a big problem. No more, Julie, I promise."

"Oh, Adrian, I'm so happy to hear that. It will make all the difference to us," I said, offering support. He had at least accepted that we both needed to change if we were to salvage our marriage, and his giving up alcohol was a great step forward. I prayed he could keep it up.

My father, an avid reader of books with a spiritual theme, had left quite a library behind when he moved to Ireland, so I used my spare time not only to write letters to Bill but also to read, with the intention of learning how to become a better person. I had been studying a book called *A Cry for Mercy* by Henri J. M. Nouwen and another on the theme of freedom called *Jesus Spells Freedom* by Michael Green. They both helped me see how I must treat Adrian. He must feel God's love through me and know that he is loved, even if he feels undeserving of it.

I gained strength and inspiration for the road ahead from the continued connection to Bill, through the letters and phone calls.

> *11 Dyrham View*
> *Pucklechurch,*
> *BRISTOL*
> *Jan. 2nd 1988*
>
> *Dearest Bill,*
>
> *It is almost midnight and I can't sleep for thinking about you. Perhaps after writing this letter I will be able to settle.*
>
> *The wind is howling outside, we have had a couple of very stormy days—definitely not weather to venture out in.*
>
> *I was so happy to catch you last night. Do have a happy 1988. Wish that with all my heart. I would have stayed up till 4am if necessary in order to talk to you. There are so many things I want to say to you that words aren't enough. I can't eat, sleep or concentrate on anything. What have you done to me?*
>
> *Even when I make a real effort to put you out of my mind, something happens to bring you straight back—a tune, a picture, a television programme. Guess what's being shown all this week? Yes, The Thorn Birds, definitely compulsory viewing!*
>
> *I have been on my own with the children for a couple of days as Stephen has gone to Switzerland and Sean is spending the weekend with friends.*

The weather has been so dreadful we haven't been able to go out. I am finding it difficult to keep myself occupied. The boredom is getting to me. I keep remembering all the things you and I packed into Friday afternoon and Saturday, what a blissful time that was. I will never forget it. I can't even recall being happier or more at peace with myself. Everything was so good and right. Thank you.

Although it was only a fortnight ago, it seems like another time, another world, almost unreal, I can't explain it very well.

Perhaps it was a little taste of Heaven, yes, that's what it was. We are so fortunate, you'll never know how grateful I am for you changing my life. If nothing else ever goes right for me, I'll always have those three magnificent days. I know now what happiness is thanks to you.

I came across the following verse on a card last year and sent it to Stephen as he was in need of comfort at the time. He keeps it on his desk.

It is pretty good advice, I could certainly do with heeding it. Hope you like it.

Live each day to the fullest,
Get the most from each hour,
Each day and each age of your life,
Then you can look forward with confidence
And back without regrets...
Be yourself—but be your best self.
Dare to be different and to follow
Your own star...and don't be afraid to be happy.
Enjoy what is beautiful.
Love with all your heart and soul,
Believe that those you love, love you.

When you are faced with a decision,
Make that decision as wisely as possible—

Then forget it. The moment of
Absolute certainty never arrives.
Above all remember that God
Helps those who help themselves.
Act as if everything depended on you,
And pray as if everything depended on God.

                        S. H. Paver

It is now past 1am and I am beginning to feel more inclined toward sleep. You are probably just finishing your evening meal and preparing to go out somewhere. It seems strange to think of you at this moment not in the time I'm in. Somehow it emphasizes the distance between us. I miss you so much, you make me laugh and that is so good.

Pictures of us keep flashing through my mind. Mass on Sunday, kissing your hand at the airport, sitting by the river at night, looking for Pilate washing his hands, wondering where the wandering mummy had got to, opening presents in the confessional, losing each other in Harrods, retracing our steps to look at The Kiss for the first or second time! Not to mention the artist and his second wife. Admiring the gentle man with long hair on the tube. Rubbing the wrong knee better, St. Paul's cathedral and nativity. Discovering the artist wasn't a drunk but a baron, seeking out the haunted house, playing Trivial Pursuit, watching the wedding video, touching…and so on and so on.

I will always remember.

Take good care of yourself and have a wonderful 1988. I will think of you every day and pray for you.

Goodnight, God Bless.
                    Your ever loving tie straightener.
                                        Julie x x
                                        Time 1:35

11 Dyrham View,
Pucklechurch,
Bristol,
10-1-88

Dearest Bill,
Thank you for your beautiful letter written New Year's Eve. I wish I was sitting in your rocking chair in place of the teddy bear too!

I also received Karen's letter to which I have replied, it was very kind of her to write to me, she has suffered too. There was so much I didn't write in the letter, I could have gone on for ages.

You were in my dreams last night again. At first you weren't happy with me but then we made up which was the best bit! When I woke up it was a great disappointment to realize it had all been a dream.

"Brief Encounter" was on the television the other night as a tribute to Trevor Howard who died during the week. I stayed up especially to watch it. All the way through it my visit to London with you was flooding my mind. What a blissfully happy time that was.

Mam's letter arrived a couple of days ago. She has my best interest at heart I'm sure but the letter left me in rather a quandary. I shall just keep praying for guidance and remember it's my life.

Just six days before we return to Newtown, I'll admit to being a bit nervous. Vincent was here last night offering advice, he has been very helpful.

There are definitely going to be some major adjustments in my marriage.

Adrian's pledge to give up drinking didn't last long, he was drunk on Friday night and out again on Saturday, his excuse was he was saying goodbye to Derek. When I get back he will have to abstain permanently.

He has suggested we attend a Marriage Guidance bureau which is a good sign. It will have to be outside Newtown as Theresa's mother is the counsellor in Newtown. Adrian would feel uncomfortable with her.

Why are you a priest? Sorry, that was out of order. If you hadn't become a priest we would never have met would we? And what a loss that would have been in my life.

I love you so much it hurts. You must tell me to be quiet if that is what you want, it's just how I feel.

God has been so good to me allowing you to bring so much happiness into my life. My prayer is that you are especially happy because of me.

Words aren't enough.

Sean and his girlfriend Nicola went up to London for three days—they stayed with Edel.

They visited Harrods, Covent Garden, St. Paul's and the Tate Gallery (after consulting me of course).

They missed the Turner wing but saw Rodin's kiss first time!

Sean was impressed mostly by the enormous painting of The Deluge. Remember? You and I sat down to gaze at it. They didn't seem as enthralled with it all as I had been. It was obviously the com-

pany I was keeping at the time that made all the difference.

You mentioned working out in your gym. I'll be taking up swimming or some kind of "keep fit" or "get fit" in my case, when I return home. At least your knee isn't causing you too many problems. That rubbing I gave it must have done the trick.

Think of me particularly next week when I'll be beginning another chapter in my life. I need to know you are thinking about me, it will keep me courageous whenever circumstances become difficult.

Keep praying and smiling and know that you are special to me in a very good way.

God is bombarded with prayers of thanks from me, for you.

Take care of yourself and drop me a line at home. I've told Adrian you will be writing to me.

All my love,
Julie xx

Jesuit Community
Xavier University
3800 Victory Pkwy
Cincinnati, 45207
Jan. 11, 1988

Dear Julie,

Your first letter arrived on Jan 8—two weeks after you mailed it. I guess at this time of year that's about average. Be sure to put the postal code (45207) on address, that might help. I'll write once a week. I hope the postman delivers the mail to Teresa—he's likely to see your name and will put it in your box.

In any event, I certainly hope your arrival back home has been a peaceful one. You certainly deserve a peaceful and happy marriage. My prayers will be with you.

Enclosed is a picture of Mary Margaret and her family. Her two boys are 7 and 5—not too different from Michael and Sean. Her girl is 1 ½. They live in Louisville, Kentucky—about 100 miles from Cincinnati. It's an easy drive since it is expressway (motorway) all the way. I went down there last week and showed them the slides I took this summer. Mary thought you and the kids look great (I agreed!!). In about a week I'll have some prints made of the best of them and will send you copies. As I said before, the one of the two of us came out pretty good though we're tilted –gives sort of a dynamic quality.

The weather here has been <u>COLD</u>——close to 0 degrees F. but very little snow. That often happens to us – the snow usually goes north of us and sometimes even south of us. I miss it a bit.

Speaking of missing—I miss you constantly. You became so much a part of my life and will always remain so. In a real way though you have become not just a part of my life but a part of ME and therefore you are with me constantly. So while I miss your physical presence I am in touch with you in a beautiful and special way. I agree one week-end every 20 years is not enough (especially since I would be 73! next time) so let's hope for the best— who knows what the future will bring.

I spent most of last week sorting out the slides of the trip and after seeing them on the big screen at Mary Margaret's will do some more weeding this week. I may go down there again next Saturday to see my brother John and his wife who will be visiting. It's easier seeing them there than in Chicago (where they live but is 350 miles from here).

I haven't been doing much walking (too cold) but I have been swimming a bit plus working out 3 times a week on some nautilus machines. They are nice—each one works a different muscle. I figure I better stay in shape if I'm going to be 73 the next time we meet!

Everybody tells me I'm changed (for better!) and for most part I let them believe it was the 3 month program. I have told a couple of people about our love for each other and it feels good to talk about it. They were quite sympathetic. The main thing is that God I think blesses it and will bring good for both of us out of it.

I miss you immensely and think of you often— especially when going to bed and waking up. I so often can sense your touch and your smell. That can never be taken away.

I sincerely wish you and Adrian every blessing in the world. My one wish is for your happiness— now and forever.

Love,
Bill xx

11 Dyrham View,
Pucklechurch,
BRISTOL
11-1-88

Dearest Bill,
I hope you're well and happy. I have been thinking about you today and about our so special time together. It prompted me to write a poem.

Everything, including the weather, was just so right. Things appeared more beautiful, events had a mystical quality and only because of love.

Only a few days before I go home—think of me and include me in your prayers.

Yet again it is past midnight. It is very rare for me to get up and go to bed the same day!

My brother Sean and I have been singing and dancing in the kitchen most of the evening, just fooling around, Amy was enthralled and a bit bemused by it all. It was good fun and I laughed a lot. The neighbours will be wondering what sort of a house this is!

I look forward to Sean coming home from work in the evening as the days are lonely despite the fact I've got the children for company.

During each day I pray and while I pray, tears start to fall. Each time I pray this occurs. Perhaps it's God's way of releasing the tension in me.

Do you ever cry? (apart from when you are saying farewell). I'm sure you do as you are such a softie. Oh how I miss you. As I write this perhaps you are thinking about me. It's about 8:30 pm your time.

Don't forget to send the photographs to "150." I'm looking forward to seeing them.

Remember you are constantly on my mind and always in my prayers.

Be happy and God Bless you,

All my love,
Julie xx

London 1987, December 18–21

This London on December day,
Dreary, damp, and dismal gray,
Since pre-Dickensian days we're told
Saw Mother Nature's wintry hold.

CHOOSING EROS

With what splendid, spectral ease
Our earthly mother did deceive
Not only us but others too
With her majestic vision new.

Did not the golden sunlight bathe
Our hearts with warmth from piercing rays?
Chilled not the wind but gentle breeze
Caressed the skin with graceful ease.

And night's encircling cloak arrayed
With stars, celestial charms displayed
While yet again by riverside
Did beauty in all and us abide.

Were we in some ethereal place?
Love's captives lost in time and space,
Where Turner and Rodin enhanced the scene
While we discovered what we had not seen.

Within your eyes the truth revealed,
A love so precious and so real.
Gaze into mine on occasions rare
That perfect love is reflected there.

To dearest Bill, all my love, Julie

Chapter 13

Keep up the courage.

And so the day to return to Adrian arrived. I was resolved to work hard at our marriage, filled with renewed courage and confidence. Bill had assured me that I was loved in an undeniable, tangible, and mysterious way, and this revelation had expanded my capacity to love. In my mind, Adrian would benefit from my friendship with Bill, and my hope was that our marriage would recover, and one day Adrian and Bill would become friends. I believed that with love, all things were indeed possible.

Adrian arrived in Pucklechurch to take us home on the same day that Derek left for Australia. It was to mark a new beginning—"a fresh start" for us all.

It was clear that Adrian was making great efforts to be a better husband. We had discussed on the phone how life must be different and what adjustments had to be made if we were to enjoy a happy marriage. We were making progress. Adrian was full of promises he intended to keep when he made them. No more violence, no more drinking, more involvement with the children, and repeated assurances that he had changed.

"I agree with you that we'll need to go for counselling, Adrian. We need help to get back on track," I urged.

"Oh, absolutely, love. Whatever you want. I really have changed, you'll see. I really want this to work this time. I promise to do *everything* in my power to make it work. I promise." His voice revealed his sincere commitment. "Only not in Newtown, okay? Theresa's mum is the counsellor there, and that's too close for comfort for me."

"That's fine. I'm sure there are other counsellors there too we can go to. Don't worry. It'll be fine." I was encouraged by his willingness to seek outside help.

I had become brave—setting boundaries and commanding respect. Bill's love propelled me forward, sustaining me and spilling over into my marriage like waves of soothing calm. I knew that I was loved. It was empowering and filled me with hope.

"What else, sweetheart? Tell me what else you need," Adrian invited.

"Well, I don't want you to ask me to borrow money from the neighbors anymore. It's too embarrassing, and I hate lying to them."

"No problem. I can do that. No more asking to borrow money. Got it. Anything else?"

"Well, yes, there is one more thing," I added.

"Name it! It'll happen. I want you to see that I've really changed, Julie." His voice was upbeat, and it suited him.

"Well, I want to be able to meet my friends at Evans Café for coffee from time to time and not be worried that I can't afford it. So I'll need one pound a week spending money that I can use just for me." Although to some one pound may seem like a paltry sum to be asking for, it was a significant victory at the time.

"Absolutely! You deserve a break once a while. Are you sure one pound is enough? You can have two pounds if you like," he offered magnanimously.

"No, no, one pound is plenty for coffee and a Chelsea bun. Thank you, though."

The verbal contract was agreed, the conditions clearly expressed, and I wanted to believe that, this time, our marriage would survive.

The next few days passed with Adrian, like a glittering firework bursting with energy and light, immersed himself wholeheartedly into the domestic arena of cooking, cleaning, playing with the children, and enquiring after my well-being. I was impressed by his zeal but also recognized the familiar behavioral pattern from previous reconciliations. I wondered how long he could maintain the effort before his energy fizzled out, and his spark would be replaced by smoldering, dangerous heat.

Although I was appreciative of his attentiveness, for him there was only one way I should express my gratitude of his renewed commitment to our marriage, and that way was through sex.

But I was not ready, and my hesitation annoyed him. From his perspective, he had made so many changes for the sake of preserving our marriage, and I had made none. To him, it didn't seem fair.

I was still recalling the natural concern, tenderness, and care with which Bill had treated me in our brief time together, only a few weeks earlier. I had been spoiled. Adrian was dealing with a different woman than the timid girl he had dominated for twelve years.

In the past, when I had left and returned, eager to believe the promises to reform, proof of my renewed pledge was expected by agreeing to have another baby. This had always satisfied Adrian, who saw it as "sealing the deal" and guaranteed that I would be around for at least another couple of years. "Barefoot and pregnant and chained to the sink" was one of his familiar refrains.

This time was different. I was not prepared to provide the same assurances. My reluctance elicited a familiar response, one of suffocating possessiveness, where Adrian's need for constant physical displays of affection consumed his focus. He expected keen reciprocation, once we were in bed, to his amorous advances made earlier in the day, whether it was a kiss on the back of the neck while I was washing dishes or cuddling on the couch, as in our courting days.

"Oh, for God's sake, Julie, can't you see I've changed?" His exasperation was surfacing as I recoiled from his touch. "Come on, will you? You're my wife!"

"I know, Adrian, I know. I'm trying, but I'm just not ready yet." My feeble response served only to exacerbate the issue.

"Well, you'd best get ready soon, or it will be too late. You're killing the love I have for you with this nonsense! Do you realize that?" His implied threat was evident.

"I'm sorry, Adrian," I offered. "I can see that you're trying so hard, but it's going to take a while to rebuild the trust. Please be patient with me. I do want us to figure this out."

"Well, my patience won't last forever, so you best get a move on," he snapped.

"Perhaps the marriage guidance will help. We've got our first meeting on the twenty-sixth," I said optimistically.

"Well, something better help, or you'll have ruined our marriage. I've changed, like you wanted, so you need to do your bit too."

"I do see how much effort you're making, and I am grateful, Adrian, honestly. I need you to be more patient, that's all."

"Well, I blame Theresa—you spend too much time with her, and I think she has it in for me," he said, reaching for a cigarette on the bedside table.

"Oh, don't be ridiculous. Theresa's got nothing to do with this! She's a good friend, that's all. This is *not* about her." I took a deep breath and turned to face the wall, praying that silence would descend.

Our arguments became predictable and exhausting, chipping away at the same jaded issues daily, eroding our marriage's already flimsy foundation.

109 Lon Gerylli,
Maesydail,
Newtown,
Powys SY 16 1QH
Mid Wales
19-1-88

Dearest Bill,

Many thanks for your letter which arrived at Theresa's today, that's where it will stay. Theresa brings the letters into town and I sit beside the river to read them before returning them into her care.

I have put her address at the top of the page, though I am writing this at home. The photograph of Mary Margaret and her family is lovely. Her hair is beautiful.

Well, I have been back four days and it has been very strained. Adrian has made a real effort which I do appreciate, he is helping around the house, we went swimming as a family, and he only had one pint of beer and a shandy when we went out together Saturday night. He couldn't come to Mass on Sunday as he was called into work.

I pray every day that this is the way it is going to be from now on, (which he is constantly reminding me).

The main problem which we still have to overcome is sex. I don't feel ready yet, I am afraid to give myself totally to Adrian just to be hurt all over again. He doesn't understand this and is putting pressure on me the whole time with such words as "Say you love me," "Can't you see I've changed?" He is always holding my hand and asking me to kiss him and sit beside him the whole time, (which I do) but when he wanted to make love and I asked for more time to get used to us being together again he got very upset and said I was destroying our marriage and killing the love he has for me. He also said it mustn't go on too long or there won't be any love left in his heart for me.

He has also said he will take his own life if I leave him again as he loves me so much life wouldn't be worth living without me.

I have spent <u>hours</u> trying to explain how I feel, he really doesn't understand. Perhaps the marriage guidance counsellor will help us sort these things out. We have an appointment at 2pm on Tuesday 26th. Adrian has asked me to stop seeing Theresa, he thinks she is trying to break us up. He thinks because he has given up some things I should give up Theresa.

There is no way that I'll stop having Theresa as my friend. She is the only person I confide in.

I have suggested that Adrian takes up some sport or keep fit, but he insists that he only wants *to be with me. That from now on we should do <u>everything</u> together. There should be no need for outside activities or interests. I am beginning to feel smothered.*

I will be going swimming on a regular basis during the day time. Adrian doesn't object to this as he will be working. I am beginning to wonder what his reaction to my taking up some evening activity will be, We shall see.

Enough on that subject!

I'm so glad you are here for me. I miss you greatly. During the day the housework gets done to the strains of Zamfir, Tchaikovsky and Mozart. You are on my mind and suddenly the chores are a pleasure to do.

I was thrilled to receive your letter this morning. My heart missed a beat while I read it. You've no idea how you've affected me—I am so looking forward to seeing the photos, especially the one of you and I together, which I shall always treasure.

Remember you are <u>always</u> on my mind.

I love you,

Julie xx

Jesuit Community Xavier University 3800 Victory Parkway Cincinnati Ohio 45207 (513) 745 3591 1/28/88

Dearest Julie,

Your letter of 1/19/88 arrived yesterday, reflecting many of the things you talked about on the phone. I hope the visit to the marriage counsellor helped things out a bit in clearing the air. Make sure he/she gets your <u>honest</u> feelings and <u>facts.</u> You might *want to schedule a private session if it's too difficult to talk in front of Adrian. Perhaps you already have.*

A few of my thoughts on what you said. Your feelings of suffocation are honest ones—any successful marriage must allow "space" for both partners. Adrian's desire to monopolize all your time is decidedly unhealthy and reflects a very poor self-image on his part (undoubtedly from his childhood)—so too his constant expression of suicide if you should leave him. He definitely needs counselling help in a professional way. But unless he does improve (very questionable!) your choice seems to be whether you want to offer up your happiness and probably the happiness of the kids just to satisfy his needs (which are totally unreasonable). Once love is gone (and did you ever really love him?—or was it pity?) it seldom comes back. Pity is no base for marriage. Don't forget every marriage counsellor and psychologist I spoke to at St. Bueno's said you should have left long ago so unless he does show decided improvement (not just surface concessions) make plans and get out. I hope the numbers I furnished (and the counselling you're getting) do provide some assistance. Don't let the suicide threat ever stop you. Even if it were serious, it's better to take the chance than condemning all of you to a long, unhappy life (just a slow form of death!). Still, I'll pray for the miracle and let's hope for the best (but at least plan for the worst!). Deep down I don't think he loves you—he needs you. That is not love. Love is openness.

Happier news—I did send the Anthony De Mello tapes and the background materials in one package and the photographs to another (both to Theresa's address). By the way, don't ever give up Theresa as a friend—sounds like you both are very good for each other. I liked her the minute I met her.

Also stick with your swimming and whatever other activities you need.

I hope you enjoy the tapes and like the pictures. I'm glad the one of us turned out reasonably well— even if tilted! How do you like that burst of light over Amy's head in your backyard? I also really like the one of Brian and Amy and the one of the three boys framed in the church window. I have the pic of you and I plus you and Amy on my desk.

I too am thrilled every time I see a letter from you in my box and you are <u>always</u> in my mind and in my heart.

The temperature today is supposed to go up into the mid 50's so I'm putting my bike in a car and heading to a bike trail about 20 miles away. It's 13 1/2 mile long (paved) old railway path that goes along a river and through a forest—<u>very</u> beautiful. How I wish you were joining me. Ever thought of getting a bike? You could even get a carrier for Amy. <u>Great</u> exercise.

I'll be anxious to hear how the counselling is going. In the meanwhile, keep up the courage and your gorgeous smile.

You are <u>treasured</u>.

<u>Deepest</u> love,
Bill
Xxx

Chapter 14

"Mr. and Mrs. Long. Welcome!" greeted the counsellor cheerfully, ushering us into her office. "Please, have a seat," she invited as Adrian and I tentatively smiled in response. "Let me explain the process, and if you have any questions, any questions at all, feel free to ask, okay?"

"Yes, thank you," I replied. Adrian nodded.

"Well, today will be about getting to hear from you both as a couple, what you see as the main areas that need help in your relationship. Then later we'll set up individual appointments where you can each speak privately about—"

"Oh no! That's not going to happen!" Adrian interrupted sharply, his anxiety exposed by her suggestion. "Anything she's got to say, she can say in front of me. We've got nothing to hide from each other."

"I don't mind if we do that," I interjected, hoping that two against one would win out.

Ambushed by his outburst, the counsellor conceded. "Well, that's usually how it's done, but we can be flexible and revisit that possibility another time perhaps." She was being politely assertive, establishing the expectations for healthy discourse, but the quiver in her voice betrayed her. She too was being put in her place by Adrian.

We discussed the tension in our marriage, which Adrian attributed to my refusing to have sex. "I've no problem," he said. "She's the one with the problem. She's as dry as a stick." I felt embarrassed by his description of me.

"Would you like to respond to your husband's comments, Mrs. Long?" The counsellor seemed eager to move on.

"Well, I've just recently returned to Adrian, and I need more time to prepare for that level of intimacy," I explained.

"Tell her where you were. Go on! Tell her how you ran off with a priest!" Adrian goaded.

"I didn't run off with a priest, Adrian. I was with my sister and then my brothers. Father Bill is back in America." I was on the defensive.

The counsellor, though a volunteer, helped us to return to a civil exchange, although the discussion at times seemed to be in danger of spiraling downward into a sparring match about Father Bill, my relationship with Theresa, my "galivanting," and my frigidity. She skillfully brought it back to a more reasonable conversation. I worried that the whole session had seemed like a wasted effort, but the counsellor had a different perspective, setting up a second appointment for the following week. "Now we have a place from which to move forward," she said confidently. "I look forward to seeing you both again soon."

150 Lon Dolafon,
Vaynor
NEWTOWN
Powys
27-1-88

Dearest Bill,

Thank you, so much for your letters (four in two days)—one arrived at above address and two at Theresa's—unfortunately I won't be able to read those till next week when Adrian has returned to work. I shall look forward eagerly to that (reading your letters that is!)

We had our first encounter with the marriage guidance counsellor yesterday—we have agreed to have three separate hourly sessions to begin with, we may need longer. Adrian didn't find it as daunting as he had imagined, we talked well with one another. The counsellor asked Adrian if he had been badly rejected as a young man, when he became rather intent on impressing on her how important it is for me to be at home for him at all times, even though he is at work.

We also discuss _you_ at length—needless to say! Also my "obsession" (his words) with Theresa. He has accused me of being a lesbian during one argument this week.

The counsellor suggested we have separate meetings as well as joint ones, but Adrian said we should both be present at all times, so I have agreed. I said I didn't mind speaking alone, so perhaps we will broach it again at a later stage. We have had quite heated rows each day since my return, except Sunday, but we have also apologized to one another afterwards each time. So, we are making progress, slowly. Enough on that subject!

It seems a long time until Monday, when I can read your letters, patience is going to become one of my finer points, it's got to be if twenty years are going to pass before I see you again!

Theresa is now reading my book, "Friendship in the Lord." She says it is a Godsend. It has helped her come to terms with a few problem areas in her own life. It certainly clarified my own thoughts on relationships, particularly the very special relationship you and I share. You can never know how much I treasure you.

The parliamentary bill that David Alton introduced reducing abortion from 28 to 18 weeks, has been voted in which delights me. It still has a few stages to pass through hopefully it will be successful. With our prayers it is sure to win through. The weather here has been very cold. We had our first snow last weekend. The coat you bought me protects me from the elements—it was a good buy! Derek is enjoying much better weather in Sidney. He cer-

tainly chose the best time to go to Australia with all the celebrations, etc. We expect to hear from him in the next few weeks. Adrian is busy decorating Amy's room at present. Edel and Tom bought some cute animal wallpaper in a sale last year and gave it to us. It was very kind.

We waited to do the room as we didn't want Derek to feel uneasy. It will look lovely when it's completed. The boys room will have to be next. This must all sound very dull to you. My life isn't very exciting, or is it?!

I wish you were here, sometimes, with my eyes closed I imagine we are together, or if my eyes are open that you are in the next room, or round the corner in the street and that any moment I'll catch a glimpse of you, oh if only...

Just believe that if I could be with you, I would.

I love you to pieces and have gained so much pleasure from knowing and being with you. I was listening to Barbara Streisand yesterday singing "Snowbird" (one of Theresa's records that I've borrowed). You must be my snowbird. Afterward on the radio I heard "A Nightingale Sang in Berkeley Square." Always something to remind me. Not that I need any reminders. The way I feel about you will never change. Except perhaps to get stronger. You make me so happy—right now it's what's keeping me going. Only a couple of hours ago, Adrian was banging his fist on the table and shouting at me "I demand that you love me." I cannot reassure him enough by the way I am so he still shouts at me every day and says I have got to love him. You on the other hand made no demands. Thank you. While I was crying today and praying for guidance, I was shouting at you in my mind asking "What have you done to me?!" (I really don't think Adrian knows how to love and he makes it so hard to reach him) and though I was cross with you momentarily, because you love me I was soon calm again and counting my blessings.

Pray for me, as I do for you. God knows we need each other, and I thank him daily for you.

I will love you always.

Julie xx

Jesuit Community Xavier University 3800 Victory Parkway Cincinnati Oh 45207 (513) 745 3951

Dearest Julie,

Your letter of 25/1/88 arrived today with the Regent Palace brochure. It did indeed bring back gorgeous memories—a truly magical one as you so beautifully put it. I hope my letter to the Lon Dolafon address finally arrived—If not, Adrian probably tore it up. Anyway, I also hope tapes and pictures have arrived (at Theresa's).

I just reread one of my favorite books "The Road Less Traveled" —a new psychology of love, traditional values and spiritual growth—by M. Scott Peck. I'd highly recommend it. Good section on character disorders might help you figure out Adrian. Super section on love (helped me figure out what happened to us!. He has a great definition of love: "The will to extend one's self for the purpose of nurturing one's own or another's spiritual growth." He explains it beautifully and of course this encompasses all kinds of love. I think we had this ever since we met 20 years ago (and indeed we do still have it—more than ever). A good quote from a few *pages on – talking about <u>too</u> much togetherness in a marriage, "Ultimately, if they stay in therapy, all couples learn that a true acceptance of their own and each other's individuality and separateness is the only foundation upon which a true marriage can be based and real love can grow." So stick with your need for doing things on your own!! I would hope the marriage counsellor would support this.*

To another point—to add to our love we complicated (in a wondrous way.) by "falling in love." As Dr. Peck points out, "The experience of <u>falling in love</u> is specifically a sex-linked erotic experience"— (as we began to be aware as our weekend wore on!!) "We fall in love only when we are consciously or unconsciously sexually motivated." I think both of us were unconscious of it at first. Secondly, he points out (maybe good in long run for you!) "that the experience of falling in love is invariably temporary. No matter whom we fall in love with we sooner or later fall out of love if the relationship continues long enough. This is not to say that we invariably cease loving the person with whom we fell in love."

Maybe this helps explain those sinking feelings in our stomachs, etc. etc., Anyhow the distance between us will complicate things a bit but who cares—God did arrange things and all will indeed be well. I guess it is good to distinguish between the two. Even if we do slowly <u>fall out of love</u> (<u>no sign of it yet!</u>) our <u>love</u> will still continue—always!

It's been a dismal two days here, very warm (60) but very rainy. I was really hoping to get one of your letters—a feeling of joy and warmth comes over me just to hold something you held.

I was glad to see what the Baron looked like. I do hope you can get back there to finally get that portrait painted. I'm looking at the picture of the two of us now – plus the one of you and Amy. Both are in front of me as I write this. (I took the desk pictures before I got the prints!.) Anyway, just thinking of you and looking at you fills me with an indescribable love—and I feel God blesses us and will bring each of us to greater and greater love because of it.

You are special—gorgeous—wonderful and I love you deeply (I'm still working out!!)

Bill

P.S. Hope you got my message on the tape.

Our second meeting with the marriage guidance counsellor followed a week after the first, where the discussion was mostly about our lack of intimacy and what, or who, was to blame. Adrian, incensed by the counsellor's suggestion that we slowly build up to full sexual intercourse, first beginning with a few preliminary exercises as a couple, refused to listen. For him, it was all my fault. The counsellor persisted until Adrian begrudgingly agreed to take home a book containing the exercises and other related topics rather than face the humiliation of having a woman telling him how he should behave with his wife in bed.

150 Lon Dolafon
Vaynor
Newtown
Powys
2/2/88

Dearest Bill,

Many thanks for the letters, the photos of your room and the tapes which all arrived at Teresa's today. I look forward to listening to them. I told Adrian that the tapes had arrived and the photos. We have been getting along much better since last Friday, in fact on Sunday night we had a really good talk mostly about my trip to London. It was the first time I had been able to discuss it with Adrian. I was able to tell him how I felt about you, how safe, happy and loved while in your presence and just how much I love you.

He understood that the love I have for you is real but separate from the love I have for him, and that you are not and <u>were</u> not a threat to our marriage. After our talk he said he felt really at peace for the first time in years. In fact he said he could probably grow to love you himself if he got to know you better and that you would always be welcome in this house. Compliments, eh?!

I said a silent prayer of thanks to God and was convinced that a miracle was taking shape. I appreciate your concern for me regarding the very "special" love we share. I promise you it has <u>not</u> interfered (except to make me more loving towards people) or more importantly not prevented me from being totally loving toward Adrian. The problems we are experiencing in the physical side of our relationship are not as a result of my association with you, far from it! This thought may have crossed your mind, I know it has mine. Be assured that nothing but goodness and beauty and happiness have stemmed from our love for each other. All positive aspects. And I certainly count myself blessed to be loved by you, who are incredibly good and selfless (and modest!).

We had our second meeting with the marriage guidance counsellor today. It was disastrous. Perhaps that is too strong a word, it certainly wasn't fruitful.

Neither yourself or Theresa were mentioned, you'll be glad to hear. The whole hour was taken up discussing the absence of sex in our relationship at present. The counsellor was very sympathetic *towards Adrian and understood why he is feeling so frustrated with me. We discussed my attitude—she also understood how I felt. Her suggestion for solving what I consider to be a temporary stage seem totally acceptable to me. There is a program where for one week, say, we would stroke each other in the <u>non</u> erogenous zones and then the following week progress slightly further until after a few short weeks we could be enjoying a completely satisfactory and mutually beneficial sex life. To my dismay Adrian went almost berserk. He refused to even consider it saying it was <u>all</u> my fault we were in this mess and I was the one who should be putting things right. All through the hour long session he was reminding me of how I was to blame. He told the counsellor that she had no right to tell us how to behave, that she was just there to listen.*

Eventually, when calm was restored, she asked if Adrian would mind reading a book about sex therapy, rather than have her instructing him, to which he reluctantly agreed, while muttering "it won't do any good, It's her, she's to blame." I felt helpless. I do so want things to be right between us. Adrian makes it so hard. Anyway we have the book on loan for one week, so who knows maybe we can get it together. Say a prayer for us.

The tapes you sent have arrived at an ideal time. Theresa, her sister Mary and myself have decided to meet regularly to discuss books we have read regarding our faith. Only minutes after finalizing the details we discovered the tapes in Theresa's hall, so we shall all be listening to them together and following the accompanying script (don't worry. Your personal message to me will not be heard by anyone but me!).

Your room is very much as I imagined it, at least now I will be able to visualize you while speaking on the telephone and think of you listening to music and visualize myself in your rocking chair. I am so fortunate to have you as my trusted and beloved friend. I don't disclose to anyone else but you (because you understand me) my deepest thoughts and desires. Thank you.

The weather has been extremely cold (thank goodness for my nice warm coat!) just one small detail—no hood! I shall have to invest in a wooly hat to keep my ears warm!

The snow looks lovely from your window— you are quite high up too! What I wouldn't give to help you build a snowman.

Take care my dearest man and remember I'm praying for your happiness which is just as important as mine but more deserving.

God bless you,

Love,
Julie
Xx

"You can carry this," Adrian directed, handing me the book on sex on loan from the counsellor. "It's not going to do any good, though." To my relief, the rather sturdy book, containing myriad pictures, both photographic and illustrated, of people in various stages of physical intimacy, had been placed discreetly in a shopping bag. I knew it would take more than a few novel and exotic sexual positions to bring us closer.

Adrian's curiosity prompted him to examine the book closely once the children had been put to bed. Its contents were presented much more clinically than the pornographic magazines he purchased and shamefully hid in various dark recesses in our home, knowing of my disapproval.

"Hey, Julie! Look at this! I didn't know people could bend like that," he said, holding the pages open towards me before flipping to the next image.

"I think we're supposed to be reading the directions, Adrian, not just looking at pictures." I was annoyed by his lack of sensitivity and knew that later he would want to assuage his lust on me.

"Hey, don't blame me. I'm just following orders. Blame the counsellor woman—she gave us the book," he said smugly.

"Well, I want to follow her guidelines. It might make a difference if we take it slowly as she suggests. Can I have a look at it, please?"

"Well, it can't hurt to give a go, I expect," he conceded, handing the book over.

My encounter with Bill had motivated me to be even more loving towards everyone. So I knew that I must also be more loving towards Adrian in a way he could receive it, through tangible expression of affection. So while he was out tinkering with a friend's car, I played the tapes on *Silence* by Anthony De Mello which Bill had sent. The soothing message drew me into a meditative state, where I prayed to be the sort of wife that Adrian needed me to be.

"So what does it say then, this book?" asked Adrian once we were in bed.

"Well, it tells us to touch each other gently on our arms and backs to begin with." I inhaled deeply and exhaled silently. "I'll go first, if you like," I said, reaching up to the inside of his arm, which was crooked behind his head, and began stroking his soft skin with my fingertips. He puffed on his cigarette, blowing smoke rings, as I repeated the motion.

"That feels good," he said encouragingly.

"I'm glad. It's meant to feel good," I replied. For the next few minutes, we didn't speak as my fingers told Adrian what he had wanted to know—that I was slowly becoming more willing for sex.

"Okay, your turn!" he said, extinguishing his cigarette and turning on his side, his hand reaching for me and tracing the same pattern of movement on my arms that I had drawn on his. His touch could be gentle, I discovered.

"Relax," he coaxed. "You're so tense."

I drew in a deep breath and expelled it with a loud *whoosh!* which caused us both to chuckle. A surge of affection for him swept over me as his hand continued to glide back and forth delicately on my arm.

"Okay, this side is done. Turn over!" he declared, resting his palm gently on my stomach. As I turned, my wedding ring slipped from my finger.

"Oops! Hold on—stay still!" I said. "My ring's fallen off. I don't want to lose it in the bedclothes."

"Could turn it into a game of hide-and-seek," Adrian suggested mischievously.

"No, thank you. I got it. Now where were we?" I said, inviting him to resume stroking my back. I was proud of him for being so attentive to me and respectful of the process and surrendered to his touch.

"Uh-oh, you've woken up Cecil," announced Adrian, using his pet name for his penis. "What are you going to do about it, hmm?" His tone was cheeky and mischievous.

"Well, don't light up another cigarette just yet," I responded, letting him know that I was ready to prove my love in the way he needed it proved. A few minutes later, his appetite sated and oblivious to the tears I had quietly shed, he asked, "What caused you to change your mind?"

"Well, I've been listening to the tapes that Father Bill sent and reading a lot about being more loving, so I knew I needed to be more affectionate towards you," I explained. He drew me close, my head leaning on his chest, the only light in the room the red glow from his cigarette.

"Well, thank you, Father Bill!" he said to the darkness. "Maybe I'll listen to those tapes myself."

"I think you'd enjoy them. I also prayed to be a better wife," I went on. "I know that we're starting over, and I'm trying to remember that the past is the past and should stay there. This is our new beginning." I so wanted to believe what I was saying, realizing that it would take continued prayer to keep me focused on how I must be in the future.

"It *is* a new beginning, love. We both need to work harder at making each other happy. I can't imagine life without you. I think I'd kill myself if you were to ever leave me again," he added.

"Oh, don't say that anymore, Adrian, please. That's from the past." I was tired of hearing it, especially since his sister, Julia, had taken her own life just a few years earlier.

"Sorry, love, but it's true. But you're right. We're making a new start. Wait and see. Things are going to be different." He pulled me closer, his strong arm wrapped tightly around me—the pressure of the squeeze conveying the measure of his resolve.

We were defying the typical cycle of abuse. With a new start, we expected to feel like we were once again in the honeymoon stage. *It's a miracle*, I thought to myself. *A miracle*! *Thank you, Jesus.* Could this be his turning point? I asked myself. The answer was to come a few days later.

> *150 Lon Dolafon*
> *Vaynor*
> *Newtown*
> *Powys*
> *4/2/88*

> *Dearest Bill,*
>
> *Thank you so much for the lovely photographs and letter which arrived at Theresa's yesterday. I am particularly fond of the one of Michael and Amy – he is a very gentle child—the picture portrays this very well. It is wonderful to have a photo of you and I together, I can look at it and remember. You look good in it, but I look a bit rough! Enclosed is a small picture taken of me the Sunday before our London trip --keep it safe.*
>
> *Adrian likes the photos, too. I didn't say they had arrived at number 109 or that the tapes had gone there either. Feel free to send material like that, which I want to keep at home, to this address.*

The tapes have helped me a great deal so far. On Tuesday evening after our rather unsuccessful meeting with the M.G. counsellor I listened to the silence tape alone. Afterwards, as it was late, I flicked through the accompanying text and my eyes rested on "Freedom." I began to realize it was my reluctance to let go of my fears of the past with Adrian that were hindering our progress. I prayed for help and made a decision to be everything I should be for Adrian. Needless to say, he was delighted. I cried but he didn't notice.

He asked what had prompted my change of heart and I explained about the tapes and my prayer. He then went on to say he might listen to them himself, so this might be his turning point.

Anyway, how are you?...really. I hope you are happy and well. Right now I want to hold you close.

You mentioned putting your bike in a car and setting off. You would be better off riding the bike you know! Don't worry, I'm just being silly again. Ever thought of getting a tandem?

On March 5th I'm going on a day retreat to Pen Maen Mawr in North Wales, not far from where you were. Adrian has agreed to look after the children. I was out last night at a UCM meeting. A local vicar was showing slides of his church's visit to the Holy Land. I felt as though all the monuments and shrines have spoilt it. The nearest I will get to the Holy Land is a pilgrimage to Walsingham on July 5th. It will be my first visit there. I am really looking forward to it.

Adrian is taking more time off shortly—12th—18th February—I don't know what he intends to do for those few days.

It is just midday. You will be getting out of bed now. I am at Theresa's writing this, she is listen-

ing to the tape on Silence, her sister will be joining us shortly to discuss a book we have all read called "Adventures in Prayer" by Catherine Marshall. We all choose a book in turn. I would be grateful for any suggestions you'd like to make. Do you know how much I love you? What I wouldn't do for you.

You are the most loving person I have ever met and very much cherished. God keep you safe.

All my love,
Julie xx

Chapter 15

Only a few hours after I had posted the letter to Bill sharing the news of our marital harmony, Adrian arrived home from work having forgotten to withdraw money from the bank, which had now closed. He had run out of cigarettes and was noticeably agitated.

"Julie, go next door and borrow a fiver till tomorrow. Tell them it's for bread," Adrian demanded in his familiar authoritarian tone, a habit he had yet to break.

"Sorry, Adrian. I'm not doing that anymore, remember?" I said, reminding him of our recent agreement. "You'll need to go yourself."

"Oh, for Chrissake, just do as you're told!" he barked, reverting to the old bullying tactics.

"No," I said firmly. "I'm not doing that anymore. I'm not going back to the way it was!" I was adamant and proud of myself for insisting he respect my answer. His simmering fury at my defiance, in the past placated by my subservience, was released in a tirade of verbal abuse. But I was not to be deterred in my resolve.

Finally, exasperated by my resistance to his will, he bellowed, "If that's how you're going to be, you can get out!" As he yelled, the wedding photo hanging on the wall dropped to the carpet. We both looked over at it, stunned. It may have been the vibrations of his voice, but I took it as a sign.

"All right, I will," I replied, surprising him with an abrupt response. He was used to me pleading, cajoling, and begging him not to be angry, but I was different now, imbued with newfound courage. I knew that I would no longer be dominated.

I called Melvin, Theresa's husband, and asked him to come and pick me and the children up. I grabbed my handbag and waited by the front door.

"Don't be so stupid!" mocked Adrian, annoyed at my continued defiance. "Where are you going to go? Who do you think is going to put you up?"

"I'll figure it out," I said as calmly as I could muster, though my heart was thumping fiercely. I had already posed the same questions to myself and had no answers.

"So you don't love me anymore then?" he pushed. "Say you don't love me. Say it! You can't, can you?" I didn't answer.

"Ah, you can't say it. 'Cause you *do* love me." He was forcing me to back up my actions with words.

"I don't love you anymore." I had said it. He stared at me, unconvinced.

With Amy balanced on my hip, I called out to the boys playing in the garden, "Come in, boys, we're going over to Theresa's." As we climbed into Melvin's car, I knew that I was leaving Adrian for the last time, that I never again would live in that house with him. What I didn't anticipate was the terror awaiting us as the reality of my decision dawned on Adrian, who would swiftly descend into despair.

Melvin and Theresa generously opened their home to the five of us for the night, the boys sharing with their children while Amy and I settled on the living-room couch. Adrian rang repeatedly, pleading with me to go home, and my answer remained a clear *no*. I called Bill briefly on Theresa's landline, conscious of the cost to her, and told him what had happened. He promised to pray for us all and encouraged me to "stay strong." Something had shifted in me, and I knew this was what I needed to do.

Sleep eluded me as I pondered our future. I was not naïve enough to assume that the path I was forging would be strewn with rose petals, but I was also ill equipped to deal with the challenges ahead. A letter from Adrian was waiting on the mat when I got up Friday morning.

4-5/2/88

Julie, I have a proposition to make. If you came back to live in the house with the kids—and I were to move into Brian's room, we would live under the same roof not as man and wife but as a mum and dad. No sex—no kissing ect. This way the bills would be paid. Housework could be shared. Decorating could be finished and the children will have a dad that they need so early in life—there would be no ties between us what so ever and we could come and go as we both please. I promise not to make any advances towards you what so-ever and after say 6 months if it doesn't work I'll leave you to live your life as you see fit—we could still go and see the marriage guidance if you wish. I'm sorry it has come to this as believe me my darling I don't want to hurt you. I'm also sorry for the things I said last night—I have not gone to bed tonight as I have been trying to listen to your tapes on love ect. Darling I'm begging you to think seriously about this—I'll be in town this afternoon to the bank etc. and if we could meet and discuss this without arguing (I PROMISE) and come to some agreement please give me a ring at work. I honestly think this would work and then we could rebuild our lives from the beginning. I promise with my heart that there would be no argueing what so ever. It's that I thought with all the depts ect. that we have, the rent, bank, catalogue ect. it would be very hard for you to manage as we find it difficult some weeks—and if I were to move out and pay someone £30–35 a week alone and you £45.00 per week rent. £40 food for you and £20 for me, taxis, milk, school dinners, gas-electric and the various others I'd have to be earning say £200 a week so in the end we all suffer including the kids, please darling—all I have said I promise not to break, and I think that between us we can lead as normal life as possible—it's up to you my love—on your decision—please ring me this morning and let me know your feelings——yes or no and to arrange a meet this afternoon.

I'm sorry. Remember Julie there will never be anyone to replace you in my heart—and if you wish as you asked in Bristol if it doesn't work after 6–9 months I'll move out I promise and I'll Also put that in writing.

I love you,
Adrian xx

Poem with letter 4-5 /88 Adrian
It has come to a head now = I can't take no more
*   pain*
I've gone over our lives = time and time again.
I've tried my best = but all was in vain
I couldn't love another = I'm going insane
This hurt we've both caused = maybe gods way
Don't leave me my darling = please will you stay.
Let's start from the beginning = let's start anew
But not as a married couple = but as two
I've always wanted what's best = my love
I've tried very hard to understand = the god above.
I'm just learning to except = that there is someone
*   there*
I've prayed every evening in bed = when you were
*   not there*
Let's live together = no sex to be had.
No kissing – no cuddling = let's not be sad
If only for the children – and give deserved love.
No smoking—no bullying = let's get help from him
*   up above*

*My darling—I'm begging = please don't do this to
    me.
I love you so dearly = I wish you could see.
We were getting on great = till this Thursday night
When I opened my big mouth = we had a big fight.
You said you don't love me = deep down I believe
    you do
I want our love to happen = oh how I love you.
With this poem = is a letter I've written you
Please my darling = remember, love you I do*

*   Darling here is a few so called verses that I
wrote while thinking of the hurt I put you through.
    Oh yes I'll give you your letters back should you
come home and believe me my darling I wouldn't
of caused Father Bill no harm as it is not him that
caused all this only I am to blame.*

*I love you,
Adrian*

*   I did not come around last night for an argument just to bring Amy's bottle around.
    Honestly.*

I was not persuaded by the letter, though it did arouse feelings of pity for the man who had written it. Later that day, after meeting with a solicitor and getting some advice, calling the women's shelter and being told that there wouldn't be a space there for us till the following Wednesday, I set off to secure alternative housing for us while the children stayed in Theresa's care.

"So you need to be rehoused?" repeated the council man after I'd explained that I had left an abusive marriage.

"Yes, please," I said.

"Well, it's not quite as simple as you think, Mrs. Long. Do you have an idea how many women come in here and ask for the same thing you are asking for?"

"No, I've no idea," I answered truthfully.

"Well, a lot. They come in here bored with their husbands and expect us to provide a house for them, just like that," he went on.

"Oh, I'm not bored with my husband. I'm afraid of him. He can be very violent," I explained.

"Well, I don't mean to be rude, dear, but you look fine to me. Has he hit you?" He was assessing my need and saw nothing to suggest I should be making such a request.

"He hasn't hit me recently, but he has in the past, and he has the potential to, if I make him angry."

"So you have a home to go back to then."

"Well, no. I left him." I couldn't figure out why this seemingly kind man was unable to understand my predicament. "He told me to get out. So I did."

"Yes, but you can go back, can't you?"

"No, I am afraid to go back. He can be extremely violent."

"Yes, you've already said that. But you've got to understand, I only have your word for it. So without any proof of actual physical harm, you've made yourself what we call *voluntarily homeless*, and we are under no obligation to house you."

Voluntarily homeless. I recalled the term that the solicitor had used earlier, which confirmed what he was telling me. "So you're saying that if I go home and provoke my husband so that he loses his temper and then come back here with a broken nose, cracked ribs, and bruises, you'll be able to help me?"

"Yes, in essence, that's about it," he said, somewhat embarrassed by my straightforward description. I felt deflated. I hadn't expected to meet such an obstacle. The emotion must have registered on my face, for a moment later, he said, "Do you happen to have a sister in the Metropolitan Police Force in London?"

"Yes! Yes. My sister, Edel. I was with her at Christmas."

"Well, I received a phone call from her in December enquiring about the services we provide to battered housewives." He seemed relieved that he had recalled that conversation. I was delighted to know that Edel had discreetly made enquiries on my behalf.

"Oh, good. Then you believe me." I was encouraged by our conversation. He could verify the facts now and offer assistance.

"Yes. I believe you. Now let me see what I can do. Problem is, it's Friday. You're better off leaving him on a Monday actually. Then we have all week to work something out."

"I'm sorry. It wasn't planned." My apology elicited a sympathetic nod.

A few minutes later, he was escorting me to a women's shelter, where a resident, under the influence of drugs, had barricaded herself in, denying us access, assuming we were the police and shouting at us from the upstairs window.

"We're not the police," I called up to her from the street. "I'm just like you." Our efforts were in vain.

"Well, now for plan B," the council man said. "We'll put you up in the Bell Hotel for the weekend. It's a pub that does B-and-B for us from time to time. Then on Monday, we'll sort you out proper."

"I've no money," I told him.

"Don't worry, the council will pay. Where are your children now?"

"They're with a friend on Maesydail. Thank you for all your help."

"Well, it was your sister's phone call that sealed it all for me. I can see you're an honest person. Let me take you to the Bell now and get you checked in. Then we'll go and get your children."

The landlady at the hotel was sympathetic and kind, showing me the room, giving me a key, and explaining that as it's a B-and-B, we are expected to be out of the building between 10:00 a.m. and 6:00 p.m. I was relieved that temporary accommodation had been secured, at least for a few nights. It would provide me with time and space to clear my head and put together a plan. Theresa would also be relieved. I didn't want to impose on her any further either. "I'll see you all soon then, dear," said the landlady cheerfully as I climbed into the council man's car and headed to pick up the children from Theresa's.

As we headed back to Theresa's home, I felt empowered. There was a tough road ahead, but it was not daunting enough to dissuade me from my course towards independence. I had made progress by standing up for myself and felt in my core that there was no retreating. The lightness in my heart ended abruptly as we pulled up outside Theresa's house behind a police car.

She ran to greet me, crying, her mother following close behind. I held my breath as my mind tried to fathom why the police were there.

"Oh, Julie, I'm so sorry. I'm so sorry." Her tone was penitent.

"It's okay, Theresa. Don't cry." I was speaking out of habit. It was clearly not okay. I was trying to comfort her while scrambling to figure out what had caused the commotion—the sick feeling in my stomach telling me it had something to do with Adrian.

"What's happened?" I asked.

"Adrian took Amy and Brian. I'm so, so sorry." She was bereft. "I tried to hide their shoes so they wouldn't go," she added, sobbing.

"Adrian took Amy and Brian." My repeating of her statement was somehow necessary as I processed the information. Panic surged through me. I knew what Adrian was capable of when angry—what more might he do when desperate? "You did the right thing to call the police, Theresa. It'll be okay. Don't worry. In offering her comfort, I was also trying to convince myself.

"Mrs. Long?" the policeman enquired as I stepped into the hall.

"Yes, I'm Mrs. Long." I was relieved that Theresa had the good sense to enlist their help.

"Is your husband Adrian Long of 150 Lon Dolafon?" he continued as he scribbled in his notebook. Part of the procedure, I thought.

"Yes, that's our address."

"Mrs. Evans here called us to report an incident regarding your husband."

"Yes, she told me. I'm very worried about my children. My husband is unstable and may do them harm. Can you help me get them back?" The urgency in my voice revealed my distress.

"Do you have a custody order?" he asked officiously.

"No, I don't. I only left him last night," I explained.

"Well, our hands are tied if you don't have a custody order. I'm sorry, but it's the law."

At this, Theresa lurched towards the policeman, screaming, "You have to help her. He'll hurt those children!"

"Please stay out of this, Mrs. Evans. This is between Mrs. Long and her husband." He was clearly irritated by her outburst, which shamed me as I maintained an outwardly calm demeanor, trusting and hoping that reason would triumph.

"Don't make him angry, Theresa," I whispered, hugging her. "I need him."

"I do plan on getting a custody order," I assured the policeman. "I just haven't had time yet."

"Well, sorry, love, the law's the law. Until you can provide us with a custody order, your husband has as much right to those children as you do."

"Well, I'll call my solicitor and see what we can do to get one," I said with growing anxiety. "Her office is shut now. Can you give me her home number, please?" I told him her name, which he recognized.

"Sorry, we can't give out home numbers." I wasn't sure if he was being deliberately obstructive, but I was growing increasingly frustrated with the seeming lack of concern and support.

"Well, will *you* please come with me so I can talk to my husband?" I begged. "Please!"

"I'm sorry, Mrs. Long, I can't do that," he said apologetically while glancing at his watch, his shift for the week probably coming to an end. "You get a custody order, and we'll be happy to help you out." It was his final word as he headed towards the door.

Now it was *my* desperation that erupted. My children's lives were at risk, and I had to save them.

"Do you have children?" I yelled after him, my tone demanding an answer. *That was the wrong question to ask*, I thought. *He is more likely to sympathize with Adrian than me.* But it was too late; the question rang on the air.

"Yes, I have two," he replied, turning to make eye contact, startled by my tone.

"Well, I want you to think carefully about the fact that on Monday morning, when you come in to work and read a report that two children were murdered over the weekend—and you had a chance to prevent it but did nothing about it. I hope you sleep well for the rest of your life!" I could feel the adrenaline rushing through me, my heart palpitating rapidly. *Oh, God, please*, I prayed.

With an audible sigh, the policeman surrendered. "Look. I'll do this much for you. I'll come with you and stand next to you as you speak to your husband, but I have no power to intervene, unless he strikes you. Do you understand?"

"Yes! Thank you. Yes, I understand. That's all I want—a chance to speak to him. Thank you." The relief and gratitude was apparent in my voice.

A few minutes later, I was back in my living room pleading with Adrian to release Amy and Brian into my care. It was futile. The policeman stood and watched as I spoke, and then he listened to Adrian's litany of complaints about me: that I had left the house in a dreadful state, the dishes still unwashed in the sink, that I was cruelly preventing him from seeing his children, and then resorting to insults; that I was a slut.

We argued in circles for three hours, his anger and volume increasing with each rejection, always coming back to the same point: that I was to blame for the mess we were in, and I had the power to fix it.

"Just come home, Julie," Adrian said in his most patronizing tone for the umpteenth time. "You're the one who's causing the problems here. You can end it right now by coming home."

"I can't, Adrian. It's just not working," I said, exhausted, but unrelenting in my efforts to get the children back.

"Do you know, she won't even tell me where my children are staying?" he announced to the policeman, with incredulity.

"They're staying at the Bell Hotel, mate," offered the policeman, probably feeling sorry for Adrian, who was almost in a frenzy. I was flabbergasted at his breach of trust, which had just put me and the children in greater peril.

Brian, who had witnessed our exchange, told the policeman that he wanted to go with me. He explained that he had felt sorry for his dad when he saw him crying on Theresa's doorstep and wanted to make him feel better. Amy was too young to make the same decision and remained firmly in Adrian's grasp.

"Go and get in the police car then, son," directed the policeman once he heard Brian's request while I continued to try to persuade Adrian to also give me Amy.

"Take a long look at her, Julie. It's the last time you'll see her, unless you come home," Adrian said menacingly. I locked eyes with the policeman, willing him to speak out on my behalf.

"Now, don't do anything foolish, Mr. Long. You're upset now, but there's better ways to go about this," the policeman urged, gently.

"I'm going to my brother's in Gloucester. She won't have to worry about us anymore," Adrian stated defiantly.

"Well, wait 'til tomorrow. Sleep on it," the policeman continued. "Things will look different in the morning when you've both had a chance to calm down."

A movement in the hallway caught my attention. It was Brian, who had come back in from the police car to help me.

"Amy, Amy," he called out in a loud whisper, hoping that she was free to join him, but Adrian was holding on to her possessively.

"Get lost, Brian," Adrian shouted angrily. "I can hear you."

Brian was holding up a set of keys, which he later told me he thought erroneously were Adrian's car keys. He was doing his bit to ensure that Amy didn't leave Newtown. I felt ashamed and guilty for putting my children into such danger. I also felt great admiration for this ten-year-old boy whose protectiveness of his baby sister and his concern for me showed his capacity for compassion.

"Mrs. Long, I think you've done all you can," said the policeman resignedly. "He's not going to change his mind." I knew he was right, but I was loathe to leave my baby girl.

"One long look, Julie. Take it all in. It's the last time you'll ever see her." The smirk on Adrian's face revealed his cruelty in that moment as he held Amy out towards me in a taunting gesture, her chubby legs dangling in the air and her arms reaching towards me. I reached out to her, but he jerked her back before my fingertips felt hers. "It's in your hands. Just come home."

"Come on, love," nudged the policeman, leading me by the elbow towards the door. "You've done all you can."

I acquiesced, Adrian's words echoing in my head and the image of Amy reaching out to me seared on my soul.

Melvin had found the home number of the solicitor when I returned, so I called her immediately and described what had transpired.

"I suggest that you agree to whatever he wants," she advised. "Just for the weekend. That way, you can buy time, and on Monday, we will get moving on the custody order." I thought about the ordeal we had been through already and the fear that consumed me regarding Amy's safety. I felt like Odysseus when confronted with Scylla and Charybdis. No matter what course I chose, there would be danger. But I had to rescue Amy.

"Adrian, I've been thinking about your suggestions," I said into the phone a while later. "Can we meet and talk about this without arguing?"

"I wondered how long it would take you to come around," he said triumphantly. "Sure. Come by the house tomorrow morning. Amy will be glad to see you."

"Tomorrow then. Okay, I'll be there early." I hung up the phone and let out a sigh of relief, knowing that, at least for tonight, Adrian was keeping Amy in Newtown. I needed to make sure it was the last time she and I were separated.

The landlady greeted me and the boys and did all she could to cheer us. She listened as I told her about Amy and informed me that Adrian had indeed been calling the hotel but that she had alerted the police and we were not to worry. She had forbidden him to set foot on the premises.

I made a reverse charge call to America and spoke with Bill. "This is *your* fault," I said accusingly. "If you hadn't encouraged me to be strong, I'd not be in this mess. I'm so tired of it all."

"Julie, you *are* strong. And you'll get through this, I promise. At least Adrian is prepared to let you have Amy back—that's a good sign. I'll go now to the chapel and pray for her safe return and for a peaceful outcome. Be assured of God's love for you. All shall be well." *Easy for him to say*, I thought but drew comfort from his concern.

109 Lon Gerylli Maesydail
Newtown
Powys
Mid Wales
Friday 5-2-88

Dearest Bill,

Well today is the first day of the rest of my life! Wish me luck! Thank you from the bottom of my heart for being there yesterday when I telephoned you with the news. I can't explain how soothed I was by your voice and comforted by your love. Adrian called me soon after asking me to go back. I said **NO.** *He has changed the locks on the door so I can't get in unless he is there to let me in. I rang the womens refuge centre and am just waiting for someone to call and discuss the practical aspects. I left with just the clothes we were wearing and my handbag, no money. Adrian hasn't offered to give me any.*

At 6am he dropped a letter through the door for me, asking yet again that I go back, using your letters as bait. He will return them to me if I go back. I rang him at work. (He also said in the letter "I wouldn't do anything to hurt Fr. Bill, it isn't his fault. I am to blame.") and told him it was too late for us and I was sorry it had ended this way but there's no going back. He promptly began accusing you again saying he would ruin you even if it meant writing to the Vatican.

I am sorry, if, because of me you suffer pain. I would never wish anything unpleasant for you. You are so precious to me. At the moment I am feeling a bit of a nuisance for Theresa. It is almost midday and I still don't know where I'll be sleeping tonight. I will not impose on Theresa any longer. She only has two bedrooms. Her 2 children and my boys shared 2 small beds and floor. Amy and I slept on the couch. I didn't sleep much—my mind is working overtime so I'm feeling quite drained at the moment. (I haven't cried yet, I feel quite relieved actually even though my world is upside down.)

I'm sorry for some of the things I said on the phone to you. I was applying pressure and it wasn't fair to you. I'm just grateful that you love me at all. I shouldn't be greedy. Just <u>KNOW</u> I love you dearly and want you to be happy. Until later when I write some more. All my love and thanks xx

Well it is almost midnight and it is the first opportunity I have had to write since lunch time. Today has been the worst day of my life without a doubt. I went to see a solicitor who was very helpful. She thinks it may be months before Adrian leaves my house. The department of Health and Social Security have given me an emergency fund of £35.00 for the week and the council have installed us in a bed and breakfast just for the weekend. (the women's refuge is full at present). It took me from 1.45 to 6.30 pm to sort all these things out. There were so many forms to fill in, and questions to answer and the people asking the questions aren't sure whether the truth is being told. It was pointed out by the solicitor that as Adrian hadn't actually hit me, I had made myself voluntarily homeless and the council was not obliged to rehouse me even temporarily. But God was on my side and each department in turn bent the rules to accommodate me for which I was <u>very</u> grateful.

Originally the council had arranged for us to be housed literally around the corner from the church. But when I arrived, a young girl, high on drugs had locked the door and barricaded herself in so the bed and breakfast was the only thing left. The gentleman from the council gave me a lift back to Theresa's where the children were waiting for me (incidentally, it was the same chap who Edel had spoken to before Christmas who emphasized there was no possibility of rehousing me at that time). Here he was trying his hardest to help me out.

When I eventually arrived at 109 Theresa greeted me in tears. Adrian had been around demanding to know where I was. Then he snatched Amy and left with her. He returned a short while later and asked the boys to go with him (Brian did). He was very rude to Theresa and her husband shouting abuse at them from the street. I was unaware of all this.

The police were called but would not get involved in a domestic argument. I was terrified that Adrian would do something stupid, so a policeman agreed to go with me to 150 while I talked to Adrian. He was shouting abuse telling me I would never see Amy or Brian again because he was taking them away. After three hours of hurling abuse, much to the officer's dismay, nothing had been resolved and Adrian would not give Amy back to me. Brian decided he wanted to be with me after all and said so.

Unfortunately the policeman was powerless to do anything as Adrian has as much right to the children as I have, so although he tried to defuse the situation Adrian would not compromise. He was calling me some terrible names you as well and shouting the whole time. I begged and begged him to give Amy to me but he refused saying only of I came back to him. He said he was taking her away in the car and I would never see her again. The policeman tried to get him to agree to stay the night in Newtown but he wouldn't. I was so distraught. If Adrian had hit me the police could have arrested him, but he was too smart. Eventually the policeman decided I would have to return to Theresa's with only Brian, which I did very reluctantly. As we left Adrian was grinning at me as he said, "Take a good look at Amy, it's the last time you'll ever see her." I couldn't believe that nothing could be done to prevent him driving away with her. Unless the court has awarded custody to one particular parent, the police cannot interfere. So after many prayers I decided I was not giving into Adrian or his threats. Theresa's mum had arrived to support me throughout the whole ordeal and to pray with me. Adrian rang up and she answered. He was equally rude to her. He told me he was driving from Newtown at 9.30 with Amy if I didn't go home.

Meanwhile, I had managed to get a hold of my solicitor after countless obstacles (the police wouldn't give us her home telephone number), but we discovered a friend of Melvin's knew her.

She advised that I agree to return home just until Monday (not to tell Adrian that) and then a judge will award me custody and if Adrian comes near me or the children he will be arrested.

I immediately rang Adrian and agreed to speak to him in the morning, so another friend from church will be minding the boys while I go and talk to him and <u>try</u> and reason with him. Brian had been busy while Adrian and I had been arguing. Once back in the police car he presented me with the back door key in order to gain entry and also what he thought was Adrian's car ignition key but was just the door key.

I still haven't managed to get any clothes or money from the house – perhaps tomorrow will be the opportunity I need.

I couldn't believe my ears when the policeman told Adrian where the boys and me would be staying. Later in the evening after his persistent calls to Theresa's house, her mother pretended I had left so he called the hotel I am staying in and the landlady, who has been great (plying me with alcohol and spoiling the boys) rang the police immediately and informed me that he had rung. She won't let him on the premises so we are safe here. I am missing Amy so badly. At least I know he is staying at home with her tonight as I have agreed to speak with him in the morning. I will be seeking an opportunity to run away with her if I get the slightest chance, but right now I just want to be near her and know she is safe. I love my babies so much—their father can jump in a lake for all I care now. He has hurt them and me so much today. You, on the other hand, I treasure dearly.

Pray, pray, pray for me. The next few weeks will be no picnic! I'll keep you up to date on the news. I love you and always will.

Julie xx

Jesuit Community Xavier University
3800 Victory Parkway Cincinnati Ohio 45207
(513) 745 3591
2/5/88

Dearest Julie,
It's a Friday evening (8pm) I have received your letter of Jan 30 but more importantly your phone call of yesterday. I was going…(just got your

phone call of this evening) I'm so glad I was in. Be strong and trust. By the time you get this I hope you will have Amy back and things will be beginning to work themselves out. It really is proving that Adrian is psychologically unsound (to put it mildly) and you now have quite a few witnesses. I will indeed be with you totally in spirit tonight and more importantly will beseech the Holy Spirit to wrap you in Her wings and give you comfort and strength.

At this stage of the game make sure you get a good lawyer and tell her/him everything. Maybe he hasn't hit you for two years but the mental cruelty and verbal abuse has been immense. Incidentally, shoving you (which you said he did) also constitutes physical abuse as far as I know. I'll be waiting for the good news which eventually will come. Keep phoning as often as you feel a need.

How I wish I could be transported out there tonight to comfort you and dry your tears. It's almost 0 degrees F and the windows are covered with a heavy frost. The thought of you all alone in a strange bed in a strange room really is bringing out my tears, but as I said above, be strong and trust in the Lord.

I hope by now your mother and father are backing you to the hilt—if they are not, something is wrong with them or they simply don't know the whole story.

Your recounting of your wedding ring falling off and your wedding picture falling down sounds like a real sign. It's weird I can almost sense where you are right now. I feel inside your feelings and am suffering along with you. I hope you are feeling my vibe as I sure am feeling yours. When I finish this I'll go down to the chapel and pray and then go to bed (a bit early) and try to be physically, psychologically and emotionally with you tonight.

*Your dream (in letter) was a remarkable one.
I've sent for some books on dreams and will interpret
it more when I get them. Airplanes, etc. are common
and show a desire for a different life or a change of
life, certainly accurate in your case and since this
dream centered around my choice of a way of life, it
was accurately centered in an airplane. The graffiti
in washroom, "Do you love your daughter?" may
have referred to my conversation about how old I
would be (if I married you) and Amy was finally
18. Remember I joked that I would be just about
70. I'm sure that stuck in your mind. Too bad you
woke up. Keep a record of them (the dreams)—I'm
trying to but finding it hard to recall them. I hope I
get over being <u>cross</u> in your dreams—you have had
enough of that in real life and don't <u>ever</u> deserve
any more not even in dreams. I promise you that I
will <u>never, ever</u> be cross with you in my life. I very
seldom am.*

*Maybe someday soon you will have enough
money for you and the kids to "pop over" to the USA
for a two week vacation. I'll save enough on this end
to cover the two weeks over here. Let's keep dreaming. Maybe you will meet a super nice rich man who
will marry you and bring you all over to the US and
we can rejoice together. Let's believe in the future—
far from pain and bonded in love. Off to the chapel
for some serious prayer and then to bed to be with
you in spirit. The back rub will be forthcoming. I
hope it puts you to sleep.*

I love you.

Bill

On Saturday morning, as agreed, I anxiously walked back to
our house after dropping the boys at a friend's house in town. It
was times like this that I was particularly grateful for my church

community. My only purpose was to be reunited with Amy. Adrian had already shown up at the hotel earlier alone, but the landlady, with her strong, protective instinct, had refused to give him access to us.

Forgetting that Adrian had told me that the locks had been changed, I pulled out my house keys and attempted to get in. Alerted by the noise, Adrian opened the door.

"Hello, Adrian, *please* can I see Amy."

"All in good time, all in good time," he answered as he ushered me down the hallway into the living room, where I hoped she might be waiting.

"Where is she?" I asked, dread taking hold.

"Don't worry, don't worry. You'll see her. But first we have a few things to sort out." He was letting me know who was in charge.

"Adrian, we won't be sorting anything out if you don't tell me what you've done with Amy." My anger at his manipulation revealed in my tone.

"Look. She's with a friend—she's fine. You can see her later." He was not budging, but I persisted.

"What 'friend'?" I demanded to know.

"Just a friend. She's quite safe." He was unwavering in his focus. "I have written out something for you to read and sign. Once you've done that, I'll go get Amy."

He presented me with a document that he had composed using formal, legal language, giving it an air of formality. It began, "I, Julie Long, do hereby swear that I will return to my home and not seek a divorce nor press charges against my husband, Adrian Long. That if, in six months, our marriage is not working out, I am free to leave." There was a space for my signature. I was hesitant to sign it but recalled what the solicitor had advised. The phone rang while I was considering what to do. It was my mother. Adrian had called her the previous evening in his distress. She first spoke to him and then asked to speak with me.

"Do whatever he asks you, Julie, so you can get Amy back," she urged.

I signed the document.

At this point, the phone rang again; this time, it was whoever had Amy. I listened to Adrian's side of the conversation and gathered that the friend had an appointment in town and needed Adrian to pick Amy up immediately.

"Wait here," he instructed. "I'm going to get Amy."

As soon as I heard the click of the front door shutting, I dashed into the hall and phoned Chris, another friend from church who owned a car. I had no idea how long Adrian would be gone. He could have stepped next door, gone a street over, or even had to go to the other side of town. I did know, however, that there was no time to waste.

"Helloooo." I was relieved to hear the familiar cheery greeting.

"Chris! I can't explain. PLEASE come to the back of my house *now*. Open the passenger door and keep the engine running."

"Julie?" She sounded concerned.

"Yes, it's me." I hung up and dashed back into the living room to unlock the french doors, which opened into the back garden, my hands trembling and fumbling with the keys. Then I darted down the hall to the kitchen, the only other access to the back and unlocked that door too, not knowing where I would be when the opportunity for escape presented. Then I returned to the living room—and waited. The waiting seemed interminable.

Eventually, Adrian returned with Amy, who was happy to see me. I jumped up to greet her, but Adrian was not ready to hand her to me. "Not so quick. I told you she was fine—you need to learn to trust more, Julie."

"Ah, just let me hold her for a minute please, Adrian. Please."

"Not until we've had a chat, and then we'll see." He kissed Amy's cheek as a show of dominance.

In my head, I was mentally tracing Chris's movements in her car. *She should be heading over the bridge by the church now and turning down by Crystals. Now she should be by the pub on the corner, now coming onto the housing estate...*

"Okay, I'll wait," I said, knowing that to insist would be futile. I needed to carefully manage the conversation in order to prize Amy from him. "Let's have a cup of tea and talk about this," I suggested.

"I'll make it, if you like." This was a risky offer as the last thing I wanted to do was make tea. But it persuaded him that I had accepted his decision about when I could hold my baby.

"No, you stay here. I'll make the tea," he said, handing Amy to me before heading to the kitchen. "Stay here." He repeated.

There was no time for cuddles or hugs. I had to move swiftly. As the familiar clinking of china cups and teaspoons confirmed Adrian's location, I calculated that Chris was probably rounding the corner at the back of our house. I peered out the french doors and cursed the solid wood fence obstructing my view of the street. Adrian was still busy in the kitchen, hopefully too distracted to see our dash for the gate.

I carefully opened the french doors, Amy clinging to my side, her bottom resting on my hip, and bolted diagonally across the garden, my focus on reaching Chris's car before Adrian noticed we were gone.

"Hey!" he screamed angrily before swinging open the back door and sprinting down the path after me—his route to the gate shorter and more direct. I reached the gate first and swung it open, ready to dive into the car. *Where's Chris!* I had miscalculated. The street was empty.

I had no choice but to keep running towards safety, Adrian closing on me with every step. Breathlessly, I began pounding on Isla and Rob's front door. *Oh, God! Please let them open the door. Why aren't they answering!*

Adrian had caught up with me, furious that I had disobeyed him. He grabbed Amy by the arm and yanked it sharply. Reflexively, I yanked it back as she yelped in pain and fright. I stopped. Adrian responded by jerking her arm even more violently towards him. She had become a rag doll at the center of an excruciating battle. I could no longer participate in her suffering, so I let her go to Adrian, who drew her close just as Rob opened the door.

"Come in, come in," he gently invited while processing the scenario unfolding on his doorstep. He and Isla had witnessed Adrian's temper. It was they who looked after the boys when I went to London.

I stepped into the hallway first and then turned to see Chris driving past and pulling up outside our back gate. I said nothing but knew that I needed to get Amy into that car.

Rob saw how distressed we both were and directed his comments to Adrian, putting a consoling arm around his shoulder and leading him into the living room with Amy. Isla comforted me in the hall.

"Isla, go and get Amy," I whispered nervously, "and take her to that car by my gate."

"I can't, Julie."

"Please, Isla. Tell Adrian you're taking her upstairs to play with your kids," I begged.

"He'll kill you," she said, not prepared to take the chance and place us in more danger.

Adrian, expecting me to follow him, shouted out, "What are you whispering about? Get in here!"

Isla and I joined him and Rob, who acted as mediator as best he could, soon realizing that there was nothing he could do to restore harmony between us. Finally, frustrated with Adrian's name-calling and use of vulgar language, he asked us both to leave.

As we reached the back gate, Adrian returned to his menacing script as he held Amy up in the air. "Take one last look. You'll never see her again if you don't come home. You've got till 5:00 p.m. to let me know. Then I'm out of here." He then disappeared into the house with Amy.

I stood on the street staring at the fence, exhausted by the ordeal.

"What on earth is going on?" asked Chris as I climbed into the passenger seat. I told her what had happened, and she offered to slash Adrian's tires to prevent him from leaving Newtown.

"No, Chris. I don't want to make him any angrier than he already is."

Back at her house, we prayed in her kitchen. Chris had heard Adrian state the 5:00 p.m. deadline and knew I was at a loss as to what to do.

"Dear Lord," began Chris, "what do you think you are doing? This woman doesn't deserve this! She goes to Mass twice a week, she's the president of the Union of Catholic Mothers, and she tries to be a good Christian."

"Shh, Chris. Don't scold God. I need him."

"Well, let me tell you what I think you should do. Call Adrian at five o'clock and tell him to take a running jump. He won't hurt Amy, Julie. Remember how excited he was to have a little girl after three boys?" She was being supportive and encouraging, although I was beginning to believe Adrian, that this mess was all my fault. "Perhaps I should just go home."

"Oh no! You are not going back to him." Chris was adamant. "You're in my house, you're using my phone, and you're going to stick to your guns and say no."

I was no longer confident in my decision to leave. Recalling how viciously Adrian had pulled on Amy's arm, I scrutinized every choice I had made since leaving him on Thursday and blamed myself for much of the suffering. When I was with Adrian at home, I could manage situations sensitively, knowing how to avoid angering him, most of the time. But leaving him like this had opened us all up to his unpredictable behavior brought on by growing desperation.

Time passed as though in slow motion. Clocks ticktocked more loudly as my pounding heart drowned out all other sound. At five o'clock, I picked up the phone and began dialing my home number. Chris stood in front of me, a formidable figure with her arms folded across her chest, a stern expression on her face and her mouth forming the word *no* as she shook her head, coaching me.

"Adrian?" My voice was weak.

"So you've decided to come home then." It was a statement more than a question.

"Adrian, I'm not coming back. Take good care of Amy." I hung up the phone. There was nothing more to say.

"God forgive me. What have I done?" I wept as Chris consoled me with well-intentioned platitudes. But the truth was that neither of us knew what Adrian would do now.

An hour later, the landlady at the Bell Hotel called, telling me Adrian had rung there for me, but she was not giving him my number. He wanted me to call him.

"Come and get Amy," was all he said, defeated.

"I told you he wouldn't harm her," said Chris, the relief almost palpable.

Frank, Chris's husband, took me over to get Amy and waited in the car while I went towards the house.

Adrian was subdued as he quietly handed Amy to me on the doorstep, acknowledging that the marriage was over.

"Thank you, Adrian," I said, knowing that the words could not convey how appreciative I was to have Amy safely returned. As she was placed in my arms, I breathed deeply, smelling her hair and her skin and squeezing her against my chest. She was oblivious to the magnitude of his gesture.

Adrian was crying. He was lost. A wave of sympathy for him swept over me as Frank approached and told me to go and get in the car. "I'll be right there," he said. He spoke encouragingly to Adrian, "You're doing the right thing, Adrian. This has to be very difficult for you."

A few minutes later, when Frank rejoined us, he shared that he had invited Adrian to follow us up to their house as he was so distraught and speaking of suicide. "It will be better for you to talk on neutral territory," he explained.

Chris took Amy into the kitchen and sent for the boys, who were playing at a neighbor's nearby, while Frank escorted me and Adrian into his large Victorian living room.

"Do you need some privacy?" he asked.

"I'd prefer if you would stay in the room, Frank," I said after noticing the iron tongs and other heavy tools placed next to the hearth and within easy reach. He obliged and settled with a book in an armchair near the window.

We talked for a while as Adrian's agitation increased. He couldn't understand why we were in this state. Frank, pretending to read, was carefully monitoring the tension growing in the room. "Please refrain from using bad language, Adrian," he stated after a particularly explosive rant.

"Sorry, Frank, but she's got to learn to do as she is told! In the army, we've got to learn to obey."

"Yes, but this is not the army, Adrian. This is marriage, and marriage is fifty-fifty," Frank interjected. Adrian huffed in annoyance.

"Do you think we could call Father Carson, Frank?" I asked, hoping that the parish priest, whom Adrian liked and respected, would be able to help us establish calm.

Father Carson arrived and listened carefully as we both shared our concerns. He helped us come to terms with the reality of our dysfunctional relationship and reminded us to think of the children, who needed us to be kind to each other, whether we were together or not. He invited us to participate in a ritual returning of rings to show our acceptance that the marriage was over. I assured Adrian that I had no intention of depriving him access to the children, that we would probably have a much healthier relationship apart than as a married couple. Father Carson concurred that parting was the right decision and that legal formalities should probably begin on Monday. It was the first time in three days that the tension between us had subsided.

Then we called the boys in one at a time as Adrian explained to them that we were no longer going to be living in the same house but that they were still going to see each other and that the love for them had not altered. I was proud of him for agreeing that if we were to have any semblance of a happy relationship, it would need to be as separate people. We were making progress, and I was once again hopeful that life would now improve for all of us.

After Father Carson left, Adrian offered to take us back to the hotel. All fear I had of him had been dispelled after the intervention of the priest. I gathered the children up, and we all settled into the car. A few minutes later, as we climbed out of the vehicle at the entrance of the hotel, I hugged Adrian, thanked him sincerely, and told him how happy I felt that we had reached this conclusion and made plans to discuss the details of our separation on Monday once I had met again with the solicitor.

"I feel so at peace for the first time," he shared, the strain of the past few days no longer etched on his face.

"That's because you are doing the right thing, Adrian," I said as I hugged him tightly in gratitude.

Sunday morning, after a restful sleep and reunited with all my children, I went to Mass to give thanks for the peaceful outcome. I popped in to the presbytery beforehand to thank Father Carson once again for his help and asked if I could call my mother in Ireland.

"I've left Adrian, Mam. We are both in agreement that it's for the best. The priest helped us to figure it all out."

"Are you sure you did everything in your power to save your marriage, Julie?" There was a hint of disapproval in her voice. "I feel so sorry for Adrian."

"Yes, Mam. I couldn't do any more. I did everything possible to save it for the past twelve years." I was disturbed by her comment. She didn't know the extent of the suffering I endured over years of abuse as I had chosen not to share the details. I tried to accept her perspective. "I feel sorry for him too," I added truthfully.

I was filled with peace as I received communion, convinced of God's love for us. In the crypt afterwards, where the congregation gathered to socialize over cups of tea after Sunday Mass, I anticipated a few questions from curious parishioners as news of the separation would have undoubtedly circulated. I was unable to return to the hotel until 6:00 p.m. and needed someone to invite us to lunch as otherwise we would not eat again until the next morning. Offers to provide lunch were forthcoming from a few people, and I readily accepted Jackie and Philip's invitation, who, with four children, had a relaxed and welcoming home and would understand the needs of my boys to play. Jackie was also known for her excellent baking skills, and we were assured of a hearty meal.

As we left the church, Adrian approached me on the sidewalk in tears. I inhaled deeply and closed my eyes, as though that action would make him disappear. I did not have the energy for another argument with him, the peace so recently experienced already dissipating. I opened my eyes and peered into his. He had spent the previous evening with friends, drinking, and was reconsidering our agreement. "Please, Julie, I don't want to make a scene. Can you please come over to the house for just a few minutes so we can talk?"

"Adrian, I can't come over now. We're going to Jackie's house for Sunday dinner. We already agreed to speak tomorrow—please, wait till then. I promise, I'll come and talk with you."

"Please, Julie, please. I'm going insane. I can't bear it. Please come over today." He was kneeling on the pavement in front of the church entrance, his arms around my legs, as people from church sidestepped to get around us. He seemed oblivious to the fact that he was drawing attention to himself in such a wretched state.

"Get up and go home, Adrian. I'll come over tomorrow." I felt cruel speaking to him in such a direct way. I must have appeared callous to some, who saw only a desolate man crying and a woman rejecting him.

Philip arrived with the car and the children piled in. Adrian was still clinging to my knees. "Please, Adrian. Stop. I'll come over tomorrow as planned."

"I might not be alive tomorrow, Julie. You don't understand. This is killing me. Please." The tears streamed down his face as he looked up into my eyes, pleading for mercy.

"Okay. I'll call you in a couple of hours once we've eaten dinner. But I'm not going back on our agreement, Adrian. We are going ahead with the separation." I felt weak giving in to him, but also moved to pity by the sight of him in such distress.

"I know, I know. Thank you. I just need to talk," he said, wiping his face on his sleeve and releasing his grip on my legs. "Please call me." He stood up and opened the door of Philip's car for me, knowing I would keep my word.

Jackie and Philip were very sympathetic to our situation and cautioned me against giving into Adrian, but as promised, I called him, feeling somewhat responsible for his despair. He begged me to go over to our house to talk. "That's all, Julie, just to talk." He apologized for the scene outside the church and assured me that speaking things through would soothe him and help him get more settled, so I agreed to go over at 4:00 p.m.

Father Carson called me at Jackie's and alerted me that Adrian had phoned him earlier, very upset, and sounded as though he had been drinking. "I'm off to Wrexham now, Julie, and won't be back for a few days. Please be careful."

"Thank you, Father. I will."

I asked Jackie to call my house at 5:15 p.m. if I wasn't back. (I'd estimated a ten-minute walk to and from her house to mine, giving ample time with Adrian).

"I won't be calling you, dear! I'll be calling the police!" I felt comforted that so many good people had come forward to help.

I went over in my head what I might say to Adrian to put his mind at rest and assure him that he would still be a part of the children's lives. I wanted a peaceful resolution and, perhaps naively, thought that it was going to happen with both of us willing it so much.

I was able to get into the house with my key, which puzzled me, as Adrian had told me the locks had been changed. When I entered the hall, he called out from the living room, "I'm in here, love."

He was calm and very subdued when I joined him, thanking me profusely for coming to talk. I was relieved to see him so meekly sitting in the armchair. He was making an effort to be reasonable and courteous, which I appreciated.

"I can't stay too long, Adrian. I promised Jackie I'd be back by quarter past five."

"That's fine, love. I understand," he said agreeably. I felt relieved. It was a refreshing change from the earlier in the day. "I've been thinking a lot about how badly I've treated you. You deserve better." I smiled, realizing he was apologizing.

"I'm sorry for any pain I've caused you too, Adrian. It's going to be fine. We'll be better as friends, and we will raise the children well—you'll see." I was encouraged by his demeanor, reading into it that he was becoming accustomed to the idea of our separating.

"I've written you a letter," he said, getting up from the armchair and offering the seat to me. "Here." He handed me a folded wad of paper. "Please read it. I'll put the kettle on." I took the letter and settled back in the chair and read his heartfelt words as he retreated to the kitchen.

Sunday Feb 7th 1988

My dearest Darling,

    I am writing this letter to try and explain my feelings within me.

    I know that I have never loved anyone as much as I love you. I could not live without you. I've hurt you deeply, and believe me if I could inflict the same pain to myself so it would take your pain away then I would. You admitted to me and Fr. Carson that you were giving a false sense of hope to help us get on. But darling if it wasn't for this false sense then we wouldn't be where we are today—the children need the father that is quite rightly there.

    When you came back from London I could see you had changed and I think inside you have always been wanting to come out and didn't show it. It most probally have made us better. So when you came back you let it come and it was indeed a very severe shock that my placid and quiet wife had changed so drastically—I honestly think that within my heart that now that I have accepted the fact you need to have a life of your own so what I'm saying darling is I'll let you. I don't want us to be broken up and away from our children. I'm sorry my darling for all the heart-ache I've caused and need you my darling. Please, please come back to me even if it's for a 6 month trial I want only for you to be happy. When your happy I'm happy.

    We were getting on great and then bump my big mouth let me down. If ever I get to heaven and when you die, and we meet up there and look back at our family and wonder if we did the right thing and maybe we did or didn't. What I'm saying darling is think of the childrens future and think also the problems most children that had a broken fam-

ily end up, like me for instance. Please darling give our marriage a chance not only for my sake but for our beautiful children I don't want them to end up like me. I love them more than anyone could. Please, please darling let's give it a last chance and with gods help and understanding see this trauma through. I can't say much more but by these few lines I'm trying to tell you I love you and I promise my darling that I've never ever intentionally wanted to hurt you but by this break up it will do more harm than good. We should of the right to bring the children as we see fit but if we could look into the future and see the pain and suffering they will most proably go through—we'll be up there think well should we of chosen another path. I'm begging you my darling I'm not being selfish darling as believe me I'm not I just want us to be a happy family and our kids to have a happy family.

I will never ever say to you, you can—you can't do anything I've now excepted you need more than me. Darling—I don't need anyone—anything as much as I need you.

Please come back and give it a try not only for me but for our children. I love you so very much— I'm not going to survive without you my only and truly love. Even in this situation where there is hurt—I only have love for you. Not hate not even regrets that we ever married. Please my darling I need you to be here with the children and as a family. I'll move into Brians room if need be but darling lets show our children what love is and not what love can do.

I beg you darling come back and let's start anew.

I really and truly love you.

Adrian

PS I love you so much I even had a vasectomy for you (not me) because I could not see why I should put you through any pain again. So I went through the days of pain so that you would suffer no more.

Julie don't you see that the love in me has been brought out especially since I came out of the army everything I have done is for you. Love love love love that's all I have done these past few years I got a job I got promotion and I thought you had love for me—but after this trauma I don't honestly believe there was any love at all. I can only say that there was love then within my heart and there is still so much love in my heart for you that only God will know eventually. Please darling I know you cant think of me but please please please think of the pain you will cause the children I may not be around but if you ever hurt them kids then be your conscience be in Hell.

Remember Julie I love you and will always love you till the day I die—

Adrian

PPS maybe you think "I don't know" but it may be the easiest way out for you but could you honestly have it on your conscience that <u>you</u> destroyed my life because the kids will <u>know one way or the other.</u>

Forget all the sins you've had forgiven how about forgiving the sins I've committed—and think = yes we did the right thing—but did we—its up to you darling. Even through this unsociable time believe that you did the right thing but believe my darling I believe in God and theres no denighing that I pray and cryed like a baby to God so that he may put me on the right path and as far as I'm con-

*cerned he helped me and you must admit that love
was rekindled and we were happy.*

*All I can say to finish this is please please please
please—lets try.*

                              Adrian

*Think of it this way I took my life or should I
say I stopped life by having the vasectomy my whole
life please give me something.*

I got partway through the letter before it dawned on me that Adrian was not accepting our breakup. *How could I have been so dense?* His gentle manner had been a ploy to lull me into a false sense of security. I read the veiled threat that we would be looking down on our children, wondering if we had done the right thing. Since experiencing a glimpse of joy in the love shown to me by Bill, I refused to be threatened or intimidated any longer. I knew that staying with Adrian would be sentencing myself to a slow death and that whatever happened, I could not make that choice. I put the letter down and turned to Adrian, who was now sitting on the couch, waiting, and said sadly, "Adrian, I am *so* sorry, but I can't—"

Before I could finish the sentence, he lunged at me and sat down on me, pressing his entire weight on my lap, one arm slammed across my chest, pinning me in place—the point of the butcher's knife he was clutching in his other hand resting on my neck. Dread engulfed me as his two eyes, like black tar pits of hate, peered into mine. His mouth was frothing as he spat out, "If I can't have you, then no bugger will!" I was stunned by the suddenness of his movement and certain that I was about to die. Thoughts of my children flashed through my mind as I prayed silently that they be brought up by my siblings. I was sure death was imminent. Out of my mouth, however, came the words, "Adrian, let's have a cup of tea and talk about this." My voice, with a will of its own, sounded much calmer than my body betrayed. Some survival instinct had kicked in, creating an out-of-body moment that bought me time.

"Oh my God, love, you're shaking!" he said, sounding surprised at my response to his assault. He stared at the knife in his hand and set it on the shelf next to the armchair. *I have to get out of the house,* was my singular thought. "I'll make some tea," he said, as though tea, as I had requested, would set our world right again. He got up from my lap, and my thoughts raced to the kitchen where there were more knives.

"Adrian, please, can we put the knife away?" I asked, speaking quietly. *Oh God, let me get out of this house.*

"Sure, I'll put it away now," he offered.

"I'd rather put it away, if you don't mind." I was worried that he might revert to violence with little provocation and felt safer doing it myself. It also gave me a reason to go to the kitchen, which was directly opposite the front door—my only escape route.

"Okay, you grab it then," he suggested. I picked up the knife and placed it carefully in my coat pocket, the blade pointing outward, just in case Adrian would push me against the wall. He then started down the hall in front of me. I was afraid that he might get to the kitchen first and get another knife, so I asked him to wait for me.

"I'm frightened, Adrian," I confessed. "I'd feel safer if you walked with me." He plopped down in the middle of the narrow hall, his feet and arms crossed like a pixie on top of a toadstool, and said, "I'll stay right here. You go ahead and put away the knife."

"I'd rather you held my hand, if that's okay." He stood up and walked towards me, his arm outstretched. Then hand in hand, with my other hand stuffed into my coat pocket, a viselike grip on the weapon, we slowly made our way to the kitchen, where I eagerly returned the blade to its resting place, expelling a burst of air as I did so.

He then lifted me up by the waist with both hands and plopped me on to the backless stool which he had placed in the middle of the kitchen floor, my feet dangling eight inches off the floor, as he set about the business of making tea.

I monitored his movements closely, knowing I had to escape. I watched as he took two mugs from the cupboard, opened the tea caddy, and removed the tea bags; then he rinsed out the teapot. All the while, I was waiting for the perfect moment to make a dash for the front door. It came as he turned his back to me momentarily to fill up the kettle with water from the tap. I leapt from the stool, which toppled over with the motion, and hurled myself at the front door, grabbed the latch, turned it, and pulled. I yanked on it again, my heartbeat pounding, my breath coming in short gasps. *Why wasn't it opening?* I had walked through that door only minutes earlier. I was confused and desperately tugging on the latch when Adrian, grabbing me by my neck, yelled, "I *knew* you'd try that!" He then flung me across the kitchen, where I collided with the stool I'd been sitting on, before landing close to the back door on my back. He followed, panting, and dragged me by my coat across the floor to the center of the room, where he straddled me, his fist raised and aiming at my face. "I knew those bolt locks were needed! I knew you'd try to escape."

"Adrian, please, I'm sorry! Please don't hit me." I was back to begging for mercy, my head bent towards my chest protectively. The strong, brave woman had retreated. "Let's call Father Carson and ask him to come over." I knew that the priest had left town, but I needed to do something to prevent further violence. He agreed and released his grasp on my coat. I scrambled to my feet and went into the hall, where the phone rested on a small corner table.

"Hello, Bridie?" I said, using the priest's housekeeper's name but speaking to Chris, as Adrian looked on. "It's Julie Long here."

"Julie, are you in trouble again?" Chris asked, her tone revealing concern.

"Yes, Bridie, I was wondering, could you ask Father Carson to come to our house on Vaynor?" I continued, feigning cheerfulness and trusting that Chris would understand what I needed.

"We'll be right there." She hung up the phone while I continued talking to the air.

"Thanks, Bridie. I appreciate your help. Bye-bye." I put down the receiver and told Adrian that Father Carson should be on his way. We went into the living room and waited.

I considered how Adrian has lured me to the house, knowing that I would feel pity for him while all the time he was planning to ambush me. He had placed some old magazines on the coffee table in the living room and hidden the knife underneath them before I had arrived. He had then waited for me to begin reading the letter and, on the premise of putting on the kettle for tea, had instead quietly locked the front door on which he had newly installed sliding bolt locks at the top and the bottom. All kindliness towards him, all pity, was being erased as I considered how calculating he had been. In its place was renewed determination to get away from him for good.

The knock on the front door jolted us both from our thoughts. I got up but was ordered to "stay put" while Adrian went to let in the priest. I could hear Adrian challenging Frank and asking about Father Carson. "He was called out on another emergency, Adrian, and asked that I come instead as you were in my house with him yesterday." The answer satisfied Adrian, who lead Frank into the living room where I anxiously awaited.

"So what's been going on then?" he asked. I wanted to tell Frank everything, but I also knew that Adrian could deny it, so I said to Adrian, "Why don't *you* tell Frank what has happened."

"That I had a knife at your throat, you mean?" Adrian responded candidly.

Frank, who was standing in front of me, his hands clasped behind his back, signaled with one hand for me to leave the room while he engaged Adrian in further conversation. I sidled out of the room and sprinted down the hall and out of the front door, then scrambled into the car where Chris was waiting. Now in relative safety, no longer needing to be hypervigilant, every muscle and nerve in my body began to jerk uncontrollably. It took several minutes before the involuntary shaking subsided and days before my heart rate returned to normal. I gave a thought to anyone who had ever been terrified for their life and prayed that I would never feel this terrified again.

Once back at Frank and Chris's home, I felt safer and could breathe a little more easily. Unfortunately, Adrian was unrelenting in his pursuit of me and was soon back there too, begging Frank to let him in so he could talk to me. Frank reluctantly agreed but stayed in the room with us and soon realized that Adrian, who was shouting and swearing, could not be rational.

"You'll have to leave, Adrian," said Frank, once his patience had been tested to the limit. He stood by the living-room door, holding it open. "You can't behave like this in my home. Take some time to calm down and revisit this on Monday.

Adrian stormed towards the door then stopped, leaned towards my face, and staring into my eyes, said, "I'll see you in hell. You are evil!"

Chris, anticipating that Adrian might head to where the children were, alerted Jackie to watch out for him as he was extremely disturbed and unpredictable. She had also called the police on my behalf, reporting the situation. The police had told her that they wouldn't take a complaint on a domestic issue as we women were always changing our minds after reporting our husbands. That if I still felt the same way tomorrow, I should go to the police station and make a formal complaint in person.

"I can't believe that the police won't accept the formal complaint about Adrian." Chris was incredulous. "If a stranger hit you on the street, they'd be arrested, but if your husband kidnaps your child, terrorizes you, and then assaults you, you're told to think it over before calling the police. Ridiculous!" I was impressed with her outrage. I had never called the police on Adrian, partly because I knew that nothing good could come from it. He would be livid that I had reported him and would make sure I didn't do it twice. This time, though, I was going to follow through.

Chris's prediction was correct. Apparently, Adrian went straight to Jackie and Philip's and knocked on their door, but Jackie, being charged with protecting my children, refused to open it, instead calling out, "Who's there?"

"It's me, Jimmy." Adrian was being sneakily clever by using the name *Jimmy*. Most people in Britain will have a pal called Jimmy. If you want to gate-crash a party, just say that you're a friend of Jimmy's. He was probably banking on the likelihood that Jackie too had a friend called Jimmy and would open the door.

"Sorry, Adrian, we know it's you. You can't come in."

"Open the fucking door! I want my children." His temper flared at her refusal to admit him.

"Sorry, but Julie asked us to watch the children until she came back, so we're waiting for her to come and get them," Jackie explained.

"If you don't open the door, I'll kick it in," he threatened.

"Take your time—all the time you need. We've called the police. They should be here momentarily."

Adrian didn't wait for the police, who arrived minutes later.

"Where is the mother?" enquired the policeman of Jackie.

"She's at the Geogheghans' house at the top of Milford Road. I can call her for you if you like."

"Okay, thank you. Do that, will you? I'll wait."

Frank took the call and, after speaking to the policeman, left to pick up the children from Jackie's and make a report to the police.

A short while later, Frank, accompanied by a police car, pulled up outside his own home where I was being sheltered. The boys clambered up the steps, hugged me, and scampered into the kitchen, where Chris had put out some snacks to distract them. I watched, relieved, as a policewoman holding Amy mounted the steps to the front door. As I reached out to receive Amy, a figure lunged towards the policewoman and snatched Amy by the arm. Adrian, furious at not being able to get the children from Jackie, had hidden in the bushes under the front-room windows, just waiting to pounce. The policewoman, although shocked by the ambush, having no emotional attachment to Amy as I do, did not let go of the baby but ordered Adrian sharply to "let go!" By this time, he was in the hallway, his hands still gripping Amy's arm while Frank and I looked on, helpless.

"She's as much mine as she is hers!" he cried, pointing at me.

The policewoman, spoke authoritatively as she cautioned him to be calm, but he was losing his mind and ranting about his rights, not caring what expletives he used. Still holding firmly to Amy, the policewoman instructed her colleague to radio the duty sergeant at the station for assistance. Despite their concerted efforts, they could not restore order, and the situation was rapidly degenerating into mayhem. As the radio call was made, I was relieved that, finally, Adrian was going to be held accountable.

I felt ashamed and guilty about the trouble brought on so many good people who had simply responded to my call for help. I was exhausted by the emotional toll of doing battle with Adrian, not anticipating the degree of terror he was inflicting as he dashed from place to place without any sense of propriety or boundaries.

The sergeant arrived. It was he that Chris had spoken to earlier on the telephone. I was certain that he would now see the need for intervention. But to my dismay, after allowing Adrian to share his grievances, he simply addressed him as "sunshine" and cautioned him to behave.

"Listen, sunshine. I know that right now you are upset. There's a way to go about getting what you want, and this is not it. You need to go home and cool off and get the official work started tomorrow, okay?" He was not interested in Adrian's reply, which was a rehashing of his complaints against me. "Listen, you can't be here. You have annoyed these good people enough already," referring to Frank and Chris. "If you come back here again tonight, you will be arrested for breach of the peace. Do you understand?" Adrian took heed and left quietly with the policeman escorting him off the premises, but my fear remained.

I couldn't fathom why he was being let off so lightly. Frank and Chris too mused as to the flaws in the justice system while recounting the litany of offences Adrian had committed in the past couple of days. It was clearly misogynistic. The valid complaints of a wife against her husband were dismissed as histrionics and expected to disappear into the ether by the morning. But annoying "good people" might get you arrested for breach of the peace. What about the peace he had breached in our marriage for more than a decade? Domestic violence in Newtown in 1988 was not taken seriously. Perhaps it wasn't taken seriously in any town in Britain.

I was terrified that Adrian might still try to get to me or the children. The Bell Hotel room we were in was on the ground floor, and I could imagine him attempting to climb in the window. Frank, understanding my fear, suggested we all stay with them for now and took me to the hotel to pick up the few belongings we had there. "He won't dare come back here and risk getting arrested," Frank assured me.

"Let's get you to the casualty department for a checkup," said Chris, who was an x-ray technician and familiar with the hospital. "At least then we will have a medical report to show to the police."

"I'm not too sore, but I did land pretty heavily in the kitchen," I said, feeling the bruises on my rib cage and shoulders. Adrenaline had prevented me feeling any pain at the time of the assault, but now different parts of my body were throbbing and tender.

"It doesn't matter. You need to have medical verification. Dr. Harris is the duty doctor tonight. He'll want to check you out."

"Well, you certainly took a battering," confirmed Dr. Harris after examining me, taking photographs and making notes for future reference. "There is clear injury to your rib cage, shoulders, and back and few other bruises coming out in your leg, but no broken bones luckily. If you experience any discomfort, take some paracetamol for the pain."

"Thank you, Dr. Harris. I appreciate your help," I said, unaccustomed to this sort of concern and attention.

"Not at all. Be careful."

Adrian called repeatedly, but Frank intercepted the calls, protecting me from further distress. I was being reassured by word and action that he and Chris would not allow any more suffering to occur in their home. They called friends from church and set up a companion rota for me while they were at work the next day, ensuring that I had an escort at all times. They had heard and taken seriously Adrian's threats to find us and make me pay.

Sleep eluded me. I was spent, emotionally and physically, but my mind would not settle. I was afraid of what lay ahead for us as a single-parent family. *How would I be able to protect my children? How would I keep myself safe?* The last words Adrian had spoken to me also rang in my ears: "You are evil." Doubt invaded my thoughts, taunting me and accusing me of being selfish and cruel. So much of this weekend's suffering could so easily have been avoided if I had simply put aside my own wishes and asked the neighbors for a fiver. My mother's admonishing question, "Are you sure you did everything in your power to save your marriage?" also crept back in to my consciousness. *Have I?* I tried to answer the question as though speaking to a cherished friend who was seeking advice, like in the old days, when I would consult my reflection in the mirror. *Well, you must choose life—not a slow death. Living with Adrian, his way, is sacrificing your life for his. It amounts to spiritual suicide. Are you prepared to die for him?* I wanted to agree that choosing life was what I should do, though right at this moment, lying in the dark, afraid, it seemed a most perilous choice.

Chris and Frank, both highly respected members of the community, were deft at enlisting help. I felt like a refugee seeking asylum, in dire need of their compassion. The next morning, when my first escort arrived, we took the children to school by car, a little late, in case Adrian was lurking by the gates. We also arranged to pick them up a few minutes early for the same reason. The headmistress, Sister Stella, was informed of the dangers and promised to be vigilant.

When we arrived to meet the solicitor, she greeted me with, "We need to go into the back kitchen, out of sight. Your husband has been making threatening calls and wants to know if you are my client."

"I'm so sorry," I said, appreciating her concern.

"Oh, you're not at fault. No need to apologize, but it's best to be safe." She led me to a cozy room that belied the nature of our meeting. "To be honest, I have never encountered anyone quite as desperate or quite as aggressive as Mr. Long."

"I wasn't sure that people believed me," I replied. "He is always so much fun to be around and seems like two different people. One that everyone else sees and one that's private. Now, though, he is showing his true colors to everyone." I felt able to share the details of our marriage with her, which she needed anyway to build a case. She asked question after question about our marriage, going back to the first time he was violent. No one else had been told what I shared with her.

"Now that I've witnessed his erratic and threatening behavior firsthand, I've already secured an emergency court hearing for Friday in Wrexham. Here is what we will need to ask for. He will have to leave the home, you will need a restraining order against him for you and the children, and you will request *full* custody of the children."

Her tone was matter-of-fact; she had clearly dealt with similar situations before. Part of me wished it didn't have to be quite so harsh, but as she stressed, Adrian's most recent behavior negated all previous agreements. The necessary legal paperwork was drawn up, identifying me as the petitioner and Adrian the respondent and was to be delivered to Adrian later in the day. It was becoming real.

I felt both brave and vulnerable, but mostly vulnerable. I wasn't always going to have a posse of guardian angels with me day and night. The realization that I would need to be permanently vigilant, forever looking over my shoulder out of fear, consumed my thoughts. But what other choice did I have but to move forward, one exhausting tentative step at a time?

Adrian was relentless in his efforts to contact me and persuade me to go home. He called my friends, he called other solicitors, he called my family. My brother Vincent, who is most compassionate and always willing to advocate for the marginalized and those in distress, called me in the early evening asking me to speak with Adrian. He had listened in length to him and was worried for his mental state. "He's threatening suicide, Julie. Can you not just talk to him and offer him some sort of hope?"

"No, Vincent, I can't. I'm tired." I was worn out justifying my decision to leave to everyone who thought they knew the history of our marriage. It was clear that the onus was on me. It was my duty and my responsibility to ensure my husband's happiness, as my mother had so often stated. My peace and happiness seemed insignificant. The fact that for twelve years I had been struggling to keep Adrian happy was irrelevant in the current crisis. But I simply didn't have the energy to fight anymore.

"Not even on the phone?" His voice was laden with concern. "He's in a terrible state." Vincent was honoring his word to Adrian that he would try on his behalf. He may have thought, like many well-meaning family members and friends, that he had the whole story.

"No. I just can't do it anymore." Vincent accepted my response without any further prodding. I was getting so weary I no longer cared if people misjudged me as callous and cruel. God knew my heart.

Frank monitored all the phone calls that evening, understanding that I needed some respite from the barrage of pleas and threats of self-harm coming through from Adrian. He had received the affidavit, which had been delivered to him at work in the afternoon, and reading the official document had plummeted him to new depths of despair. "I'm going to kill myself, Frank. I'm going to slit my wrists."

"Well, a longitudinal cut is best," Frank instructed, irritated by the repeated calls and the now familiar desperate script. He too was getting tired.

Chris, wanting to provide me with some restful space, had given me a private room. At any other time, I would have relished the quiet, but all-consuming fear prevented me from relaxing into sleep in the dark. I felt so childish requesting that the landing light be left on and my door remain open. I was thinking about Adrian alone and forsaken in our home and the threats he had made earlier. I imagined him still trying to reach for me in the darkness. I prayed that he find peace and acceptance. Sleep was restless and erratic. Frequently, I was startled awake by the natural creaking and groaning of the old house, or the wind whoo-whooing in the chimney breast—ordinary sounds that, because of their unfamiliarity and my delicate state, became harbingers of danger. When sleep did come, it was filled with nightmares. I vacillated between yearning for sleep while interpreting every noise as a possible threatening intrusion, and fighting to stay awake to avoid the terrors that sprung to life in my dreams. I longed for the sun to rise and herald a new day.

Tuesday was like Monday, in so far as good people appeared to accompany me while taking the children to school and back and to keep me company during the day while Frank and Chris were at work. About four o'clock, I spotted Theresa and a fresh-faced, red-headed policeman, not one I had met before, walking up the path to the Geogheghans' front door. It didn't make sense. *Theresa should be at home with her children. Why is she accompanying a policeman? Something is wrong.* I sensed it.

"Mrs. Long?" enquired the policeman gently as Theresa stepped over to my side, sympathy shining from her eyes.

"Yes. That's me." I noticed the pained expression on his face as it lost color. He was struggling to continue. I thought he might faint. "Do you want to sit down?" I invited, offering him the armchair I'd been occupying.

"Yes, thank you." He sat and inhaled deeply.

"My husband has committed suicide, hasn't he?" I stated, trying to help him out. I don't understand how I knew. But I had no doubt that was the news they had both come to share.

"Yes, he has. I'm sorry to have to bring you such bad news," he said, regaining his composure. He told me that a local farmer on the Dolfor road had seen a car late Monday night near the entrance to his field. As the windows were steamed up, he assumed it contained an amorous couple. When he returned in the morning and the car was still there, he looked more closely and discovered Adrian's body slumped over the steering wheel. He called the police, who discovered that he had cut his wrists and fed a hosepipe from the exhaust into the car.

In an instant, death had halted time and altered lives. A person who had walked and talked only hours before no longer existed. The truth of this reality was tantalizingly out of my grasp. *How could that be?* The policeman would go home and have his dinner of sausages and mash, the busses would still pick up passengers on schedule, the Boy Scout meeting would still be held in the scout hut. The men would still show up in the pub for their after-work pints, but death had already altered me and gifted me life.

A great sadness enveloped me. *It did not have to end so tragically.* The sadness mingled with an emerging sense of relief at the realization that the catalyst of my fear was no more. Then macho guilt muscled its way in, shaking its fist at me for feeling relief, temporarily overshadowing all other emotions. It would be some time before I reveled in my new state of freedom.

Part II

Chapter 16

Bill comforted me on the phone once I shared the news of Adrian's death, encouraging me to continue to be hopeful and brave.

"You are so loved, Julie. God has great things planned for you. Be strong and know that I love you too."

"I know, thank you. I just don't know what to feel right now. I can't believe that I'm actually a widow." I wasn't able to think clearly. My emotions were in flux, and I was physically drained.

"Well, let Chris and Frank take care of you. I'll call again soon. I'll go and mail the letter I wrote earlier. Just remember you are loved."

> *Jesuit Community Xavier University 3800*
> *Victory Parkway Cincinnati OH 45207*
> *513 745 3591*
> *2/9/88*
>
> *Dearest Julie,*
>
> *Just received two letters from you (Jan 20 and Feb 4) plus the phone-call from Theresa asking me to call you this evening which I will do. Poor Theresa sounded <u>very</u> downcast and <u>frightened</u> which certainly gave me a sinking feeling in my stomach. I take it Adrian is threatening people (including himself) on all sides. I feel so responsible but will just have to hope and pray that everything will be for the best.*
>
> *On that book I mentioned (The Road Less Travelled by M. Scott Peck, M.D.) Adrian's con-*

dition is almost perfectly described on pp. 98 on ("Dependency") He is a passive dependent of <u>classical</u> proportions. He really does <u>not</u> love you—he depends—or is dependent on you. I really suggest you read it.

I'm enclosing a check for £100.00 which I hope will come in handy for emergency purposes or whatever. Wish it could be more.

Speaking of more, the possibility exists. A fairly wealthy couple in the parish who I told your story to expressed a desire to help in any way. They particularly said later on if you need help going to school, getting a sitter for Amy, even starting a small business!! They would be glad to send you the money to do it. Hopefully, they won't forget (I won't let them) so be specific later on if you need some monetary help and I will pass it on to them. They do seem to have <u>plenty</u> of money and <u>really</u> want to help, so please ask.

Thank you, for the picture—it's in my wallet. As always—you are <u>LOVELY.</u>

I'm looking forward to phoning you tonight but dreading the bad news. I would <u>truly</u> <u>give my life</u> for your peace and happiness. Let's still believe in God's plan for all this. Stay brave and count on plenty of love.

Deepest love,
Bill
Xxx

The next few days were consumed by a battery of activities which required me to make choices, something unfamiliar to me. I had not been allowed to make choices as Adrian's wife as he had made all decisions. Now expected to make choices, I was overwhelmed. I was asked to select Mass readings, choose hymns, decide what type of flowers, notify family members, compose the obituary notice, find out whom to contact about housing concerns, speak to police, buy a funeral outfit, pick a color for the burial shroud, select a casket (the list goes on ad nauseam)—all from the home of Frank and Chris, who invited my brother Vincent to come and help with whatever was needed.

The toughest challenge was notifying Adrian's family. He had called his brothers, sisters, and parents over the weekend, as well as calling members of my family. They, understandably, were suffering now too and needed someone to blame. With Adrian's older sister committing suicide only a few years earlier, it was particularly painful for them all. For some, I was as evil as Adrian had labeled me, and they wanted me to feel their rage.

It was agreed that it was unreasonable for me to be expected to speak to each person in turn as everyone wanted the answer to "What happened?" Frank took over the organization of informing family and left me to meet with the funeral director, who made suggestions about what might be written for the newspaper column.

"You might like to say 'sorely missed by his wife and children,'" he offered.

"No, that won't work," I replied. "Can we say he was *loved* by his wife and children? That is more accurate."

"Yes, we can do that."

And so decisions were made one at a time, each demanding attention and sensitivity out of respect for all who were connected to this desperate man. Adrian had been loved, and the funeral was for us all.

I was worried that there may be a scene at the funeral after receiving menacing phone calls from one of Adrian's brothers and his wife.

I didn't want the children to be exposed to any unpleasant outbursts, so I arranged for them to have their own children's prayer service the day before the funeral, which was still over a week away. It had been tough knowing how best to explain their father's death but decided to have a conversation with them geared to my youngest son, Sean.

"You know when you had chicken pox and your body got covered in spots, Sean? Well, that let me know that you were sick and needed a doctor," I said gently.

"Yeah, those spots were itchy!" he recalled.

"Yes, it wasn't nice was it, being sick? Well, your daddy was sick too. It was like he had chicken pox on the inside, but because we couldn't see the spots, we didn't know he was sick and weren't able to get him help." It was a feeble explanation but one I hoped would suffice for the time being.

Sister Stella gave out invitations to the boys' classmates, encouraging them to attend the funeral service, and we modified the Bible passages so that they would be easily understood by the younger ones. Brian, Michael, and Sean were each invited to write a letter to their father, which was to be placed on the top of the coffin in church. Great care was also taken that Adrian's family, though not Catholic, would feel welcomed and comforted through the familiar hymns and the homily at the adult funeral, which I asked Father Carson to deliver with a focus on sacrifice and resurrection.

The police asked me to go to the station and pick up Adrian's "effects," which included his vehicle, wallet, etc. Vincent came with me, first stopping at the house to get some clothes. The police had been there before us and told me later that they removed a noose from the landing ceiling where Adrian had contemplated hanging himself. It was eerie, stepping back into the home in which so much had happened in a few days. On the record player, Adrian had been playing the Pet Boys' "Always on My Mind." I ran through the melody and lyrics in my head and was overcome with sorrow. Nearby, on the coffee table, in the place where the knife had been, was Adrian's diary and a note addressed to me.

1

My darling I'm so sorry it has to end like this but to live without you would be unbearable. You have killed all the love I have for you even up to this moment is so strong. Please please bring the kids up

*well and explain to them that I could not live with-
out your love. I love them dearly but I know that
within your heart you love me also.*

*Please please please darling forgive me for this
I love you truthfully Ive tried getting a flat but to
no avail. I tried to talk but you ignored this. Please
explain to my family that I'm sorry But darling I
can't live without your love.*

The £50 is for the kids.

I love you

Adrian

Xxxxx

I needed help and you ignored me.

2

*You are all I ever lived for and I love you now
even though I am taking my life.*

*There is no drink inside of me and there is no
malice towards you. Please my love do not ever tell
the boys and Amy and boys that I never ever loved
them I am doing this because I love them and I will
always love them—we were getting back on good
terms and the love in me then was as strong as it has
been for quite some time.*

*Time will heal the scars that I have put in
your heart, but time will never ever make me love
you less. My darling please forgive me in your heart
it's the only way I could have had the peace and love
kept in my heart. Good-bye my love*

May we meet somewhere

Heaven or Hell

Adrian

Nothing prepared me for loss. Yes, Adrian had been abusive, but I had also loved him. I made *that* choice, even when he was most resistant. I couldn't articulate my emotions—I really didn't fully understand them either. I just recognized the sadness that was settling in my bones, sadness that he had felt so abandoned and alone. I never wanted him to suffer but couldn't explain that to anyone. Some friends wanted to prove their love of me by being angry at him on my account; others told me I was much better off without him. They may have been right, but the part of me that loved cried for him.

At the police station, I signed the necessary papers to retrieve Adrian's belongings. The policewoman on duty handed me a clear plastic bag with my rosary beads, his wallet, his keys, and a de Mello tape on love.

"I don't imagine you want the hosepipe and knife that he killed himself with," she said, sensitive to my circumstances.

"No, I don't need those, thank you," I replied, shocked. I had not even thought that they would be returned.

"Well, you'll need to sign here to say I offered them to you, but you didn't want them. It's the rules," she added by way of explanation. "We have to make sure everything is given back to the next of kin, or at least offered back."

"Oh, I understand," I said, taking the small bag from her and thanking her.

"Well, I'm sorry for your loss," she said, almost as a formality.

I nodded my head in acknowledgement. "Do I pick up the car here? My brother has a driving licence." Vincent was going to get the vehicle cleaned up and then maybe sell it or give it to someone who needed it.

"The car?" she sounded puzzled.

"Yes, the car, an Austin Allegro, that my husband was in when he died."

"Oh, let me have a look for you. Hmm…" She flipped through a log on the desk and then said, "Oh, the vehicle has already been picked up."

"By whom!" She had just informed me that the rules stipulated that all effects were to be returned to the next of kin.

"Here's the signature. It was signed for yesterday." The signature was illegible. I was getting annoyed. The police had repeatedly mishandled my situation from the first day they had known about it.

"Who is that? I can't make it out." I wanted an answer.

"I'm not sure." The poor woman was embarrassed. She had so diligently followed the regulations, but it was obvious that someone else on duty yesterday had not. "Let me go and ask. I'll be right back."

Vincent examined the signature in the book while she was gone in an attempt to decipher it. "This looks like an *M* or maybe an *N*. Know anyone with those initials?" he asked.

"Mickey Mouse! Noddy!" I answered with irritation. "I can't believe it, Vincent. That the police would claim to be so careful, making sure I get all his belongings but then hand over the car to the first person to walk in off the street and ask for it."

"I'm sorry, Mrs. Long, I have no information on who took the vehicle," the policewoman said apologetically a few minutes later.

"What do I do now then?" I asked.

She shrugged her shoulders sheepishly. "I'm really sorry."

"Can I make a formal complaint?" I was getting stronger and standing up for myself.

"I suppose you can do that," she said.

"Well, where's the form I fill in?" I picked up the pen on the desk and waited.

"We don't have a form. You should probably write a letter."

"Unbelievable!" said Vincent. "I presume you will look into who has stolen my sister's car?" he spoke with authority, something I was still learning to do.

"It's not stolen, sir. It was signed for," she corrected.

"It may have been signed for, Officer, but not by the owner, and definitely *without* the owner's permission. I think you'll find that constitutes theft." He was showing me how to be assertive.

"I'd like to report my car stolen," I interjected.

Back at the Geoghegans' house, as we discussed readings for the funeral, Frank received a phone call from an anonymous male caller who told him to "tell the slut that her car has been crushed, and if she wants it, she should go to the scrapyard and fetch it." The caller clearly relished that he was causing me distress.

"What's wrong with people?" Frank said rhetorically. "What pleasure is there is being so insulting and cruel?"

I was still trying to figure out who it was that took the car, so I got Adrian's diary and skimmed through the pages. He knew of my habit of keeping a page-a-day diary, though lately I had been more sporadic, so he too had adopted the practice at the beginning of the year. I discovered that the person with whom he had spent most time over the previous weekend was Martin Keenan. He and his wife, Penny, had been good friends to us both, but it seems that Martin, at least, had chosen loyalty over truth and taken Adrian's side. He had also accepted the judgement that I was evil and decided that I needed to be punished. It was to them that Amy had been given when I went to our house on Saturday morning, and it was Martin who had signed for the car. I shared my discovery with Vincent, who then called Martin to ask why he had felt the need to do that and how had he persuaded the police to hand over the car to him so readily?

It transpired that Martin was acting on behalf of Adrian's brother, Kevin, who was extremely angry at me for causing his brother's death. Kevin had contacted the police and authorized Martin to take the car and crush it after emptying it and sending him the contents. I still don't know how Kevin managed to do that. What was exposed, however, was the decision of the police to obstruct my access to my husband's property and then lie about it, claiming ignorance of the facts. It was a deliberate cover-up. I didn't want the car. It was not about that. In fact, I was thinking about offering it to Kevin. What incensed me was the outright refusal of the police by their actions to afford me respect. I asked Vincent to come with me to the police station where I insisted they contact Kevin and have him return the photographs I knew were in the car. I had no interest in the tools and other mechanical gadgets; he could keep those, but I wanted them to know my days of being pushed around and bullied were at an end.

A few weeks later, I received a call from the police inviting me to go to the station and pick up my photographs. By this time, I had discovered that Martin had been regularly reporting to Kevin any news he had on me, sharing gleefully the "good news" of the challenges I faced with my new home, finding it "highly amusing" when the pipes burst and flooded the house, damaging the new carpet, which was put outside to dry, draped over the dining-room chairs and all mistakenly removed by the garbagemen. I was exasperated by him and wanted to lash out, but instead bought a blank card with a dove on the front and wrote out Kipling's poem "If." I added the message, "Father, forgive them for they know not what they do," and left it unsigned and mailed it. Only then could I let the anger I felt towards him go.

I met with the housing authorities and expressed my reluctance to move back into our house. They understood and relocated me to a house the other side of town above the train station, closer to the school and church. I was grateful and looking forward to having a new start in a new place. I didn't care that the house, with its stained yellow walls and reeking of stale tobacco, was in dire need of redecorating. I would enjoy making it a home for the children and myself. Men from the church and from Adrian's workplace, Laura Ashley, offered to do the necessary work of painting and laying carpets, etc. There were so many good people ready to help. It softened the pain caused by others who delighted in my difficulties and who were eager to spread malicious gossip. I was given the keys, but it would be a couple of weeks until it was habitable.

2 Brynllys
Fron Lane
Milford Road
Newtown
14-2-88

Dearest Bill,
Please forgive me for the delay in replying to your two letters and Valentine's card which Theresa gave me a few days ago. (Happy Valentine's Day).

Things have been happening so quickly, my mind is just a whirlpool of thoughts and I haven't had a spare minute to myself. Today was spent painting my new house, 2 Colwyn. It was left in a very dirty condition by the previous tenants. Three men from the church and one lady helped me sort it out. Father Carson gave me £100 to help out. People are so kind. I spent £80.00 on paint alone, nothing spectacular just necessary.

It was my first Mass since Adrian died. I felt quite strange facing the people in church, everyone was sympathetic to my plight and made it easy for me to cope. The people I am staying with Frank and Chris Geogheghan have been absolutely fantastic the whole week. They have made me feel welcome and also the children.

Apologies if this letter seems disjointed. I don't feel as though I'm thinking straight. I am so tired and have lost 10lbs even though my appetite is fine. Night time is a bit difficult I can't sleep well so I deliberately try to stay awake reading until I drop off.

Vincent is sleeping in the same room as me while he is here which is some consolation—I feel afraid on my own.

Adrian's family have been ringing me up and been very unpleasant. They came to view the body in the chapel of rest today. The undertaker told me of their plans so that I could make myself scarce. They are filled with anger and hatred which they are directing at me. If only they could believe that Adrian is happy at last and in the safety of our loving father's arms. I expect them to be upset at the funeral on Wednesday—I pray they will find some comfort from the service. I have chosen as a reading part of St. Paul's letter to the Thessalonians and the

*Gospel is the Sermon on the Mount (well maybe not
all of it!) Also Psalm 102. The hymns are "Do not be
afraid," "Lay your hands gently upon us" and "Let
there be love shared among us." I am looking forward to the children's service the night before when
the body is received into the church. If I can cry all
I have to then I should feel better.*

*On Wednesday I shall feel so vulnerable all
alone – please be with me in spirit.*

*I want to thank you again for all you have
done for me by talking about me and bringing my
predicament to the attention of your friends. I am
overwhelmed with people's generosity and kindness.
It fills me with hope and joy knowing there are so
many good people about. You are one of those good
people and I love you dearly.*

Think of me often,

Much love,
Julie xx

The day of the funeral arrived. A babysitter took care of the
children, who had already had their prayer service the previous
evening. I greeted people at the entrance to the church as they
arrived, the music from the organ wafting through the air and setting the tone. Many were friends and work colleagues of Adrian's,
whom I had never met, others pals from the pubs or from his army
days. I was happy to see such support for him and for us. I was
anxious about facing his siblings and his mother, who arrived at
different times. Some of them hugged me; others glared and took
their seats. I reached over and put my arms around his mother as
she came in. She did not resist. I was relieved that at least, on the
surface, all was calm. Adrian's old army pal Taff arrived, leaning
on a cane. I remembered how he had protected me from Adrian's
violence when we lived in Northern Ireland. I moved towards him,
smiling, and was stunned when he spat at my feet. His loyalty to
Adrian was fierce.

My mother, one of the last to take her seat before I was ushered to the front of the church by Vincent, noted my mood and scolded me, "You're too happy." I didn't know how to respond. I had never been a widow before; *how was I supposed to be?* She, concerned about what other people would think, wanted me to assume a more solemn expression. Self-consciously, I linked arms with Vincent as we walked down the aisle to our seats for the beginning of Mass and worked hard on making my mother happy.

The Mass was all I had hoped it would be, an affirmation of life, acceptance, and love. The choice Adrian had made to end his life presented as sacrifice rather than selfishness, a gift of resurrection for him and for me so that I could have new life. I believed that Adrian knew that he would not be able to leave me in peace if he lived. By committing suicide, he was liberating me too. He could not harm me if he was dead. I chose to interpret his death as a loving gesture and took comfort from knowing that he had been playing the de Mello tapes in the van and had my rosary beads in his possession, suggesting that he died with a prayer on his lips.

Later, when deciding on the inscription for his headstone, I recalled the allegory of the hind from *Hinds Feet on High Places*. The hind was crippled and struggled daily to get closer to the top of the mountain in search of love, many times falling but persevering. Once the mountaintop was reached, the hind was perfected by love and made whole. I saw Adrian as crippled, emotionally and spiritually, but wanting to be a better man. I believe he, like the hind, at the moment of his death, was perfected by love.

Chapter 17

I moved in to my new home on Treowen with the children, adjusting to life as an out-of-work single parent. Fortunately, the Social Services provided financial assistance by paying my rent and also providing me a weekly allowance that matched what Adrian had allotted me, so my years of being frugal prepared me well. Bill also sent me money from time to time.

Gossip was rife. Adrian had intercepted some of Bill's letters and had photocopied them and distributed them at work and in the pubs. When the representatives of Laura Ashley came to offer condolences and assistance with decorating my home, one handed me the contents of his work locker, explaining timidly, "Your husband handed out these letters telling people they were from your boyfriend," while placing in my palm a stack of photocopied letters which Bill had written, expressing his concern for my safety. I was mortified to think that strangers in the town had access to my private correspondence, and even more concerned that the gossip would affect the boys. I shared my concerns with Bill in my letters and looked forward even more to his now that there was no longer any danger of them being confiscated.

Jesuit Community Xavier University
3800 Victory Parkway Cincinnati Oh 45207
513 745 3591
2/18/88

My Dearest Julie,
    It's such a relief sending this letter to your new home and with the funeral finally out of the way.

You can truly begin to live life anew with freshness, freedom and grace. I'm so deeply proud of how you reacted throughout the whole ordeal. You got stronger by the days, keeping your self-esteem high, handled the children in a healthful, life giving way, and even diffused the anger of Adrian's relatives.

Now, as I say, you begin the rest of your life! What will it bring? Who knows—but God has directed things up to now and we can be sure He will lead us on. Will there ever be a chance for us— to see each other again, to marry? Well, God has proved full of surprises up to now, so who knows. One way or another He will show us the way.

What I want you to do now is savor life and the freedom it now brings. Take advantage of the offers to get away for a while—meet people and be open to friendship and love. Don't let your love for me prevent you from being open to falling in love again. I am such a long shot and a big risk item that I want you to have plenty of time and freedom. Enjoy yourself, and maybe Mr. (or Dr.?) Right will come along and sweep you off your feet. Hopefully, he will be super nice, gentle, rich (or moderately so) and be filled with the wonder of life (like you are!!) How about a 35 year old doctor, recently widowed with 2 or 3 children!!! There will be plenty of guys with just sex in mind, but you have handled them up to now so why worry. You are a beautiful woman so this will be expected. But there are guys with more than sex on their mind so let's hope you meet them.

Just for the heck of it, I drew up a list of the problems you'd have to face in even thinking of me as a husband. (I'm sure you've heard them from your relatives).

Priesthood—I can be layicized (LAYICIZED) thus able to legally marry. But the present Pope is *slow about granting this (about 1 year?) An ex-priest is no great stigma anymore, especially in USA and England but for the <u>Irish</u> is still would be a BIG DEAL! I've been a pretty good person up to now, but <u>not</u> an especially good priest, so I have given thought before as to whether I would be better off to leave and get married.*

Age—I'll be 54 in March, so I <u>am</u> old enough to be your father (in fact, I'm just younger than your Mum if I recall rightly). When you are my age now, I'll be <u>78</u> or else dead!! On the other hand I am in fairly good shape (except for some arthritis—knee!) so with today's health standards no reason why I_ <u>can't</u> be vigorous into 70's. (God willing!).

Money-security prospects—probably the <u>biggest</u> difficulty. It is <u>possible</u> I could still stay teaching here, but it would take a bit of a fight. Since I make about $16,500 for 8 months of teaching the fight would be worth it. If I do leave the Jesuits, I would get about $5,400 (severance pay) room belongings and that's it—starting from scratch almost. I probably could dig up a job (other than university teaching) but it would prove a challenge. If you married me, you would probably have to work too.

USA – England—Since I could only find work here, you and kids would have to change countries (and leave relatives and friends).

Marriage is probably the furthest thing from your mind but I thought it interesting to speculate on it anyway. <u>Enjoy</u> your freedom, savor it and enjoy life and be open to love. Take plenty of time, let's pray a lot, and ask God to help us figure out His will. I want nothing but your happiness—you certainly deserve plenty of it. I thank you for your love and assure you I love you with all my heart. Enjoy *your new home. Love to the children—may God bless and keep you.*

Love,
Bill

Jesuit Community Xavier University
3800 Victory Parkway Cincinnati Oh 45207
513 745 3591
Feb 19, 1988

Dearest Julie,
    I still have the letter I wrote last evening on my desk and decided to continue it a bit—hence part II—after all, you sent a three parter! I'll mail them together, so hopefully they will arrive that way.
    I guess that what I'm trying to say is that marriage-wise I am a <u>BIG</u> risk (especially for you) while you are the closest thing to a sure thing I have ever come across. Even with 4 children you are sure to attract every eligible man in the British Isles—and rightly so. You are beautiful, gentle, lively, loving, caring, <u>passionate,</u> and on top of everything else—still young! So enjoy your freedom and have some fun and don't even think about marriage for a good while.
    How I wish we could manage to see one another again—just to get to know each other a little more. What we have (and it is plenty!) are those wondrous, emotion-charged, six / seven days together in Newtown and London. I have every second etched on my memory. It was emotion-charged, wondrous, dangerous and a great risk, which reminds me of something in one of my text-books.

To laugh is to risk appearing a fool
To weep is to risk appearing sentimental
To reach out is to risk involvement.
To expose feelings is to risk exposing your true self.
To place your ideas and dreams before the crowd is to risk their love.
To love is to risk not being loved in return.
To live is to risk dying.
To hope is to risk despair.
To try is to risk failure.
But the greatest hazard in life is to risk nothing.
The one who risks nothing, does nothing and has nothing—and finally is nothing.
He may avoid suffering and sorrow,
But he simply cannot learn, feel, change, grow or love.
Chained by his certitude, he is a slave, he has forfeited freedom.
Only one who risks is free!

You have risked everything, Julie. You are indeed free and if God points the way, I too, will risk everything.

Martin Luther King has a great sentence, "When the chains of fear, and the manacles of frustration have all but stymied my efforts, I have felt the power of God transforming the fatigue of despair into the buoyancy of hope."

Finally from Erich Fromm,
"If I truly love one person,
I love all persons,
I love the world,
I love life.
If I say to somebody else,
"I love you,"
I must be able to say
I love in you everybody,
I love through you the world,
I love in you also myself."

I do truly love you, Julie and indeed all these things have happened—I know it is the same for you. For this let us rejoice in God and keep our trust in Him to point the way. Enjoy that freedom.

> *I love you,*
> *Bill*
> *xxx*

"Enjoy that freedom"—a concept that would be a while taking root. What I was free to do now was to give voice to my feelings for Bill and accept his declarations of love for me. The letters provided courage and fueled my optimism that life could become a joy. Although Bill presented logical reasons as to why marriage may not work for us and encouraged my being open to loving others, I basked in the love we shared.

I was so protected by my church friends and showered with kindness by them that I wasn't prepared for the reaction of the remaining townspeople, many of whom had never met me, to seeing me out and about in town. While walking to pick up the boys from school, I would hear a whispered, "That's her!" from a passersby who had heard a sordid tale of my running off with the priest and causing my husband's death. A lady I knew by sight stopped me in the street one day to caution me that rumors were being circulated that I'd had an affair with Father Carson since he and I were both away from town at the same time. I assured her it was nonsense and didn't mind if she put people straight on that point. "They're calling you the *scarlet woman*," she added, leaning in and lowering her voice, unable to hide the pleasure she was having from spreading more gossip. I didn't read Nathaniel Hawthorne's novel *The Scarlet Letter* till years later, but when I did, felt great affinity with Hester Prynne.

My four younger brothers wanted to ensure that I transitioned to living alone and decided, each in turn, to spend a week with me. I was glad of the company, especially as it afforded me a few nights out while they were here. Friends of Bill had generously offered to send me money for one night out a week to cover babysitting costs, so I looked forward to a change in scenery and an evening spent without small children. As my brothers all lived out of town, they were not known to the locals, and it was not long before I realized that it didn't matter what the truth was, the gossips and curtain twitchers were eager to spin a juicy yarn with a sprinkling of fact to give it an air of credibility. I was seen out on the town with a different man each week, so of course all my husband had claimed about me was true—I was indeed a slut.

My brother Sean recalls our entering the Castle pub on Broad Street as resembling a scene from a cowboy film, where the gunslinger saunters through the swing doors of the saloon, silencing the customers in midsentence, who turn to gawp until he reaches the bar and asks for a whisky. Only then does a slow murmur of voices resume conversation, as though suddenly aware of how conspicuous they are.

"So who's this then?" asked a stranger leaning on the bar, assuming the role of inquisitor on behalf of everyone present.

"My brother," I replied, feeling somehow compelled to respond, even though I know I should probably tell him to mind his own business. It took a long time for me to care less about what people thought of me. Only then did I really experience true freedom.

The same scenario was repeated with my brothers Stephen and Vincent when they too accompanied me to the pub in later weeks. But when my brother Donald, who is adopted and black, walked into the pub with me, instead of asking, "Who's this then?" I was greeted scornfully with, "Don't tell me this is your brother!"

The gossip increased with plenty of people ready to pass on the latest scoop, believing they were fulfilling some civic duty by alerting me, nearly always prefacing the information with, "It's none of my business, but I think you should know..." Much of what they shared was an embellishment of what had already been told to me by someone who had beaten them to it. My curt interruption, "Yes, I know," nearly always elicited a poorly disguised expression of disappointment that they weren't the first to tell me, deflating their zeal.

I became most disturbed by the comments that were made to my boys by children at school who had heard their parents discussing us. Michael came home one day upset by the remark, "Your daddy killed himself because your mum was sleeping with a priest." I assured him that had not happened and that people were going to repeat unkind things that they have heard, but we must forgive then because they didn't really know the truth. Brian was affected differently, drawing a disturbing picture of me and Adrian with broken hearts and a knife with a note attached that read, "My dad loved my mum, but she broke his heart, so he killed himself. That is why I hate her. I might just run away. Brian Long." I told him he was brave to hand me the letter and drawing and spent an hour talking with him, reassuring him that he was loved, as was his father. We hugged, and I prayed that he was feeling consoled, but the suicide had deeply impacted us all in ways we were unable to comprehend or predict.

Life was not settled or routine. Apart from the daily appearance of at least one airmail letter, my readiness to pen a response, and the anticipation of a weekly phone call from Bill, all else was still in flux. I was keen to establish order in our lives for the sake of the children and myself. At least they could depend on the familiar routine of school, which provided a sense of normality.

My mother had been faithfully calling to check that we were doing all right and planned a visit to "talk." In our phone conversations, she quizzed me about my relationship with Theresa and asked if Adrian was "justified in his complaints about her," using that question or a similar one as a lead-in to ask about Bill. She was not going to be satisfied until we had a face-to-face meeting to discuss the issue of my relationship with Bill to her satisfaction. I was hoping to get to see her in Ireland later in the year, but a trip to England for medical treatment gave her the opportunity she wanted to pay me a visit. "I'll bring your sisters with me. They need to see you all too."

2 Colwyn
Treowen
Newtown
Powys
23/2/88

Dearest Bill,

Many thanks for the last letter you sent to Theresa's which she handed to me this morning. (you can use "Long" on the envelopes now instead of Manning since you'll be sending all mail here from now on). I have just written to the McDaniel's and Fr. Edward to thank them for their kindness. It is 11pm and my first night in my new house, I am feeling quite nervous and alone. The children are all soundly sleeping.

I have not been sleeping well lately—mainly because of bad dreams.

In one, Adrian is chasing me, and no matter where I go for refuge he appears before me, forcing me to seek shelter, only to discover he is there too.

In another dream I am sitting in what appears to be a waiting room—plain clothes police officers are present dusting the walls for finger prints. I know I am dead and just waiting for the certificate to confirm it. I think to myself, "If this is what being dead is like it's not so bad. What a pity I won't be able to speak to my kiddies or friends again."

Then I put my hand on my chest and feel my heart beating and realize I am not actually dead and ask to leave and come back later when I am dead!

These were the dreams I had last night and the night before. I would like to dream something pleasant for a change. Are there any suggestions in your books for choosing the subject you dream about? Let me know if there are.

My Mam rang last night. She is going into hospital for a minor operation on Sunday next. She wants to pay me a visit and "talk" so she may pay me a visit this week.

I have told her I will go over to Ireland at Easter with the children, so perhaps you can send on that money, recorded deliver, which will allow me to make that trip. I'll probably go for a fortnight.

Dad will be glad to see that I'm not falling apart at the seams!

They may even line up a few of the local bachelors, good, decent, hard-working Catholics of course. Oh I do hope not.

Mam is still quizzing me about Theresa and you. The fact that she mentions Theresa at all is just a cover. I wish it wasn't so difficult to admit how strongly I feel for you—they just couldn't handle it.

Michael came home from school yesterday, quite upset. Apparently a boy at school had said to him "Your Daddy killed himself because your mum was sleeping with a priest."

He isn't the only one saying this. That particular story is running wild throughout the town. Adrian had made several remarks to his colleagues and girls in the office about me running off to with you to London, and backed them up with copies of your letters so most of the people who knew him are choosing to believe that.

I wouldn't mind so much for myself but it isn't fair on the children.

So when I read your letter and saw your suggestion to come and visit me here in Newtown, I was upset. It is something too difficult to contend with right now. The thought of seeing you in August fills me with joy, but how and where are the questions filling my head.

My priority must be the children <u>not</u> myself. I'm not sure how they would react to a visit from you.

I cannot imagine anything more ideal than you, me and the kiddies in a family situation. Unfortunately reality isn't always as accommodating as we would wish.

It's all so frustrating. Why is doing the right thing always so difficult. I'm sure God intends for me to be happy but I wish he would let me see it. Perhaps patience is what I am lacking. If so, please God help me to accept your will and in your good time.

Thinking today about you, I was picturing you in your home environment— nothing changes for you, the routine, the friends, the security are all there, constant and reliable.

Here am I, my life upside down, being persecuted by malicious tongues for something I haven't done…unable to reach out and grasp the one thing that would make me happy. WHY?

I'm sorry. This self-pity is so destructive. It just all seems so unfair. Why did God let me fall in love with you knowing it would cause so much soul-searching and heartache?

I don't want to offend him, but I love you and he allowed that.

Do you know what I'm going through? I wish we were talking instead of me just waffling on and on. Your voice is so soothing. You mean so much to me, I don't want to lose you—the little I am allowed, if only letters is sufficient. I won't be greedy.

I'll think about August. You decide what you want to do and I'll go along with it. I'll suffer what-

ever consequences. It will be worth it. I do love you
so very much.
     God bless us.

                                        Julie
                                          xx

"I'm very concerned about you, Julie," my mother began once the first cup of tea was placed in her hands.

"I appreciate your concern, Mam. But I'm fine, really." I wanted to reassure her but knew that she would persist with the questions until she was satisfied. My sisters were entertaining the children in the back garden, no doubt at Mam's insistence, so that she and I could have a "private" chat.

"Have you heard from Father Bill since Adrian's death?" she said, fishing.

"Of course. I called him to let him know what had happened."

"Well, be careful. You're in a very vulnerable condition right now, and when I brought him to see you last August, I was very aware of him as a man and not as a priest." She stressed the word *man* as though it was taboo.

"Well, he *is* a man!" I answered, putting emphasis on a different word.

"Did anything improper go on while you were in London?"

I was transported back to my teenage years being scolded about the sins of omission not recorded in my sin diary. "No. We behaved impeccably. We spent a lovely couple of days reconnecting as old friends." She wasn't ready to hear how deep that connection had become, and I wasn't ready to tell her. Yet.

"Anyway, I've loved Father Bill since I was a child. That's no secret." I went on, "That hasn't changed except that I'm now a woman, and even if we did grow closer, there's not a lot we could do about it with 3,500 miles separating us. He loves me too and has been an incredible source of strength for me throughout this whole ordeal." It was as close as I dare go at this point.

"Well, I think he has filled your head with notions of an alternative fairy-tale existence," she continued. "It's a good thing he's back in America."

"Well, struggling as a single mother of four children on a meager allowance is the only existence I know right now. Hardly a fairy tale."

"Well, I wonder if he may have influenced your decision to leave Adrian, contributing to his suicide."

"Mam, Adrian and I did *not* have a healthy marriage, as you know from all the other times I left him." I was becoming defensive, wishing she would drop the subject. "It was not Father Bill's fault."

Almost as though summoned by my will, Father Carson arrived, unless my mother had called him and told him she would be visiting me, which was a possibility.

"Just popping in to see how you're settling in, Julie."

"Oh, welcome, Father. You've met my mother, Ena. Let me get you a cup of tea. It's just made."

I left the two of them chatting while I went to get another cup and saucer. "Help me!" I mouthed to my sisters through the kitchen window. They smiled back, shrugging their shoulders, knowing that I had to endure the interrogation and that they were powerless.

Father Carson, like the cavalry, had arrived just in time to intervene and reassure my mother. It wasn't a marriage, Ena, it was ownership. Julie should have left him years ago."

I felt vindicated. And also felt the remark shifted responsibility away from Bill.

"Well, I don't want you doing anything stupid on the rebound, like throwing yourself at the first man you meet. You need to remember your morals and self-respect." She seemed to be relishing giving me this advice in front of my priest.

"Of course I won't, Mam. I've no interest in 'throwing' myself at anyone. Can we talk about something else. Please?"

Mam handed me a note from my father, who had written only one other time to me when I was eight, and he was training to become a prison officer. The note read,

For the moment all I want to do is reassure you of my fondest love for you Julie. There is no doubt that years of prayer on your behalf have not gone unanswered but will bear fruit. He has gone to "his place" through God's merciful judgement and we must rest content in our loving Father's design in what lies ahead.

I look forward to hearing all when Ena returns. You are always on my mind and in my prayers. Love to the children and my special love to you.

Dad.

No questions, no judgement, just reassurance and love.

Chapter 18

Letter writing was a priority after the funeral. Adrian's youngest sister Patricia had not felt able to attend, so I wrote and offered her his Bible. She wrote back thanking me, expressing her sadness at Adrian's choice to kill himself but assuring me of her love. I also wrote to Adrian's father, Den, and his partner, Jenny, who also stayed away from the funeral to avoid causing a disturbance. He too was affirming and gracious in his reply, wishing me a good life and acknowledging that Adrian could be difficult. Even Adrian's mother, Sybil, wrote a thank-you in reply to a letter I had sent on her birthday. The only members of the family who continued to bear animosity towards me were Adrian's brother, Kevin, and his wife, Sally. I did not write to them. But it was Bill's letters and weekly phone calls that sustained me in those first months after Adrian's death while I figured out my new status. It was a way to share our thoughts, concerns, doubts, and dreams of a possible future together but also to confirm that the love we felt for each other was genuine and life-affirming. How to act on that love was the quandary.

3/7/88

> *Dearest Julie—*
> *I'm out in the country – 1ˢᵗ night of retreat—*
> *just took a walk—fresh air and stars—thought of*
> *you. Your letter (written after phone call) arrived*
> *when I left today. I agree—the joy of loving and*
> *being loved by you far outweighs all the problems. I*
> *choose it all (and I mean all) again.*

I think I can replay every second of our evening on the couch—and in fact, often do. The <u>most</u> memorable thing, (after that magical first kiss) was that indescribable, powerful, musky, lovely <u>smell</u> of you—I'll never forget it. It made every perfume pale in comparison.

How I wish you were here with me—to walk hand in hand through the starry night—but could it match that evening along the Thames, or the walk beside the river in Newtown. Wherever you were— it was magic and memorable. It was you who made it so not the scenery.

So let's trust God in His (Her) goodness—He's carried us this far and will take us through to the end.

I want you, I need you, I love you, and besides nobody kisses as good as you.

Especially on sacred couches!!

With black dress on with 268 buttons!!

I loved you at 10 and have never and will never stop.

Love <u>always</u>.
Bill

I was discovering truths about human nature that I had not experienced before. Now that I was a young widow, many people I once considered friends were more distant. I thought at first that it was because they were at a loss as to how to speak to me about the suicide. Talking about taboo topics is very hard for some. I was getting used to seeing familiar faces coming towards me in the street, who, on seeing me, dashed across the road or ducked into a shop so as to avoid talking to me. It was not only discomfort of the topic of death that caused folk to flee from me, as though I had a contagious disease. It was fear.

I was a threat. I expected to be shunned by those who believed the malicious gossip but didn't know me. But I was deeply hurt by the rejection of those I once considered friends. Married women were now more possessive of their husbands, thinking I may want to steal them, so invitations to homes, which had once been a regular occurrence, ended abruptly. Married men prevented their wives from keeping me company on a night out as my one goal, they erroneously assumed, was to pick up a man, and that would lead their wives astray. I had no single women friends and didn't feel that it was a group to which I would easily adapt as those ladies, besides being a decade younger than me, probably *were* out on a weekend looking for someone to love, if even only for the night. So my loneliness increased, along with my yearning to connect with people. I cherished even more the loyalty and friendship of the few who knew me and stood by me.

"We need to get you out of Newtown for a night out, away from the stares and the gossip," suggested Lynn, a friend who had recently separated from her husband. "I know what it's like."

"I need a change of scenery for sure. Okay, let's plan on it!"

We set of for the Buttermarket in Shrewsbury, renowned for its nightlife, my first visit to that town only twenty-eight miles away. I was entrusting all to Lynn as she knew the area well. It was abuzz with people out for fun on a Saturday night, and its biggest appeal, and such a refreshing change, was that I knew no one. So grateful to be included in someone's plans, I didn't consider Lynn's goal, which was to "get lucky," as she explained it later. I was content to spend a few relaxed hours chatting in a cozy pub, but Lynn was on the prowl. It was like a reconnaissance mission, she setting the pace, leaving me on the pavement while she popped her head around a pub door to assess its suitability for her purpose. "Nah, it's dead in there. Let's go to that one across the road and see if there's any action going on there." We would eventually find a pub that met her criteria: lively music, busy, but not heaving with bodies, lots of good-looking young men, and easy access to the bar. "We'll have one in here and see how it goes." Sometimes it didn't go as she hoped, and only halfway through my drink, I'd hear, "Drink up! Time to move on." I would have been content to stay in one place all evening. I was not prepared for this marathon event at which Lynn seemed so adept.

"Lynn, I'm not used to this, sorry. Can we find one pub to stay in for more than one drink? I'm out of practice, and I can't keep up." The fact was I had never done this before as my social life had been dictated by Adrian.

"Oh, I forgot, you're still a novice," she teased. "Oh, all right, let's find somewhere to park ourselves and see who shows up."

We found a pub with a fairly lively mood and settled in for the rest of the evening. She pointed out the different men who caught her eye, which was a waste of her time with my poor eyesight as I couldn't see or appreciate whatever attributes she was noting. Then she spotted a pair of young men sitting at the bar. "Ooh, the one on the left—he's yummy. He's mine. You can have the other one. Time for another drink, me thinks," she said, raising her glass to her lips and gulping down the contents. She stood up, empty glass in hand, and approaching the men at the bar, began a conversation, inviting them over to our table. They grabbed their beers and sauntered over, engaging us in entertaining banter for the remainder of the night after introducing themselves as Chris and Mark from Newtown. I noted the irony.

Lynn and Chris had already left together as Mark and I continued chatting easily.

"You should come out on a weekend. There's a group of us that hang out in Newtown," he invited as we parted ways.

"Thanks, I might just do that," I responded, happy to be included and making a mental note to never go out alone again with Lynn.

The following Saturday, at the Buck, Mark introduced me to his six pals, all single, unattached men ranging in age from twenty to thirty-five. I met Eddie, Ted, Humbug, Clive, Pea, and Ozz, none of whom seemed to mind that I had been invited to tag along from time to time. In fact, they were the safest group to belong to as I posed no threat to any of them; and at the end of each Saturday's revelries, they would take it in turn to escort me safely home. I was so relaxed in their company and grew so fond of them that I invited them all to be guests at our first Christmas in our new home. I bought a bookmark for each of them so that after dinner, when presents were unwrapped, they would be able to join in. It was great for the children too to have someone there to play with them other than me.

Of course, this all proved fodder for the gossips with whom I was growing more irritated. One market day, I bumped into Mark in the center of town, and we decided to go for a coffee. Bridie, Father Carson's housekeeper, saw us together and asked in her distinctly Irish accent, "Ah, hello, Julie. Is this your new boyfriend?"

"Oh no, Bridie. This is Tuesday. I have a different one for every day of the week." I was using humor to halt her questions. She had no reply but a nervous chuckle. I could now add Snow White to my list of nicknames.

A few days later, I received a visit from Father Carson. "Julie, there are rumors going around town about you that you've been entertaining many different men in your home." He sounded genuinely concerned.

"Father, I don't entertain *any* men in my home. I have some friends who make sure I get home safely on a Saturday, but they don't come in to the house," I replied. "Some people just want to cause mischief."

"I know, but please be more careful in what you give them to work with." His admonishment was clear.

My brother Donald later added to the gossip when he and his wife, Louise, came to babysit in May while I spent a week with my cousin Yvonne in Dundalk, Ireland. He, always keen to snap up a bargain, shopped voraciously at Pryce Jones, a warehouse store near the railway station. As I alighted the train on my return from my holiday, I looked up in horror at my house on the top of the hill. Donald had bought a supply of reduced-price lightbulbs and installed them in my home, the rosy glow emanating from each window usually associated with ladies more generous with their sexual favors than me.

"Donald! What on earth were you thinking!"

"They were cheap," he answered, as though all other considerations would be outweighed by his fiscal savviness. No wonder people were talking!

An inquest into Adrian's death was scheduled for April 25, for which my presence was required. I made tentative plans for Easter and summer holidays but kept that date free. Bill and I were considering a visit from him in August but were sensitive to the scandal that might cause more distress for the children. We explored all sorts of possibilities, weighing the pros and cons of each and always through the letters. We were developing more trust that God was the driving force and, in his time, would show us the way. In the meantime, we shared our feelings of affection and hope, sometimes in letters and other times on a beautiful card.

March 10, 1988

My Dearest Julie,

The thought on the card caught my eye—how true. I look through my mail each day and am thrilled when I see your handwriting.

Glad to hear you're enjoying the "Somewhere in Time" tape—Somehow it catches our love and its frustration—and let's hope—its ultimate fulfillment.

Sorry to hear about that bad dream about your father, but glad to hear he came through with such a nice letter. He does love you—as does your mam, but of course find it difficult to understand. My parents would have been the same way had they still been alive.

Speaking about dreams—a weird one from one of the men (a policeman) that I gave a retreat to. When I was leaving the place, I found an anonymous letter which stated the writer had a dream the previous night. He saw a guy with a cockney accent (like Eliza Doolittle in "My Fair Lady") who had a message for me. The message was "Go back to Wales and seek "Eros" and turn away from "Thanatos" before it is eternally too late. He said he didn't understand it but there it was. Strange, but true.

It was surprising since "Eros" and "Thanatos" are terms not usually in the vocabulary of your average policeman (maybe in England they are!)

"Eros" as I understand it is the life principle—wish—usually having to do with sex and/or the erotic side of life. "Thanatos" on the other hand is the death wish—keeping everything on a pure intellectual level—refusing the affective side of life.

I had talked about my stay in Wales and mentioned you <u>briefly</u>, but that's all. Do you think God is telling me something? I could go along with the Eros—Thanatos bit, but don't think God would talk in "eternally too late" terms. But I'll take it for what it's worth and see if I can whoop up a message dream. I've had another great one with you and me—just as potent as the ones I described. Please remind me to tell you about it on the phone.

Don't let Kevin and Martin get on your nerves—they are "small" mean-minded people I don't think they are going to change. As you say—keep your head high—you deserve it.

I'm glad you "survived" your mam's visit. I think she knows we love each other on the man/woman level. Twas super you were able to say we behaved "impeccably" —tis pretty true all things considered and what could easily have been (and almost was!!) I see it all in my dreams. (I hope you get the wavelength.)

Men of Milford Jesuit Retreat League
9.3.88

Dear Father,
I'm very sorry to be the messenger of this news but I have been awake most of the night and many

thoughts have been running through my mind, vivid pictures of events and places, and of people that I once knew. My best friend, may he rest in peace! Don Martin, asked about his son, that he and Gail were going to adopt, the week after he was shot and killed. I shall try to look her up and find out for him.

    Then I had the vision of a hackney sort of bloke, with an accent like that of the gallery-maid, before she became, "My Fair Lady," in which he stated: "Return at once to Wales and choose Eros—give up your thoughts of Thanatos, before it is eternally too late!" I don't know what this all means. May heaven help us all—to do the right thing!

    May God be with you and give you Peace.

I interpreted the letter that Bill received from the police officer as a sign from God that our love was a blessing. I was encouraged to extract all the joy I could from it and worry less about what other people thought or said. I was becoming stronger and confident that God was indeed directing us.

Jesuit Community Xavier University
3800 Victory Parkway Cincinnati OH
45207 513 745 3591
April 21, 1988

My Dearest Julie,
    I just got off the phone with you and I'll start the letter right away. I'm imagining already what you said you would wear to bed (here's hoping I visit again) this time I won't knock.
    I guess the plan for the Summer '89 visit has the "advantage" of giving us 16 months to fall out of love. If it (the love) continues to increase (as in the past 4 months) things are going to be interesting to say the least! I'll still keep some time open this

*August, just in case a miracle happens, but <u>please</u>
don't let this keep you from any August plans. It's
a long shot—and I may blow any chance of going
over in '89 if I go over this year. It's a confusing situation isn't it (but I wouldn't miss loving you for the
world!). I promise you, if I do marry, (a big if!) it
will be <u>YOU!</u> God works in mysterious ways!!*

*You are a gem, my love, and I still can't figure
out how you could love someone on the <u>near</u> verge of
getting <u>old</u>. (But I appreciate it). For your sake I still
hope a <u>young</u> suitor will come along and sweep you
off your feet and bring you happiness and a true and
lasting love. You deserve it so very much.*

*As I told you on the phone, you were with me
every second on the trip. I was showing you this and
that, checking out houses, lying on the beach with
you, smelling the dogwoods, etc. It made the trip,
especially the driving, really speed by. You would be
fascinated by Florida. It is a tropical island (almost).
It has 8,462 <u>miles</u> of tidal coast because of its countless deep bays, islands and inlets. I hope someday we
can visit it together with the children.*

*I was amazed at how good my brother looks
(except for letting some bottom teeth fall out). He
drinks far too much, smokes likewise and doesn't get
too much exercise but he still is just the right weight.
My sister in law looks good too (she is 66—he is 68)
but is having lots of problems with her hip (operation screwed up the nerves. I'll be seeing my other
brother and sister in law this weekend in Louisville.
I'm going down on Saturday to Mary Margaret's
and stay overnight. Kevin (her oldest) is making his
first Communion. It's good to know Mary Margaret
knows about us.*

*Well, it's time (10:40 pm) to get my wash out
of the drier and get to bed. I'll think of you (4am in*

Wales) and imagine again how you are dressed and come into your room. If one of the boys is in with you, I'll just look and admire, but if they are not... be prepared!!

You are lovely, Julie, beyond imagining. I adore you. Give my love once again to Brian, Michael, Sean and Amy. How lucky they are to have such a mother as you.

God bless you my darling, sleep tight, and in God's arms. You are precious.

All my love,
Bill
xx

The day of the inquest into Adrian's death, took place on April 25, the day after what would have been his thirty-fourth birthday. I didn't know what to expect and asked Theresa to come with me. When we arrived, there were only three others in the room: the coroner, the clerk of the court, and a journalist from the *County Times*. It was in marked contrast to the large crowd that had attended the funeral. The coroner spoke kindly, but I was startled when, without any warning, he presented me with an enlarged color photograph of Adrian slumped over the steering wheel of the car in the blue-and-gray sweater I had bought him for Christmas—blood stains on the car seat, on the knife, and on his clothing—and asked formally, "Is this your husband, Adrian Long?" Reeling a little from the shock of the ambush, I answered meekly, "Yes, that's him," the image instantly and permanently seared on my mind. Perhaps the coroner didn't know that I had never seen Adrian's body, that the last time I saw him, he was in Frank and Chris's house, accusing me of being evil.

Frank had been the one to assume the burden of identifying his body, knowing that it would have been traumatic for me to have to do it. When Frank returned home that day, we said no words to each other as, leaning his back against the kitchen counter, he nodded solemnly, his arms outstretched, inviting me to take comfort in his strong embrace. His arms wrapped tightly around me while, with eyes closed, I prayed silently for Adrian's soul to be at peace.

On the other hand, maybe the coroner *did* know I had not seen the body and knew that in order for me to move forward, I needed to see evidence of the death so that closure could be reached. I had been having distressing nightmares in which Adrian pursued me relentlessly, popping up wherever I sought sanctuary and safety. If I ran from him and knocked on a door, it was he who opened the door. When I escaped him and ran down an escalator, he was waiting at the bottom of it, ready to do harm. In one disturbingly vivid dream, Adrian appeared and told me menacingly that he wasn't dead, that he had watched the funeral from across the road at the petrol station and was going to catch up with me one day, so I should be ever alert. I even questioned sometimes if he was really dead. I would see someone drive by in a truck and think it looked just like him, or hear someone speak with his inflection and intonation and turn, expecting to see him standing there. I was afraid to sleep because of the terrifying dreams, from which I would suddenly awake, shaking and sweating, my heart racing for minutes afterwards. Even in death, he was still able to fill me with dread. Perhaps now, after seeing the tragic picture of his lifeless body, I could accept the finality of his death, and he could finally rest in peace.

Jesuit Community Xavier University
3800 Victory Parkway Cincinnati OH
45207 513 745 3591
April 26, 1988

Dear Ena and Danny,

Forgive the long delay in writing—I guess I wanted to give the traumatic/emotional events of the past few months, time to settle. I certainly was the prime mover in the whole event, but looking back on things, if I had to do it over again, I would act in the same manner. Adrian was psychologically a very disturbed person and had the marriage con-

tinued, I think both Julie <u>and</u> the children would not only have been <u>very</u> unhappy but would have been in both physical and mental danger. Physical violence and bullying was simply a part of Adrian's make up. I think all of this was programmed into him as a child, so he probably was not responsible (morally?) for his actions, hence, as I told Julie, I'm sure God forgave him and has now welcomed him into Heaven. So the total result didn't (I hope) turn out too badly. A very disturbed man has now found ever-lasting peace and Julie and the children are free to face a life without fear and oppression. I think the rosary found around Adrian's neck was a pretty good sign that somehow finally he was doing what <u>he</u> thought was the best thing for Julie—somehow a final act of love to somehow set her free. He simply was unable to love correctly in life but maybe he managed it in dying.

Regarding our (Julie and I) final weekend in London (which you <u>may</u> have been wondering about), it was filled with wonder, appreciation, fun, the zest of living and love (in the <u>widest, truest, spiritual</u> sense.) I guess Julie and I have loved each other in this way since I met her as a 10 year old. So I treated her with a sense of loving joy (as she did me) and we had a ball—museums, restaurants, walks, talks, shops, games, church, prayers, tube rides, etc. I think (hope) she realized all this <u>was</u> a part of life and should have been her <u>right</u> in any normal marriage. At the airport on the day of my departure, after eating breakfast, we spent our final hour together praying in the chapel at the airport—to ask the Lord to guide both our lives and to thank Him for guiding our destinies.

Do I love her still—indeed I do!—but it's a love that wishes her only a continued spiritual growth and happiness. I would literally give my life for her. I really don't know anybody in their right mind who wouldn't love her once they meet her. She is a gem in every sense of the word.

Well I hope that answers some of your questions—on to other things.

I hear you are quite happy in your new Irish surroundings. I still hope I can visit you there some day. You are two of my favorite people and will always remain so. Julie told me what a source of strength you have been to her in her time of distress. She will still need much support as she faces her newer and freer life.

I'm beginning to work on my fall courses and have gotten into retreat work at a nearby retreat center. I miss Wales—it was a time of grace, security and new relationships. God works in strange ways.

Please, (along with Julie), remember me in your prayers! That I may continue to find God's will in my life. I have always counted on your prayers and will continue to do so. God bless you and keep you.

Love,
Bill

I received a copy of this letter from Bill so that I would know what he had shared with my parents. They had great respect for him, so although they may have considered me naive and vulnerable, his being so open with them validated me too.

Now we had to figure out whether we were meant to be together permanently. I had no doubts about the love I felt about Bill and was confident in his love for me but wanted to do God's will. I looked for more assurances that we were on the right path. The letter Bill received from the police officer was one sign which I interpreted as an endorsement of our relationship, the fact that we had been close in spirit for decades was another; but were we, as my mother had suggested, being swept away by fairy-tale notions?

27-4-88

My Dearest Bill,

Talking to you last night (early morning) was wonderful. I called you feeling frightened and alone and your love encompassed me and dispelled <u>all</u> my fears. Within half an hour I was sound asleep feeling completely secure. Thank you for everything.

Theresa noticed I was tired today so I told her of our conversation. (not the details, just that we had been speaking to one another). I shared with her some of my doubts and fears, she was very helpful.

She pointed out that because Adrian was unkind to me I am unsure of myself and as a result find it difficult to trust people completely. In fact she told me off (in a nice way) for not being totally fair with you. I know that I have hurt you by some of the things I've said about your age etc. I won't be so insensitive in the future. I really do love you and would never intentionally upset you, please believe that.

There are lots of things going on in my mind, all the time. One fear is that you have an idea of me that isn't real and if you did come in August, or even next year, for that matter, that I would be a disappointment to you. I can safely assume that you've had more dealings with ladies "romantically" than I have with men. Adrian was the only man I ever became intimate with. As a result, I'm afraid of embarking on a sexual relationship, as while I kept Adrian at arms length he treated me fine, but once we were married everything altered. I realize it is unfair to you, but it would be awful if you did come over and expected everything to fall into place automatically, it wouldn't be that simple. Perhaps things will develop, who can say, but I'd hate for you to feel you'd wasted your time if you were expecting more.

This is a very difficult subject to write about. I only hope you can understand what it is I am trying to say. I do know for certain that I love you, and need you, that you are the man for me. I want everything to be right between us. I guess this is one reason it is so important that we get together and TALK *things through, all vital issues.*

You are probably exasperated with me by now, I don't blame you in the least. I manage to confuse myself at times.

Please try to understand what I've found so hard to put down on paper. I <u>never</u> want to hurt you or let you down. I suppose my greatest (and totally irrational fear) is that I will lose you, something I pray fervently never occurs. You are so important to me.

God has to have us in his care, I realize we must trust and hope in him.

Always know that I love you,

God bless you,
Julie
xx

What was becoming evident was that letters and one scheduled half-hour phone call a fortnight were not an effective way to discern our destinies. We each wrote once a day, the letters taking about a week to reach us, by which time we had chatted at least once. So ideas were shared, issues presented, love expressed, but without time in each other's company, the process of making a decision was slow and stilted. Bill had more time to ponder our situation and more to consider with regard to his own circumstances. At fifty-four, marriage to me, with my four small children, would be a significant adjustment in lifestyle.

Bill had shared with me during our walk back from Crystals in November that there had been two other women with whom he had been in love while in the priesthood, but he had lacked the courage to leave and marry. I listened as he opened up to me about them, appreciative of the fact that he was being so honest with me regarding these relationships, one of which he had since ended because of us. I also felt some jealousy, which unnerved me, as it is such a destructive force. I recognized that it came from a place of insecurity and prayed for strength to manage it.

So it was clear that we had to have more time together. The difficulty arose from the fact that Bill did not earn his own money. He also had to ask permission to travel, giving justification for it, and the expense, which is why summer 1989 seemed the most likely opportunity for our next face-to-face encounter. In the meantime, we continued to write out our thoughts about the future.

Jesuit Community Xavier University
3800 Victory Parkway Cincinnati OH
45207 513 745 3591
April 28, 1988

My Darling Julie,
    Your beautiful card (flowers on front) arrived today. Your thoughts so well expressed really reflected my own and as you say, prayer has to be the answer so we can recognize God's will. I was beginning to let up a bit in prayer but I began to read Hannah Hurnard's, "Hind's feet on High Places" and was able to pray quite a bit with that. It's a beautiful allegorical book, (I'm sure you have read it). Reminds us of our lives' difficult journey.
    Your thought on our 16 month wait (Summer 89?) to see each other was also well put—we're 1/5 of the way there! I really weighed the pros and cons of coming this summer and the cons certainly were stronger. It simply wouldn't be fair to you (or either

one of us). You and I both need some time to think, plan and get settled – we are so moonstruck that if we saw each other this summer we'd never be able to part nor probably be able to keep from making love. (Well, maybe we would but it would be diffi-cult!!!) So, barring a miracle, I guess we begin to aim for summer '89. I also think by that time I have to decide whether marriage is a viable option. It would simply not be fair to you to postpone the decision any longer. No matter what the choice (ours and God) marriage or not, I will continue to love you till my dying day.

The three options seem:

1. *Our marriage—still the longest of long shots—I have so many negatives, it sim-ply doesn't seem fair to you.*
2. *I stay a priest and you marry someone (a nice guy!) I can handle it because you will be happy. I'll still be able to see you occasionally.*
3. *I stay a priest and you don't marry. You may feel this way now but I'm sure God will point out the way. Again, summer visits possible (both ways)but we'd have to be careful of feelings (though by this time I'd be so old the kids might have to pro-vide a wheelchair for me").*

Anyway, we're in the Lord's hands—Let's pray! Your love has changed my life, forced me to take some concrete steps to find out just who I am and where I'm at (and going!)

I do have an idea of how precious I am to you because you are the same to me. Our love has grown for 20 years in spite of little tangible contact and it will be forever no matter what.

As Hannah Hurnard comments at the end of her preface to her book "It (the book) may help them to understand a new meaning in what is happening, for the experiences through which they are passing are all part of the wonderful process by which the Lord is making real in their lives the same experience that made David and Habbakuk cry out exultantly, "The Lord God maketh my feet like hinds' feet and setteth me upon mine high places." (Pr. 18:33 and Hab. 3:19) Let us pray, Julie, my darling, that the Lord grant us our hinds' feet so that we both may find our high places in His company. You already are God's exaltation!

I love you more than my own life. Hugs and kisses to my favorite four children.

Bill

xx

Option 3—that Bill remain a priest and I remain single, with intermittent visits, was an option I was not prepared to consider. There was simply no way I was going to be his long-distance mistress. We definitely needed to talk.

Chapter 19

Our house was beginning to feel like home. No more mismatched army issue furniture, no more cheap carpet remnants from the market stall, no more "make do with what you're given." I was now free to select paint colors that suited my taste. I couldn't wait to put my mark on the haven I would share with my children. Thanks to Laura Ashley, as Adrian's widow, I was entitled to £5,000; £3,500 went to settle his debts, but the rest, more money than I had ever had at one time, was going towards style and comfort. The relaxing peach and cream hues in my bedroom, the new bedding for the single bed I would occupy, the matching curtains, and the frilly cushion (an added indulgence) made it a heavenly sanctuary. Similar attention was given to the rest of the house, and a professional family portrait was taken to complete the decor. As I placed the picture of the five of us over the mantelpiece, I thought to myself, *Now this is home.*

The garden too needed attention. The weeds and overgrown shrubs and flowers, vying for space and sunlight, were to be tackled next. I hired a landscaper who took on the task and learned from him how to care for the plants so that they would thrive. I wanted to ensure that every living thing in our home was nurtured and loved. The liberation had begun.

My life, which had been so restricted once I married, was now my own to determine. I had discovered the fragility of life and how swiftly it can end, so I chose to embrace all that life offered, exhilarated by my new independence. I had learned from the recent terrifying experience and the years trapped in the cocoon of fear that life is a wondrous gift to be lived to the fullest. I was indeed reborn, filled with wonder, curiosity, and unabashed joy at the possibilities that lay ahead. I had emerged transformed and ready to take flight.

I was eager to explore the myriad ways to expand my mind and my experiences. My one night out every weekend with the lads was a welcome distraction from the responsibilities of motherhood, but it didn't satisfy my yearning to do something worthwhile. I had been in the dark for so long all I wanted now was to dance in the light. I enrolled in a psychology class at the local college that met weekly and also volunteered with the probation service as a home visitor. But the work that made me most proud was the bereavement counselling I was privileged to do for CRUSE, a charity that assists people stuck in their grief. I looked forward to the time devoted to each endeavor, drawing energy and joy from every minute as I rediscovered what it means to be alive, to be a part of something bigger than myself, to be relevant.

The weeks developed a comfortable rhythm that offered a sense of stability and permanence to our lives. Letters continued to pass back and forth across the Atlantic. I learned to ignore the guarded whispers of the townspeople and relied on my close friends for companionship and support. Life was good. Even the challenges that arose from being in love with Bill were teaching me to be more patient.

Bill, impatient to tell me the news, called on the phone.

"I was going to write a letter—but I just needed to tell you immediately. We will be together in August."

"*This* August?" I didn't trust what I'd heard.

"Yes, this August." I had accepted that it would be summer '89 that we would next see each other, so knowing that it would be happening twelve months sooner made me giddy with anticipation. Now we could look forward to making a decision about both our futures. I felt a mix of excitement and concern.

I was glad that the months between the phone call and the reunion were busy. I had planned a week's holiday for me and the children at Butlins, a popular holiday camp with lots of activities for youngsters, and also a restorative trip to Ireland on my own to stay with my cousin Yvonne.

With so much to discuss and discern, we needed privacy, at least at the beginning of his visit. I would have to find babysitters in whom I had confided for the boys. It would be an imposition to ask anyone to have all three for a week, so different members of the family each agreed to take one child.

I found a secluded place called Glan Gwna, near Caernarfon, away from the inquisitive, which rented out self-catering cabins, so I booked a week there for Bill, Amy, and myself, then sent Bill the directions on how to get there by train.

2 Colwyn
Treowen
NEWTOWN
Powys
SY16 1NA
2-7-88

Dearest Bill,

Enclosed find train tickets and seat reservations—please don't lose them. Only four weeks before you set off, it will seem like twenty four!

The weather here (unlike yours) is very mixed, today we have had three or four heavy showers and it's very chilly. I advise you to include a couple of sweaters when you pack your suitcase.

Brian is off to Ireland for the summer on the 20th. I shall be taking him up to London on the 17th. There is a day trip that day that works out considerably cheaper than the train, also more convenient, so I shall be going over the ground exactly a fortnight before you. Needless to say, you'll be on my mind. (When are you not!). I do so love you. Daily I give thanks for the gift of your love. Don't ever allow me to spoil what we have. It is so special and must be nurtured.

I came across a poster today with the caption "Against All Odds." That's how I see us.

Love is <u>all</u>, nothing else is important. God is love, what else matters.

I wish at times it was possible to tell everyone how I feel (well my parents in particular) what a pity they wouldn't understand. Maybe one day with God's guidance we'll find the right words.

Come and give me a cuddle. I haven't had a decent cuddle since our farewell at Gatwick. (There don't seem to be as many "touchers" about as I would like).

Till our phone call on the 5ᵗʰ.

Take GOOD care of yourself.

God bless you.

He loves <u>us</u>.

Julie xx

With plans made and the children dispatched to various households, I set off on the train to Bangor with Amy, praying that my careful attention to detail would enable the fates to align so that Bill would "return to Wales" and find us in the cabin by the stream.

I caught a taxi from Bangor station to Glan Gwna, traveling through picturesque villages dotted with colorful gardens spilling over with blooms, past fields of grazing sheep on undulating hillsides, my thoughts focused on our reunion, which was to take place in just a few hours.

The cabin was rustic and basic, but I couldn't care less. For the next week, it would be our retreat. After checking out the accommodation and plopping my luggage against the bedframe in the room I was to share with Amy, we took a stroll to get to know the place and to fill up the time until Bill's arrival. I came across a shop on site that printed semicustom T-shirts and selected an image of two teddy bears with a large red heart between them. I added the words "LOVE IS US."

I harbored a fear, unfounded though it might have been, that I would prove a disappointment to Bill, that he had created and fallen in love with an idea of me that exceeded reality. I didn't have the vocabulary or the insight then to consider the impact of sexism and the "male gaze." I only knew that for twelve years, I was repeatedly reminded of my inadequacies with regard to my general appearance and sexual appeal. Names Adrian had called me such as "bucket ass," "Doris the docker," "the dragon," "skank," "no-tits, I still owned. Echoes of comments he had made about my lack of sexual prowess still haunted me: "Having sex with you is like screwing a pound of liver," "You're dry as a stick," "Who would want you?" No amount of affirmation from others or positive self-talk could erase the damage inflicted by years of subjugation.

Bill had better find out now that I'm flat-chested, I thought as I put on my new "LOVE IS US" T-shirt and decided to greet him braless.

As the time of his arrival drew closer, I imagined every possible scenario that could interfere with our plans. *What if he missed his flight? What if his plane crashed? What if he missed his train? What if he missed his connections?* The what-ifs this time encroached on my joyful anticipation and required great effort of will to dispel. However, I never once entertained the *what if he changes his mind?* That question would be answered at the end of the week.

The taxi pulled up outside the cabin, and Bill, in the familiar gray Mackintosh he was wearing when I alighted the train in London, stepped out. It was real. No words were needed as we held each other, realizing that we were indeed meant to be in this place at this time, together.

"Hello, my darling." His voice was a caress.

"Hello, Bill, I can't believe you're really here." I gazed up into his eyes and hugged him tightly.

"Believe it, my love." We lingered in the embrace that enveloped us like a loving mist, breathing in each other's essence, reassured by the peace emanating from our touch.

"Julie, I want to sleep with you. Can we?" The request, so simply stated, was redundant.

"Yes, please," I responded as all concerns I'd had about being physically intimate faded with the sunlight.

That night, a prayer I had made years before was answered. I experienced how two souls, released from fear and shame, exquisitely and tenderly merge in the full glory of passion when love is the reason for their existence.

The week was spent in blissful harmony as we explored not only the beautiful countryside around Caernarfon—its castle, the slate mines, the waterfalls, the small quaint towns—but also our futures. We prayed together, laughed together, sung together, slept together, and often walked in silence together, content in the knowledge that our hearts, like our feet, were in step with each other. Amy's presence added another delightful element of family. At not yet two, she needed constant attention. Bill shared that his heart leapt when, during a visit to Caernarfon castle, Amy stepped dangerously close to a ledge as he cautioned her, "Amy, step away." A lady nearby, being helpful, said gently, "Listen to your daddy." *Daddy*, a name he had not yet been called but for which he yearned deep in his being.

As our time together came to a close, the one thing we were certain about was that we were both truly in love with each other. There was no doubt in either of our hearts about that. We discussed the practical challenges like money, work prospects, and location. Bill explained that his salary was not his own; that, as a Jesuit priest, all money belonged to the community and went into a common fund, which eliminated payment of tax but, in so doing, also stopped payment to Social Security, which provides retirement benefits.

"If, by some miracle, God wants us to marry, He better make it *clear!*" he said after one tedious summary of the fiscal challenges facing us. "But whatever happens, Julie, 'all shall be well.'" He was using the well-known phrase from the teachings of St. Julian of Norwich, a medieval mystic, whose faith instilled a powerful optimism in the goodness of God and the certainty that "all shall be well, all shall be well, all manner of things shall be well."

"He *will* make it clear, Bill," I replied, confidently. "Why would he allow us to fall in love like this, otherwise?" I had more to gain, and Bill had more to lose by our committing to marriage now. He was still not sure he could leave the priesthood and keep his job. He was being practical and sensible, and I was believing in the power of love to conquer all.

"And God did direct you back to Wales, didn't he? That's a sign, I'd say," I added encouragingly.

"Yes, and I am exceedingly glad I heeded the message. So let's trust and have confidence that all shall indeed be well." He had been relying on that phrase as encouragement whenever we discussed our options.

By the end of the week, we still had not made a firm decision about what to do next. What we had confirmed was that our love would endure. We were returning to Newtown more in love but still in a quandary. It frustrated me that we were unable to make plans other than to arrange surreptitious meetings.

As we climbed into the taxi for our ride back to the train station in Bangor, our beautiful time together in Glan Gwna ending, I was overcome with sadness. We sat silently side by side, staring out of the window, the memories of the past few days and nights being summoned to improve my mood but instead compounding my melancholy. I felt as though I was entering limbo.

"Look!" Bill blurted out in amazement. "Slow down, driver!" He pointed out the window on my side of the taxi. "Do you see it!" There, in the largest letters I had ever seen, written in white, on the side of a large red brick building, were the words "ALL SHALL BE WELL." My immediate reaction was one of wonder and delight. Then the skeptic in me surfaced as I thought about how this could be possible. Had Bill, in the middle of the night, trekked four miles with paintpot, brushes, and ladder to create this message? No. Had he hired someone to do it? No. How could it be explained? The mystery of it perplexed us, until we both came to the same conclusion: that this was simply another sign from God that we were meant to be together. My hope and joy was restored, and all fear evaporated. It was a turning point in my life, helping me accept the mystery of God's timeline and let go of my impatience to have answers and plans. From that point on, my own conviction has been that "all shall be well." No matter what troubles, suffering, or pain we experience, in the end, *all shall be well.*

We returned to Newtown infused with confidence and impervious to the slurs of the gossips and naysayers. We didn't flaunt our love; neither did we hide it. I had finally let go of the anxiety about what other people thought and met each day with the excitement of a child, renewed and ready to discover what the next chapter of my life with Bill would reveal.

> *My Darling,*
>
> *Thank you, again, for a gloriously happy three weeks—I have never had such a vital and lovely time in my life. As I told you over and over—you are a treasure and I love you as much as life itself.*
>
> *I go over every day and really can't decide on a favorite. Maybe our excursion day with Amy on the train, or maybe our final day in London, or maybe our famous day in Coventry and the missed train and Golden Memories.*
>
> *I took the photos of our stay at Caernafon to be developed. I asked for two prints of each so I should be able to mail you some in a few days. I'll pick out the best. The rest are slides which I'll send out.*
>
> *I spent most of today getting my new office in shape. I'm about half way there.*
>
> *After phoning you the first night back, I went back to bed (feeling your cuddle) and slept another five hours—so a total of 11 hours sleep! It worked. I felt fine from then on.*
>
> *If possible I'll try to phone you on Friday, Sept. 2nd at our usual 11pm your time (rather than Sept. 6th).*
>
> *I love you immensely, and always will. Till we meet again,*
>
> *Bill xx*

1st Sept. 1988

My Darling,

Thank you so much for the lovely card which arrived today. It is great being able to look forward to your letters again. (It's 5 weeks since I last received one!)

I share all your thoughts about our so special time together, and I'm so glad we didn't fall out of love, which I half expected to happen.

Like you I find it difficult to choose one particular time above another. Every moment with you filled me with joy and contentment.

Our "smiling Christ child" rediscovery and the prayers together in the oratory before Our Lady will remain cherished memories. We are so fortunate to have known such a love as ours, few can boast such total contentment, which is how I feel when with you. I've given up trying to understanding <u>Why!</u> God knows what he is doing.

To a lot of people our alliance will appear scandalous, sinful even. Thankfully, "people" are not our judge, our Father in Heaven is, and his ways are not of this world. Everything about "US" seems so right. Whatever happens I will continue to love you, never have I been so sure of anything.

Thank you for loving me. Your love has helped heal those injuries caused by Adrian's neglect. If ever I cause you any pain, please tell me. <u>NEVER</u> would I hurt you intentionally.

You mean all to me and I thank God for you daily.

God bless and keep you safe,

Love always,
Julie xx

Dearest Julie,

I sent this letter to your Mum today, <u>again</u> trying to show her that Adrian's death shouldn't be considered a tragedy (even for him). If this doesn't work, I'll give it up. I'll write you on the weekend after our phone-call. I love you <u>more than ever</u> (is it possible!!!) I hope you received the pictures.

Jesuit Community Xavier University
3800 Victory Parkway Cincinnati OH
45207(513) 745 3591
August 30, 1988

Dear Ena,

I got back home a week ago and finally am catching up on correspondence. It was very nice talking to you twice on the phone. I'm sorry I wasn't able to visit you, but I certainly hope to one if these summers—perhaps in '89. I hear you're in a beautiful spot. I enjoyed my time with Julie and the children <u>immensely.</u> Julie continues to be an absolute delight and I found her more happy and optimistic than ever. I hope you can see Amy soon—she is really learning words and putting them together beautifully. She charms anybody she meets and can coax "sweeties" out of every person. Michael is really a nice, gentle boy who cares for his sister more than any other boy I have <u>ever</u> seen. Sean is a never-ending bundle of activity. He can be hard on the nerves sometimes but is super lovable nonetheless. I missed seeing Brian, but taking care of all 4 is a tough job for Julie but she has done a remarkable job. She is firm, but lovable and gentle with the children and they are turning out beautifully. They <u>know</u> she loves them!

I hope by this time you are seeing Adrian's death as less of a tragedy. The tragedy would have been if he had lived. Julie is free and much happier—the children have one super role model parent rather than one really bad one who kept the other in fear and trembling. As I said in my last letter, I'm sure that Adrian was programmed <u>not</u> to be able to love in a positive way by his parents (mother, especially?) and when he came face to face with God, I'm sure Jesus forgave him and welcomed him, since we cannot sin in unawareness. So again, where is the tragedy. Adrian is happy—Julie is happy—the children will grow in a positive glow of love—Julie is even financially better off. I'm sure Adrian finally saw his death as the one positive thing he could do after his repeated attempts to change always came up short. As you yourself say "Julie is very positive and facing life with new zest and vitality which has been lacking in recent years." Not only that, she is now bringing that zest and vitality to others around her. The plan of God is mysterious but in this case so much good has come from it I don't think any tragedy has happened. It would have been tragic otherwise.

I enjoyed also the company of Sean and Vincent for the time they were at Julie's with me. I also saw Lulu, Donald and Stephen in my day at Bristol. You certainly have interesting children!

I hope that you have recovered from the car accident—can you survive without a car?

I start teaching tomorrow after an absence of 16 months—I'll be rusty. Wales is in my blood and I miss its beauty and peacefulness. The past 16 months have been <u>very</u> vital for me with Julie so much a part of it. Please keep praying that continued growth and love comes to all our lives.

Enclosed is a Fulton Sheen tape for Danny. Please give him my very best. I hope to see you in the not-distant future.

Love,
Bill

Chapter 20

We had received two clear signs, as I interpreted them, the letter from the police man on retreat and the writing on the wall near Bangor, that affirmed our love. Now we needed to make some decisions about what to do next. Once back in America, Bill continued to phone me weekly for a thirty-minute conversation that he never exceeded since all long-distance calls were logged and had to be accounted for.

"I'm thinking of applying for a year's 'leave of absence' for personal discernment. It will require me to abstain from all priestly duties such as administering the sacraments. I'll live independently apart from the Jesuit community but keep teaching at the university and earn my own money," Bill explained in our weekly call.

"Are you allowed to do that?" I was intrigued.

"Yes, a leave of absence is permitted when a priest is unsure of his vocation. At the end of the year, I would either renew my commitment to the priesthood or leave and marry you."

"I suppose they think it gives you time to get me out of your system." I was a little anxious that Bill still needed more time.

"That's the idea, but rest assured, Julie, you are part of me now. We have a retreat that's spread out through the school year to allow us to focus on personal growth. It will be a year of decision, and we'll have some months to pray and work out where I am going," he explained.

"Well, I hope you're going towards me!"

"Always towards you, Julie. It is you that has enabled me to love God more than ever. He has a purpose in all of this. I know this has not been easy for you, darling. I promise out of fairness to you to have made a firm decision by the end of the year. You can use this time to focus on your growth too. Perhaps this is the year Mr. Right shows up, and the decision will be made for us."

"Well, whether we are to marry or not or be together or apart or become missionaries on Mars, I'll respect your decision." I was trying to be magnanimous, but my heart would be crushed if he decided against marriage.

"Thank you. Emotionally, I'm still in a muddle. Being so much in love with you is a delirious feeling, especially knowing you feel the same way."

"I *do* feel the same way," I interjected.

"I know, Julie, but being four thousand miles away, plus having all the difficulties facing us, causes some emotional churning. I exult in your love and treasure every moment of it. Whatever we decide, I will love you for all eternity."

"Not *we*, Bill, *you*," I corrected. "I know what *my* decision is. As far as I am concerned, we're already married in God's eyes. But as I said, I will respect your choice, even it means we never contact each other again." The discussion was making me sad. Bill constantly assured me of his love; but for me, the natural next step was marriage, and the prospect of waiting another year for him to make a decision was distressing.

"I know, love. There are so many things to consider. I want you to have the life you deserve, and I want to make sure I can take care of you and the children properly. I can't do that without a job, and I don't know whether I'll be able to stay teaching if I leave the priesthood." He was justifying his hesitation.

"Why is it always about money?" The frustration was creeping into my voice. "We will manage, Bill—I can be very frugal." It was my turn to reassure. "You keep telling me to trust that God has a plan, so *you* need to trust and have faith."

"You're right. We must trust." He let out a heavy sigh before adding, "Well, can we agree that neither money—the lack of it, that is—or the official approval of the church will stand in our way of a decision to marry or not?"

"Yes! Yes! God allowed us those wonderful three weeks, Bill. He has brought us together. I can't imagine he wants us to be apart. Thank you, sweetheart. All shall be well, remember?"

"All shall be well," he repeated. I was encouraged by our optimism. "I think we are both in the flow of life, Julie. I feel totally alive since you are more alive, and so am I. No matter what our choice finally is, we *will* be okay. Our love will never end, and that can never be bad."

Two significant obstacles were no longer going to be allowed to interfere with our dreams. If Bill decided against marriage it would be for some other reason than money worries or church opinion.

"On another note," he went on, "I'm on the budget committee, and they were moaning at the last meeting about our projected spending on long-distance phone calls, so I guess maybe I'll have to limit our weekly call to twenty minutes."

"Oh, that's a pity. I so look forward to our nice long chats."

"Well, at least they didn't mention my name! Thank God we got three months' worth of free calls. Maybe God was giving us some necessary phone time."

"Yes, we needed it. I forget that you don't own a phone." It slipped my mind from time to time that Bill had no personal income.

"Well, if we are limited to twenty minutes a week on the phone, we'll just have to plan on spending more face-to-face time together. I'm going to see if I can figure out a way to come over at Christmas. No promises yet, so we can't get our hopes too high."

"Oh, Bill, that would be marvelous. Oh my goodness, I hope you can do it," I said excitedly.

"I hope so too, darling. I have told Father Bishoff, my spiritual director and a very holy man, about our love for each other, and he says love only comes from God. He will keep my confidence. It feels good to have him to talk to."

"I'm so glad you have someone you can trust to speak to about us. Oh, I do hope you can come over at Christmas," I said, already imagining how wonderful it would be to share that family time.

"I'll see what I can do about a December visit. It's a long shot. Fares will need to go down low, and circumstances have to be just right. Please don't say anything to anyone about it as it would have to be unofficial," he cautioned.

"I thought you said you were going to get a year's leave of absence? Surely, it won't need to be a secret then." I hated not being able to be open about our relationship, which I felt was being tainted by the deception.

"I'm *thinking* about asking, but now isn't the best time to do that because of the way our teaching contracts are written. Once the time is right, I will." It sounded like another delaying tactic. "One way or another, I'm dying to see you, to kiss you, to hold you. Keep praying and let the spirit guide us, hopefully to each other's arms. But wherever we both end up, be assured of my love." The thirty minutes were up. "God bless you, my darling."

"God bless us! I will say some prayers. I love you, Bill."

As soon as we hung up, I began to pray. Bill's encouragement of my social life freed me to explore other relationships, though in my heart I felt bound to him. If he was right in speculating that we might be infatuated with each other, then going out with other men might help clear that question up once and for all. So I accepted invitations to go out on dates. One young policeman, Robert, was introduced to me at a charity cheese-and-wine party hosted by Frank and Chris. We were the youngest people there, Robert sent in place of his mother, who was too ill to attend. We liked each other immediately and made plans to hang out together once in a while. He was a courteous, kind, and chivalrous man of twenty-four, his gentlemanly ways somewhat reminiscent of an earlier era in civility and manners. He spent time with my boys, taking them out rally-car racing and generally being a positive role model. I recall one of our early dates, as last orders was called at the pub, asking if he would take me to Crystals.

"Crystals? Are you mad? It's a dive. There's no way you'll get me in that place!" His loathing for the place was apparent.

"Aw, please, Robert. I don't want to go home yet, and there's nowhere else open. Besides, I'm having too much fun with you."

"Sorry, Julie, I'm having fun too, but I'll never step inside that place when I'm off duty." He was not budging. I ignored his remark, trying one more time to persuade him with an ultimatum I never expected him to accept.

"Well, we can either go to Crystals, or you can take me home to meet your mother!"

That was the night I met his mother.

Later in the month, while out to dinner, he told me that if we were to become boyfriend and girlfriend, I would not be allowed to speak about Adrian, that it was a taboo subject. I told him playfully that we would never be boyfriend and girlfriend as dating sometimes leads to marriage, and I couldn't possibly go from being Mrs. Long to becoming Mrs. Large. I then confessed that the real reason behind my flippant comment was my feelings for Bill. So he revised his expectations and chose to remain my cherished friend until his death from lymphoma at age forty-six. He never married.

Mark too asked me out separately from when we met the gang of seven on a Saturday night. We had grown close, and I had offered him the use of my shed for his woodworking. I had shared with him that I had strong feelings for Bill but did not know what the future held for us and that I was trying to be open to all possibilities. He, being much more pragmatic and living more in the moment, said he understood. He became a familiar sight in my garden, sipping the tea I supplied and then taking me out for a drink as Mary Ann, the children's favorite babysitter, came to stay the night.

I enjoyed the thoughtful attention he paid me, which had been so lacking in my marriage. I told him again of my attachment to Bill, which he claimed to understand; yet in my loneliness, I responded to the warmth of his affection and tender touch. He invited me to his flat for dinner and to stay the night, so I told Mary Ann that I would be home before she woke the children up in the morning.

When I arrived at Mark's apartment, music was playing softly, the lights were dimmed, casting a warm glow over the room, and dinner was baking in the oven. Mark opened a bottle of white wine and offered a toast, "To whatever the future holds." We clinked glasses as I sank back into the couch, every single one of my senses fully engaged.

Later, shrouded between the sheets of freshly washed cotton, I surrendered to his slow touch. It was an exquisitely sensual and pleasurable experience that brought me closer to understanding how some people can separate love and sex.

To Mark

Seeking comfort in each other
With each caress our fears abate.
Suspended,
Thoughts of past and future wait,
Surrendered,
Myself once kissed,
All else dismissed,
Temporarily

Julie Long
October 25 1988

To Mark

What am I to you?
Perhaps just one of many passing through.
What are you to me?
Sweet agony.

Julie Long
October 25 1988

To Mark
Though my heart yearns for a distant love
You are my present consolation.
Forgive me now for taking
And later forsaking.
Perhaps we should have started with,
Goodbye.

Julie Long

October 27 1988
Ode for Julie

I'm only your accomplice in crimes of passion,
Which is sort of fashionable.
Though it seems their tender crimes
Us two in our prime,
Both with soft kisses
And I suppose well meaning wishes.

Slipping away like morning stars, acting appropriately
For any circumstance, we make a fine team
You know what I mean.

For me happiness is in the hour.
When it turns sour, or to coin a phrase
You return to your ivory tower,

I know our friendship and equalities will
Keep us together, while setting free
Your requited love, not meant for me.

Mark
November 12, 1988

Night III (a poem for Julie)

A mother sleeps, warm and soft as breath
That trembles bedsheets.
Quiet as dream conversation with an expressionless
Expression she lies still, stately
A pyramid dweller.

Not my mother, but I notice a mother's devotion
Even through the luxury of rest.
I see a profile cut loose,
Troubles thawed by sleep.

I look for her shallow breathing
Almost hidden as those dreams take expression.

A subconscious rises,
Visions of a long ship appear,
Set adrift, flames rain down on her from loosed
arrows,
A mother sails away
Sand cools beneath my feet.

Mark

I had been unfair to Mark. I liked him but knew that we were not going to have a future together, so after a few dates, I told him that I would prefer it if we could just be friends. It was difficult for him to accept that my encounter with him had helped me to appreciate the depth of feeling I had for Bill. To continue to sleep with him would only be offering him false hope. His affection, understandably, turned to anger at my rejection of him, so the inevitable happened, and our friendship ended.

He was unable to accept it at first, especially as I had agreed to go to Cardiff with him for a weekend and then cancelled and, for a while, persisted in asking me to reconsider, even showing up drunk outside my house late at night months later and crying out to me in the darkness. Feelings of fear that I thought had died with Adrian resurfaced the more persistent Mark became. When I awoke to him standing over me in my bed at three in the morning, after secretly entering my home, terror took hold as he insisted I rethink my decision to end our relationship. He was drunk, angry, and unpredictable, and I needed him to leave. I leapt out of bed and rushed down the stairs to the living room, hoping to persuade him to go home. He followed me, as I expected, but was not ready to go. All the old strategies in my arsenal that I had employed in the past when managing Adrian's anger and which I thought would never again be needed were resurrected as I pleaded with Mark to go home. He was as intransigent as I was insistent and stood defiantly in front of me. Finally, with my back up against the wall and his hand gripping my throat, he leaned in, saying, "Listen, just listen!" I was defeated. There was no fight left in me, so I just slid down the wall, his hand still clutching my neck until I sank too low, sobbing. I sat there while he leaned on the wall for support, looking down at me, a crumpled mass of flesh, slumped over on the carpet, asking myself, *Why was I so reckless?* He left me there and did not return.

At first, I struggled with how to tell Bill that I had been intimate with another man. He had encouraged my venturing out into new relationships, but part of me felt that I had betrayed him. We had promised our love to each other but still had not decided how that love would manifest. I was afraid of losing him but also wanted our relationship to be based on openness and honesty. I wept and prayed for courage to confess to him what I had done and then decided that rather than a letter, I would tell him in a phone call.

"I have something I need to tell you, Bill." I sighed, the sadness seeping through.

"What is it?" he replied, giving no hint that he was aware of my distress.

"You know my friend Mark, the one who uses the shed?" I sighed heavily.

"Yes."

"Well, I've been out with him and stayed overnight at his flat." This was so much harder than I thought it would be.

Bill's silence told of his pain. "Hmm. I was half-expecting it, Julie," he said gently after pausing to think. "Not necessarily with Mark, but with someone."

"Oh, Bill, I am so sorry. It has made me realize how much I love you. I know this must hurt you, and for that I am so, so sorry."

"I understand. It was bound to happen sometime," he continued kindly.

"I have told him we can only be friends now, and he's angry. I don't blame him. I was being selfish. Oh, I am so sorry."

"You were being human, Julie. Only human." I was in awe of his capacity for forgiveness.

"I'll understand if you're angry with me too, Bill." I somehow felt I deserved to be punished for what I had done.

"I'm not angry, Julie, but it would be a lie to say I'm not hurt and disappointed."

"I promise, Bill, it will never happen again, but I understand if you don't want to continue with me." I had begun to cry. "You're being so kind right now, but you may feel differently later when you've had more time to think."

"I know it won't happen again—maybe it had to happen for you to clarify your feelings for me. That's what happened with me. To be honest, I've had a couple of close calls myself since I returned from Wales, though I haven't actually made love to anyone since you. We are both human, Julie, please don't worry. We will get through this."

"What do you mean, close calls?" My heart sank as I remembered that Bill too had relationships that needed attention.

"Well, I went over to help move a wardrobe, and one thing led to another, but we *didn't* make love. I thought about you and about us and stopped."

I listened, understanding now how he could be so compassionate in his response to me. "Well, thank you for telling me. I thought about us too, Bill, and have realized that no one else is for me but you. Please believe me."

"I love you too, Julie. We will get through this. As I said it was inevitable—better now than later." He was suffering and yet not scolding me, constant in his gentleness towards me. "Sleep well and know that God loves you, and I love you."

We were each, in our own clumsy way, searching for meaning in our personal life. We both wanted to be authentic, living life honestly; and although we had acknowledged that our love for each other had acted as a catalyst for necessary change, we were both also discovering that the path towards the light is unique to each soul—a solitary journey which we must courageously navigate alone.

12/8/88

> *My Dearest Darling Julie,*
>
> *Well, it is now almost 5 hours since your phone call and you were wondering how I'd feel then, not much different, really. A hurt has set in (I guess because I <u>do</u> love you so much), but it is a hurt I can deal with. And I <u>do</u> understand why you did it—in fact, as I said on the phone, I almost did expect it. Maybe it was the fact that you <u>were</u> taking birth control pills, plus your maternal instincts esp. w Mark) <u>and</u> your simple need to be held and comforted. Anyway, I'm glad you came out of it still loving and preferring me and I'm sure it will make our love stronger. As I said on the phone, I've avoided actually <u>making love</u> with anyone since you, but it's been close a couple of times (so I deserve to be forgiven too). It's been the same for me—it's made me realize how much I love you and how special our love is.*
>
> *In class we just watched Woody Allen's "Hannah and Her Sisters"—one of my favorite films and a good one to see tonight. It is the relations between three sisters, their parents, their husbands/lovers over a period of 2 years. There is hurt, betrayal, love, concern, feelings and ultimately happiness though all despair of it for awhile. A very upbeat film.*
>
> *Thank you for sharing your feelings—I <u>did</u> sense something bothering you (and did unconsciously guess what it was). All this has only increased my love for you <u>and</u> my trust in you—and I hope your trust in me. I was thinking the other day that*

the 3 women I have loved, have made love to 3, 3
and 2 men respectively and believe it or not, I somehow figured the number would change to 3, 3, 3
so what the heck—I'm glad I won't have to wonder
<u>when</u>.

Seriously Julie—you mean more to me than
ever and I can't wait for our three weeks from today
to be up. We have so much to discuss and figure out,
but not before I have kissed you at least 5,000 times,
and held you, and touched you, and made us one in
body and spirit.

So dry your tears my darling, life is too short
for sadness. I adore you—always have since I first
met you twenty years ago and always will—into
eternity. God <u>had</u> a purpose in bringing us together
and together we will figure it out.

Today is the feast of the Immaculate Conception
<u>and</u> I haven't said Mass yet ('tis now 10:30 pm).
I'll go down right now and say it—offer it to Mary
that she may guide us and help us. I remember our
prayer at the oratory (and I'm sure she does too). She
loves you, Julie, as does Jesus and last and I guess
least (but mightily!) do I.

You still and always will be my moon, stars,
earth, eternity, moonbeams and diamonds—all
rolled into one.

May the time fly by 'til I hold you in my arms.
Deepest love,
Bill
Xxxxxx

2 Colwyn,
Treowen
Newtown
Powys
SY 16 INA
9-12-88

My Darling Bill,
How can I ever thank you enough for being so understanding and forgiving.
After our telephone conversation last night I felt so calm and so totally loved—I slept well.
For a couple of weeks I have been trying to muster the courage to tell you what had happened but so terrified was I of losing you that I kept putting it off.
I was quite prepared for you to turn away from me—I felt it was what I deserved—this I would have accepted.
You are everything I could ever wish for in a man, if nothing else, this whole experience has only served to confirm my love for you which is without doubt the one good thing in my life.
I really am sorry for any pain I have caused you, it is the last thing I ever want to do. Your happiness is my one concern. Being 4,000 miles apart doesn't help our situation.
Thank you again for allowing me to make mistakes and still loving me. You are my only love and my life would be so empty without you. I can't wait until the 29th to hold you and kiss you.
I love you Bill, so much.
God bless you and keep you.

Julie
xx

Bill had shared his plan to visit us after Christmas with Father Bischoff, who promised not to speak of it to anyone. He had told the Jesuits he was spending the holidays in Louisville with his niece Mary Margaret, who had my number in case anything cropped up and Bill needed to be contacted. She and another cousin of Bill's had offered him money so that he could afford to make the trip.

We had a couple of glorious weeks together with the children, who fell in love with Bill almost as deeply as I had. He joined me in the pub for the regular Saturday night with my rather motley crew of "guardian angels." Mark was there and was still upset about the end of our friendship so took Bill aside to "have a word." Ozz, who had become my confidante and coach with regard to how to manage Mark's emotional outbursts, which had become part of the routine on the weekend, especially after a few drinks, watched from his seat at the bar as Bill and Mark discussed me. I knew that Bill would maintain his composure and would be a calming influence on Mark, so I trusted that Mark would feel heard. If it got out of hand, Ozz and the other lads were on standby. I watched nervously, nevertheless, feeling remorse for the pain I had inflicted on Mark. A few minutes later, both men returned to the group with an increased respect for the other. Later, Bill shared that Mark had told him that he had better marry me quick before someone else did.

Back at home, the light and joyful atmosphere was enhanced by a visit from some of my siblings, who now knew of our deep and growing affection for each other. I felt relieved to be able to be open with them and was delighted that they were there to share in the peace emanating from every corner of my home. Sean babysat so that we could get away to Chester for an overnight trip, where we fell in love with the town, in part because of the beautiful memories we created there. The more time we spent together, the more we wanted to be together permanently as husband and wife.

I was unaware that Bill had spoken to the children about his love for us all with the intention of asking their advice on where he should propose marriage. So although I was delighted to be spending time alone with him in a quaint bed-and-breakfast overnight, I had no idea that he was preparing a surprise speech for me.

We took a walk, hand in hand, around the top of the city walls and stopped to admire the streets below lined with the familiar black-beamed Tudor houses with their whitewashed facades. Then standing under the town clock, holding my two hands in his, he turned to face me. I sensed a solemnity in his demeanor that I reciprocated as we held each other's gaze.

"Julie, in your love, your touch, your voice, your spirit, your goodness, your generosity, and maybe especially in our bodies uniting so beautifully with fun, spirit, and downright joy, I certainly have found God's love and now understand more fully how he loves us. I promise to love you all the days of my life and hope that I end my days with you by my side." Tears had started falling down my cheeks as his gentle words reached my soul in anticipation of the question. "Julie, will you allow me the privilege of becoming your husband?"

"Yes, please." I wanted to be as eloquent as Bill had been, but he was content hearing *yes*. The what-ifs had ended.

There was no engagement ring, but I didn't care. I knew now that we were going to be a family. I couldn't contain my happiness. The entire world—the trees, the people, the sky, the flowers—everything living thing took on an aura of beauty that filled me with bliss. I had never experienced such utter and total contentment and peace. This was indeed true love.

"We are so lucky to have found each other, Bill."

"I've loved you since before you were born, Julie. I think I prayed you into existence."

We prayed together under the town clock, a prayer of gratitude and a prayer of promise to love each other unconditionally as husband and wife. The year 1989 was to be a year of planning, preparing, and praying.

Life had been transformed. I could now speak to the children about Bill freely and assure them that we would all be together someday. Although I longed for that day to come, I was not anxious about it. I missed being close physically as we were so in tune with each other, so I drew even more comfort and consolation from his heartfelt and encouraging daily letters. Time was measured in space between visits. How soon until we would see each other again?

2 Colwyn,
Treowen,
NEWTOWN
Powys
Mid Wales
12-1-89

My Darling,
    Almost 36 hours have passed since we said fare-
well at the airport and I am missing you desperately!
    I am so impatient to be in touch with you that
I can't even wait until tomorrow to buy some air-
mail paper and envelopes. I have taken the centre
pages from Brian's school book!

    Bill, I love you more as time goes by. Thank
you, for your visit, every day spent with you teaches
me more about love and its joys. I have never expe-
rienced such a feeling of wholeness as when we are
together. I have never met anyone who makes me so
completely happy as you do.
    Please don't worry about my being faithful to
you—I've learned that particular lesson well. You
are all I will ever want and would not put our rela-
tionship in jeopardy by being so reckless again.

Going to bed last night was a very lonely experience, particularly as I could still smell you on the sheets. I keep going over our time together in my mind, our Christmas visit, evensong in the Cathedral and the very poignant Mass at Gatwick chapel.

You are a splendid man, and I am being constantly delighted by your kindness and attention. You give me so much and take so little, I feel as though I will never be able to show you half as much love as you have shown me but I do honestly love you.

I will miss our hugs and cuddles and holding your hand. Gosh! We always have so much to catch up on whenever we manage to get together.

Don't be lonesome, I am thinking of you constantly. Around my neck there is always something to remind me of you 24 hours a day. I used to try to get you out of my mind, now thoughts of you are a welcome blessing and always bring a smile to my face.

Whatever happens, and I hope it will be in our favour, I will never stop loving you.

God hasn't let us down yet so he will guide us through to our ultimate happiness. I believe it will be a life together, sharing everything, pain, pleasure, all things. But together we can overcome any obstacles.

I love you to bits my dearest man. Take care of yourself and be happy. Remember you're my "bipple nug!"

Love to Bill Daily and Fr. Bischoff, but far more importantly my love as always for you.

God Bless you,

Julie

xx

1/19/'89

Julie, My Darling—

It is now nighttime—after my class. I posted the letter on my feelings (about your overnight trip) this afternoon but am now much more peaceful— but not <u>entirely</u> unworried! Knowing your circumstances, I do realize asking you to wait six or seven months without my seeing you is a hard thing but I know you will be faithful as you promised. There is now no question on my part—you <u>are</u> my everything.

I do make <u>all</u> the promises that this card spells out so beautifully—and I (we) will learn by each mistake as we already have.

These six months are so crucial for both of us and trust, fidelity, and faith are essential. I have given you my heart, my promise, and my life forever.

I'm off to Louisville tomorrow where I look forward to sharing our feelings with Mary M. I still haven't received any mail from you but if it comes tomorrow (the letter to Mary M) I'll bring it with me. The mail delivery will come before I leave, if not, I'll post it to her.

With each passing second!—I love you more.

May God Bless and keep you always,

Love,
Bill
Xx

2 Colwyn
Treowen
NEWTOWN
Powys
SY 16 1NA
22 -1-89

My Darling Bill,
    Though it is only a very short while since we were talking on the telephone, I still felt the need to write to you and tell you how much I love you.
    It makes me so happy to know that you feel confident enough to share your deepest feelings with me. Thank you for that—also that I am able to respond to them. It was quite difficult to tell Mark that I wouldn't go to Cardiff with him after all or anywhere else for that matter—he seemed so desolate. But now I know it was probably the best thing to do—even though it was painful for him.
    I couldn't do anything that may cause you to worry so it was not a difficult decision to make. Your happiness is my paramount concern—please continue to tell me if I might upset you by any of my actions.
    I had two dreams last night one before your call and one after both about aeroplanes.
    The first had the children and me on an aeroplane waiting to take off. When I looked around to check that the children were strapped in, they had gone. I was very anxious to find them, other passengers helped me to look and the pilot delayed take off till we were all on board again.
    The second dream had me rushing to catch a plane but getting to the runway just as it took off. I was very sad. Strange that I should have two dreams about planes.

I also dreamt vividly of looking through a window of either a car or a train and noticing an entire street of houses and buildings, large industrial chimneys, and lots of red brick buildings with white frameworks around the windows. I recall thinking, I must remember this as I may visit it one day. It was an unusual dream as there were no people in it at all—the streets were eerily empty.

I wonder what you can make of all that!

I am so glad that signs continue to be shown to you, like the music, etc. Every day something that we have shared or talked about reminds me of you, not that I need any reminders, but it is noce to have these little triggers.

I love you so much, Bill I could burst and that's not a complaint. You mean everything to me. Let's pray for continued guidance and increasing love.

Take good care of yourself please as I need you—sometimes I get so lonely and miss you desperately—don't worry though there is no substitute. You are all I want.

God bless you and love you.

ALL my love always,
Julie
xx

Jesuit Community Xavier University
Cincinnati OH
45207 (513) 745 3591
1/27/89

My Darling Julie,
With some of the legal complexities of leaving the society and still trying to teach at XU new in my

grasp, let me propose two possibilities of timing with advantages and disadvantages of each.

I will preview them by saying on my part it is now not a question of if I will marry you but only when if you continue to love me—I am committed to you with gladness and joy.

#1 Scenario

I tell the Provincial I want to leave when he comes in late March/early April (providing contracts have been signed by then).

Advantages

1. *Possibly—I could get papers of dismissal by mid-May which would enable me to start earning money with my summer course plus regular salary.*
2. *Freedom to visit you in summer for 2 months with no need for any approval.*
3. *Maybe earning enough so you could come over in late March/early April 1990 (with family) and we could marry.*
4. *Could visit you freely at Christmas.*

Disadvantages

1. *This year's current contract was a stupid one but it contained the clause "University can dismiss you if you act in a manner that will bring criticism to the university." This is pretty wide ranging and they could use it to try and invalidate contract by saying my leaving the society will bring "criticism" to the university.*

345

2. *How would your parents react to my visiting them with you as a layman and not a priest.*

3. *We would be spending our own money for the July. Aug. trip.*

#2 Scenario

I wait until current contract is up (Aug. 31) and new one (to be signed in March) is in effect – then ask for dismissal.

Advantages

1. *They couldn't try to fire me because of wording in this year's current contract.*

2. *If I get permission to come over to England for July-August, our trip would effectively be paid for by the Jesuits.*

3. *Your Mum and Dad might be more receptive to me visiting them since I will still be a priest. (At least receptive till we tell them our plans to marry!)*

Disadvantages.

1. *We have to wait longer. I'll not start earning money for myself till my dismissal papers come—maybe Oct. '89.*

2. *Our marriage date would be summer, 1990 at earliest, unless we win a lottery.*

3. *There is a chance Jesuits wouldn't let me visit you in the summer (you could still come here).*

Maybe <u>you</u> could add some advantages and disadvantages to each case and let me know what you think. If I can get some <u>good</u> legal opinion regarding the current contract (that they couldn't use it against me), then I would highly favor scenario #1! I am quite restless and unhappy without you and it is obviously beginning to show. The sooner a definite date is set and decisions are made, the happier I will be. On the other hand, jeopardizing the chance to continue teaching here would be foolish, too.

Goodness—if only life were simple.

The only thing I'm sure of—I love you and desperately want to marry you and be with you and the children as soon as possible and forever. I found a "Resurrection Prayer" by Christina Rosetti (we saw pics of her by her husband at the Tate Gallery) that I will send to you. This Lent will be a good time for much prayer, penance and petition that the Resurrection graces will shine through for us.

I love you so much Julie it is hard to express. May the Lord lead us and guide us.

You are <u>grace</u> to me.

Love forever,
Bill
xx

Chapter 21

It felt wonderful to be actually planning for our life together as a family. Life had renewed momentum, spurred on by our love. Our time with each other over the new year had inspired a firm commitment to getting married. Now it was simply a matter of when. Bill would tackle the logistical issues in the US with regard to his career, leaving the priesthood, housing, immigration, etc. I would learn to be patient.

Father Carson, who had been so supportive when I was leaving Adrian, became increasingly judgmental once Bill told him of our plans to marry. Bill had met with him privately to share our news in the hopes that he would keep a protective eye on me, but instead we, and our relationship, became a target for his public disapproval.

One Sunday, shortly after the marriage proposal and before Bill returned to America, we attended Mass and were stunned when, from his moral pedestal during the sermon, Father Carson spoke scathingly about "those Jezebels who lure the good priests from their vocations." In such a small parish where everyone knew one another, it was clear that his comments were directed at us. I closed my eyes as though somehow time would reverse and erase his words. Bill too, except for reaching to clasp my hand firmly, sat motionless, as though willing himself to disappear. Heads turned as the priest's remarks drew glances from the congregation, at least from those who had been paying attention. Some eyes, thankfully, were filled with compassion; others revealed their disgust. Although I felt no personal shame in our decision, I knew that Father Carson had just elevated those present who deemed themselves "righteous" and morally superior to the position of judge and jury.

A few days after Bill had left for the US, Father Carson asked to meet with me at the church.

"Julie, *Father* Hagerty," he said, stressing the word *father*, "has told me of your plans that he should leave the priesthood and marry you."

"Yes." I nodded, not sure what he expected me to say.

"Well, this puts me in a rather awkward situation, I'm afraid." I was confused by his comment, wondering how our plans made things awkward for him.

"Sorry, Father, I don't understand."

"Well, do you plan to go through with this marriage to Father Hagerty?"

"Yes, that's what we hope for." Naively, I was also hoping for his support, at least privately. I knew he couldn't congratulate us, but I was dismayed at such stubborn resistance to what I now considered God's will.

"Well, if you are intent on pursuing this path, then you must abstain from receiving Holy Communion in the future." He was laying down the rules reflecting his assessment of my current state of sinfulness. I was shocked at his statement and repeated my early remark.

"Sorry, Father, I still don't understand."

"You are not to receive communion," he stated plainly.

"Why?" My voice began to quiver as I considered what I was being denied.

"Because you are causing scandal," he explained.

"But he's in America, Father. How are we causing scandal if he isn't even here?" I wanted to understand the reasoning behind the punishment. He took a deep breath, as though by inhaling, he could muster up the patience to deal with a defiant child.

"Will you come to confession and say that you have abandoned your plans to marry this priest?" he asked authoritatively.

"No, Father, I can't do that," I said as tears spilled over onto my cheeks. I was annoyed with myself for appearing weak in his presence as I summoned up my dwindling courage to stand up to yet another man, wielding his power and dismissing mine.

"Well, until you do, I am refusing you communion."

Silence descended as I processed his words. I searched his face for a glimmer of compassion but met only stern resignation. It all seemed so un-Christian and cruel. My love for God had increased, not diminished, since Bill and I had fallen in love. How could this be so?

"You are also to change when you attend Mass. You can come to the Saturday night Mass instead of Sunday morning."

"But, Father, I always come to Sunday Mass."

"I know you do, but you are not to attend Sunday Mass anymore. You can return, as I said, once you tell me in confession that you no longer plan to marry Father Hagerty." He was asserting his authority, and I had no choice but to comply. I felt bullied.

I was devastated. As a devout Catholic, I received spiritual sustenance from regularly receiving the Eucharist. I felt as though Father Carson wanted to shame me publicly, and that in such a small congregation, my absence from my regular Mass and abstinence from Communion would actually become an occasion of sin, stirring up gossip.

"What do I tell people when they ask me why I've stopped going to Mass on Sundays?" I asked, anticipating the questions that would come.

"You can tell them you've switched to Saturday because it suits your social calendar better." He was not to be swayed. I left, despondent and dejected, but unwavering in my decision to marry Bill.

It hurt me deeply to be excluded from full participation in the Mass. Great sorrow swept over me each time my children squeezed past my legs to go to the altar and receive the sacrament, leaving me wanting in the pew. I understood the church commandments and knew that in the eyes of the Catholic Church, Bill and I were committing the sin of fornication. However, I was convinced that in God's eyes, we were fulfilling our destiny and His will.

I had reached a turning point in my spiritual journey. I was learning to trust and respond to my conscience rather than to follow blindly the antiquated patriarchal rules designed to control and suppress—rules made and enforced by powerful men who ignored the message of Jesus, which was to love one another with compassion. I prayed to my compassionate, all-loving, and merciful God to supply the grace denied me in communion to continue to be a faithful disciple of Christ. I received spiritual consolation and courage and was sustained by the letters from Bill.

2/5/89

My Darling Julie,

Sunday evening—listening to "Somewhere in Time" and praying, I came across these thoughts in meditating on John 5:6 "Do you <u>want</u> to be healed?"

"The truth is we are not sure. We are so used to our life of limitations that we don't rightly know what we are missing. Besides, we take pride in managing as well as we do. There is comfort in company where the fine edge of accountability is conveniently blurred. Mostly, we are scared to death of the life-changing immersion in the Holy Spirit! Why trade the known for the unknown—the shelter of our personal portico for a wide open world of risk?

Rise—the Lord can no longer tolerate the atrophy of the Church (and me!). The <u>decisive first step</u> must be taken. We either go forth in the power of the Holy Spirit or <u>we shall die inch by inch of terminal regret</u>. There is work to be done in the world and we have run out of excuses."

Imagine reading and thinking and praying about these words while listening to "Somewhere in Time"—still playing as <u>I write this</u>.

You, my love, have given me the power to take that first step—and God willing, neither of us will die inch by inch of terminal regret.

I asked the Spirit to give me a consoling memory—the one that flooded me was when I was doing the dishes in your kitchen and you came softly up

*behind me and hugged me tightly for about one
full minute. Not a word was said but I felt truly
blessed and one of the most fortunate and blessed
men in the world. I feel that same warmth now and
I rejoice in the Spirit for creating such a wondrous
lady as you.*

*With God's love—you are transforming me,
Julie—and I will never be the same and be forever—eternally grateful.*

*Two in the morning your time, my dearest,
may you be sleeping soundly and peacefully. Again,
I shall be with you in your dreams. I adore you.*

Love—

Bill

And so life continued. The sun rose and set as it always had.
The birds sang in the trees, the children played and squabbled, the
bills arrived too frequently. It rained a lot. I went to classes, to work,
and to Mass, and yet everything was altered because now I was looking forward with confidence to the fulfillment of a divine promise.
It had been one year since Adrian's death, and so much good had
happened. I felt different. I wanted to lift up anyone feeling lost
or broken. I couldn't articulate it satisfactorily, but I knew, without
any doubt, that God's love is real, and I wanted to share that good
news. I had been surprised with joy, immersed in love, and all fear
was removed from my heart. I accepted the challenges that were to
come before knowing what they would be and chose to pay attention
to each moment, glorious or messy, assured that I was not alone on
the journey. I understood fully for the first time what St. Julian of
Norwich meant when she declared, "All shall be well."

Bill had work to do to prepare for our becoming a family. I had
simply to be patient and wait and find a good time to tell my parents. Bill had asked for as few people to be told as possible, though
I was bursting with joy and wanted to shout it to the world. The
process of immigrating to the US, we were told, could take up to
two years from the time of applying. Bill was eager for me to visit

Cincinnati before moving there, so we discussed the possibility of a two-week vacation there without the children, sometime in 1990. In the meantime, while he opened a bank account for the first time and explained why, at age fifty-four, he had never had one, I maintained a simple routine for the children's sakes, got used to dealing cheerfully with the gossips, and looked forward to the next visit from Bill, whose letters had taken on a more intimate tone now that we were officially engaged.

Happy Valentine's Day
10.30 pm 2/15/89

My dearest, Sweetheart, Lover, and <u>Wife</u> (Past, Present, and Future),

After our lovely phone call (which ended with my "Julie Diviner" pointing steadily westward!) I decided to go to a movie. It turned out to be another sign—the film was "The Accidental Tourist." It's about a man stuck in a routine, easy life who meets and falls in love with a <u>vibrant</u> woman who truly loves him. His choice is to stay with the familiar or take a chance on a new life and love. How's that for a sign?

I'm always so overjoyed and revitalized after I talk to you. When it's over, I can't wait until the following Wednesday. You do indeed light up my soul. I'm glad the 1st Anniversary of Adrian's death is over. I know you dreaded it and I guess getting by with just one bad dream isn't too bad.

I'm glad you enjoyed the flowers—I wish I could have arrived with them. I can't wait to see you in the coral necklace (maybe just the coral necklace!!) —you make pretty things even more gorgeous.

The rain continues without let-up—3 straight days now and it's expected to continue through tomorrow morning. Funny you are having the same thing. Anyway, you are my sunshine (good title for a song??)

Summer dates look something like this—if <u>no</u> 60 day limit (June 29–Sept 5-7) —<u>if</u> 60 day limit (July 10–Sept 7) or possibly July 6–Sept 4-5. I'll check soon.

I hope Brian's having a good time at Edel's. With Edel's curiosity she is liable to know all about us before visit is over! Sean's good behavior with Brian gone is probably due to the fact that Michael plays with him now instead of Brian—Sean tends to be left out in the Brian-Michael duo as you know.

Anyway, time for bed (now 4am your time). How I wish I were there—coming up from the station, going in the front door, up the stairs, into your room, undressing quietly and crawling in next to you and snuggling up to your beautiful, warm body.

Julie—how I do long to make love to you right now. I've been tingling ever since I talked to you and I guess (know!) desperately need the feel of you to comfort me right this minute.

Do you know of any warm, wet, slippery silky places that can exert some rippling effects? If so, let me know! I will gladly donate the vitamin C!

I adore you,

Love,
Bill xxx

7-3-89

My Darling,

I miss you so much right this minute it hurts.

The boys are being naughty—telling lies, stealing and sneaky. Sean is OK but the other two are

*driving me nuts. I've had to confront them with it
all and tell them how sad I am at their behaviour.*

*It would be so comforting to know you were
supporting my endeavours to parent properly. If only
you were here my task wouldn't appear so awesome.*

*Roll on June when I can gain strength from
your presence here. I always feel that no problem is
beyond a solution when you are with me.—Alone, I
feel overwhelmed by it all.*

*I also feel you are going to be disappointed
with me as I'm not coping as well as I should. Please
believe me when I tell you that* NEVER *will I give you
cause to be sad. Your happiness is my desire. Maybe
I will be able to demonstrate in some small way a
portion of the great loving care you have shown me.*

*I love you more than words can say, Bill, and
will forever.*

Julie
Xx

Violets are red
Roses are blue
I get confused
When I'm around you
It's what you do to me—put my head in a spin.
I <u>LOVE</u> being confused!!

MARCH 1989

DEAR BRIAN, MICHAEL, SEAN AND AMY—
THANK YOU FOR THE LOVELY BIRTHDAY
CARD—ESPECIALLY FOR THE 'FATHER' TITLE. I
DO THINK OF ALL OF YOU AS MY CHILDREN AND
I LOVE ALL OF YOU MORE AND MORE AND MORE.

I'LL BE LOOKING FORWARD TO SEEING YOU IN LESS THAN 3 MONTHS NOW.

BE SURE AND BE GOOD TO YOUR MUM. SHE NEEDS YOUR LOVE AND SUPPORT. <u>WE</u> HAVE TO STICK TOGETHER AND SUPPORT ONE ANOTHER. PLEASE GIVE YOUR MUM A BIG HUG AND KISS FOR ME. SEE YOU SOON.

I LOVE YOU,
(YOUR)
<u>FATHER</u>

Chapter 22

Learning patience was a tough lesson. I found the best way to help time move more quickly was to stay extremely busy. Although I was volunteering with the probation office, running the Union of Catholic Mothers chapter (where Father Carson had kindly let me continue as president), counselling the bereaved for the charity CRUSE, working part time at SPAR, and taking care of four little children, I had time in my week for more. So when Ozz, seeing that I could use a little extra money to supplement the welfare I received, offered me a job cleaning his flat once a week, I accepted. He and I had developed a deep platonic friendship, due in part to his love of all things Irish. He listened as I relayed the trials and triumphs of being in love with Bill, and he was there for me when I messed up with Mark. His strong, protective, and sensitive nature was poorly disguised under his long hair, longer gray trench coat, and heavy black boots. He looked tough. Amy tested just how tough when he foolishly allowed her to brush his hair while babysitting. It took twenty minutes to extricate him from the tangled mess she created, yet he endured with grace and good humor. Sometime later, Ozz presented me with a poem he had written about us.

18-6-89

Julie and Amy

Have you ever seen a bond so close?
The crying child with arms outstretched cries for her
protector,

And there she stands emitting love,
A radiant beauty to the child's eyes (and to mine).
A fairy queen with the power to right all wrongs.
Your inner beauty shines more in this moment I see
    you
With your baby, than at any other in the past.

By Ian Austin (Ozz)

I turned up to clean the flat that Ozz shared with Humbug above the Newsagents and discovered that my job consisted of emptying ashtrays, discarding beer bottles, and washing a few dishes. They didn't need a cleaner at all. It was a ruse to assist me financially while preserving my dignity. Nevertheless, I was grateful, not so much for the extra money but for the thoughtfulness and concern. I also loved that Ozz knew the words to so many traditional Irish songs and joined in with gusto whenever an opportunity presented itself, which was any time we were out together. We were allies, drinking buddies, and good friends—and best of all, Bill approved.

Of course, the gossips were ready to spread more rumors, but by now I was becoming immune to their jibes. Soon I would be shedding the scandal mantle they had shrouded me in. I was learning to be patient.

April 4th 89

My Lover,
    I'm still rejoicing in our good news! God has been so good to us. I am filled with exuberance and joy. I have composed (3 pages!) a letter to one of my brothers and sister-in-law and will send eventually the same one to the other. They should receive them Friday, and I will call each over the weekend to get reactions. Once over the shock, they will be supportive since they really are concerned with my happi-

ness. This will take care of the last of my concerns—though this was a small one next to the others.

The days are really starting to go fast, with plenty to do and people to see and classes to prepare. I haven't taught a speech class for ten years (my summer class). And I'll have to have all 4 of my classes ready to go before I leave on the 29 June.

The lease on my apartment is not up until May 31 so I'll probably be able to stay there until then (maybe paying rent to Jesuits from May 15 on). If we try it—I'll stay later—maybe till I leave though a teacher in our department is leaving for his summer house on June 10 and said I could stay in his home here from then on until I leave. I'll save the new car and a semi-permanent apartment until I return in late August.

I rejoice in our happiness and hope the time will fly by for you. You are my life. I will love you always,

Bill
Xx
(Only 2 4/5 more months!!)

4/4/ 89

Dear Mary and John,

I hope the vacation went well and I'm sorry to have to greet you as you return home with a "bad news" (from your viewpoint, I'm sure) letter.

To get to the point quickly, I have decided (starting May 15th) to take a "leave of absence" from the Jesuits. Let me explain what this means. I'll still technically be a Jesuit, but that's all. I'll begin living in an apartment, drawing my own pay (I'll still be teaching at Xavier) and obviously start paying my *own way (rent, car, taxes, food and all!). During this time I will also <u>not</u> function as a priest (won't <u>say</u> Mass, etc.). In one year (or earlier), I can decide to return to the Jesuits or decide to leave for good and get dispensed from vows. This would include the priesthood, too, of course.*

You have probably noticed I have been extremely uneasy lately—actually for quite a few years! I can go into the reasons when I next see you or talk to you. I probably should have taken the "leave" long ago but never quite worked up the courage.

The events in Wales—Julie and the death of her husband—were certainly precipitating factors but not the main motivation for the "leave." During the time I have seen Julie after the husband's death (5 weeks) we have discovered a deep love for each other and have enjoyed each other's company immensely. I love the children too (and vice versa) and get along with them famously. Julie and I both realize that a future marriage would present innumerable difficulties—<u>but</u> may be not impossible ones. But we do have to get to know each other a bit more. With that in mind I plan to go over to Wales in July and August (after I teach summer school in May and June). Maybe I will scream in horror after a 2 month stint, 24 hours a day basis with four children—maybe she will simply feel I am too old or too bald or something! We'll see—but the point is we <u>do</u> have to see and it can't be done 5,000 miles apart.

The good news in all this is that it looks as if I can continue to teach at Xavier—no matter what! The contract we sign simply has no provision for firing us if we leave the Jesuits—or even get married.

Will I be under some financial strain especially in getting started in May? —Yes indeed! I'll get some money from the Jesuits as a primer, but it's *not much. When my regular salary ($32,000) starts coming in, I'll be alright, but I may need a little loan from you (especially in getting a car) if you can afford it.*

As long as I stay single I will survive nicely, but if I do decide to marry a penniless (but beautiful!) Irish widow with four children (11, 9, 7 and 2 ½) that's when things will get tight and I'll really need a spot of help. I'll have to work at least a year to even consider this, so there will be time to think.

In all of these decisions I have received much advice from a couple of good spiritual directors (Jesuits) and many other folks. All think the decision to take a leave is a good thing—to give me time to think, pray and plan while having a good shot at independence.

I realize your first impression of all this is "He's CRAZY*!" —throwing away a comfortable, prestigious, secure life. Maybe so, but I do feel exhilarated and happier than I have been in many years. I also feel very close to God and prayer is coming easily. So I'll ask you to keep up the prayers and will be open to further questions via telephone or on the next visit. I'll try to phone you sometime this weekend since it is a little hard to phone me (and get me in!)*

Would you spread the word to the kids and as many relatives as you see fit—maybe to Catherine Breen especially since she does send Masses somewhat regularly. I have told Mary and Russ, they have been a good support.

Hope you haven't fainted! I'll talk to you soon.
Love,
Bill

PS: Interestingly enough, there are 3 other women who seem to be in love with me (and even marriage) but since two are already married and one is a nun—and I'm not in love with them there is no worry here!! Just think what could happen if I had some hair!! I told you my life was more interesting than movies.

PPS: I sent essentially the same letter to Pat and Tom.

4/9/89

My Darling—

I returned Saturday after a one-day meeting in Dayton, Ohio of university professors. It's rather like a union meeting, I feel I need some insurance in case of later problems. It was long but fairly interesting.

I did some shopping today—bought a new pair of jeans—my old ones got a big hole in the knee -though that is how the kids like them. These already look old so I'm still "in."

I phoned my brother and all went well. They had already received my letters and both were quite kind. My older one was tremendously kind and supportive. He says he has kept my share of the 'inheritance' from my mother and will send it on to me. It won't be much, I know. They all said they weren't particularly surprised by my decision (I think they realized I was in love with you when I showed them the pictures and slides from Wales!). Now nobody left to tell privately except to make it publicly known around May 8.

I started a checking account and will upgrade it to a checking/savings account when some more money comes in. I'll have my pay checks deposited directly to the account. It feels good to have one— my first!!

I love you madly. I don't even want to go to movies, plays, concerts, etc. because you are not with me—but you soon will be—and for FOREVER.

We're down to 2 ½ months—should go fast— the past few weeks certainly have!

Enclosed is a picture of what we consider a VAN. A station wagon is more like a car except it has a 3rd seat. They both cost about the same. We'll talk about what to buy when I come over (what FUN!).

Soon we'll be together—I can't wait. Take good care of yourself (and your jeans!). Also enclosed is a stress test card—I just turned up completely relaxed—BLUE. Hope you are too.

You are now soundly sleeping (it's 1:30am your time!) and dreaming nice dreams of me.

You are my treasure.

Love,
Bill
Xx

As Bill was figuring out the best time to let his Jesuit community know of his decision to take a leave of absence, I was wondering when and how we should tell my parents about our plans. We agreed that Bill should make a visit to Ireland to speak with Mam and Dad and that Michael could go with him. I was also poring over holiday catalogues searching for a place to rent for a week in the summer so we could have some respite from the curious eyes of the townspeople and spend needed time together, simply, anonymously, as a family. I found a terraced house in the city of York, within walking distance of its magnificent cathedral and the cobbled streets of the Shambles. Bill was delighted with the choice and sent me the money for the deposit. The air was abuzz with plans and joyful anticipation.

4/27/89

My Darling,

Super <u>HOT</u> the past 4 days—85 during the day. We went from Spring to Summer. The building is really hot (my room is 82 and it is 10pm at night). I'll go to the apartment when I finish writing this— there is an air-conditioner in my bedroom.

I'm going to Detroit (about 250 miles north) tomorrow afternoon till Sunday for a reunion of my Jesuit entrance class. I really don't feel like going—especially now, but another of my classmates is counting me for a ride. I'm not sure I'll tell them I'm leaving—I am going to tell our community (by note) next Wednesday.

I went for 2 long bike rides the past two days and did a nautilus today—still am in great shape (thank goodness). Even the bloodshot eyes seem <u>much</u> better.

That was too bad about the priest and the woman in the headlines (Mirror or Sun?). <u>We</u> were lucky. Thank goodness we didn't make love that "famous" night on Edel's couch—I know I wanted to but something said no while my body was crying "yes." Leaving you on the couch was the most difficult thing I ever did. Going back on the plane I kept thinking it would have been the <u>one</u> chance to make love to you in a lifetime. Now I know why we didn't—maybe God was testing us—I don't know.

Just to be on the safe side now—make sure as few people as possible <u>know</u> about us—and those that do you can tell them that I have left the Jesuits and the priesthood. That should defuse any newspaper interest I <u>hope</u>! We <u>do</u> make "The Thornbirds" pale in comparison.

The dollar has been getting stronger (1.69 to the pound as opposed to 1.89 when I left at Christmas) so I changed some more dollar travelers checks to pounds. I'm gambling a bit that it might head the other way.

Julie—you are indeed the center—the heart of my life. You bring me joy—happiness and love. I thank God every day that we have been brought together.

Only 2 <u>months</u> to go—don't forget the B.C. pills! You can figure out the timing.

I adore you.

Love forever,
Bill xx

4/29/89

My Darling Julie,

I am writing this from our university in Detroit. It's a rather depressing place—and a rather unsafe one. It's the murder capital of the world (or it was)—more murders per population than anywhere in the world. The university is surrounded by barbed wire—so much for serenity. Another classmate and myself drove up Friday afternoon and arrived just after dinner time (6:30pm). There were about 20 of us from the entrance (Jesuit) class of 1954 (3 years before you were born?).

Anyway—we had a nice long evening recounting hilarious tales of our days in training. I was the center of many stories—I was more of a rebel than I remembered. I decided <u>not</u> to tell them I was leaving as I'm not telling <u>our</u> community 'til Wednesday and it wouldn't be fair for it to get out before that. I'm having a good time with good friends but how

I wish I could share my joy of loving you. The next reunion (5 years) will probably be our whole class (including the ones who left with their wives) so maybe <u>you</u> can meet them all then. I did tell the guy I was driving up with that I am leaving—I had told him about you previously. I think he envied me my attitude about loving you and having arrived at a firm decision—he has been having many problems himself. He is a nice gentle soul who I think was dominated by his parents.

Today we have a Mass at 4:30 pm—then a cocktail hour, then dinner at a downtown Detroit restaurant. It was 85 when I left Cincinnati but it's about 35 up here. I only brought a blue seersucker shirt—I'll probably freeze.

Once again I look back at my life and see God in all its phases and cycles. I simply can't say I should have left sooner—or else I would never have been in Wales at the time I was—would never have met you, etc., etc. It <u>was</u> destined, I'm sure. My love for you simply FILLS me, Julie—day and night. Even the reunion reaffirms my decision— everything does.

Note the date on the letter—2 months from this evening I leave for England—I can't wait. Two months from tomorrow evening I'll be arriving in Newtown and see you on the platform. Happiness is YOU.

Keep well, my love. I treasure you.

Love,
Bill

Did you hear about the cloistered nun who was only allowed to say <u>2 words</u> per year.

After one year she said to Mother Superior, "Soup cold!"

After another year, she said to Mother Superior, "Bed hard!"

After the third year she said, "I'm leaving!"

Mother Superior looked at her and said, "Thank God! All you do is complain!"

"I love you to bits" (quote from a famous Irish raven haired beauty that I have appropriated to myself).

5/6/89

My Darling,

Well, one more barrier crossed—I finally put up the notice I am leaving on our community bulletin board. Since I ate breakfast at my apartment, then cleaned more of my room up, then went shopping (and ate lunch out), then returned to the apartment and took a bath then came back here (now) and in a few minutes a Jesuit is taking me out to dinner—I haven't seen anyone all day (Jesuits that is). It will give the message time to sink in and be seen by all. The last barrier to get through will be next Sunday at my final Mass—letting the people know. I feel tremendously right about the decision, Julie—excited, prayerful, trusting—exhilarated! Less than 2 months to go—less than 8 weeks now!

I will get a good picture book of Cincinnati and either send it to you or bring it with me. I think you'll enjoy the city—it has lots of charm. It's a river city, of course, and is built on seven hills (like Rome!). There are plenty of trees, flowers, and bushes—and most streets are quite curvy (like you!). My niece Kathy rated it as tied with Boston as her favorite city to live in. It was founded (or settled I should say) mostly by German immigrants and still

is considered sort of a German city. It is quite conser-
vative in nature, all in all, I'm sure you will enjoy it.

   Some good news I was talking about in my
Mother's day card, I heard of two priests yesterday
who did receive <u>*laization*</u> *from Rome (permission*
to marry). Both came only about <u>*8 years*</u> *after the*
marriage, but at least there seems to be some case for
hope. It's not impossible at any rate. Marrying you
<u>*twice*</u> *will be* <u>*really*</u> *neat.*

   I saw two films this week both excellent—"High
Hopes"—a British film set in London—a satire of
the class system. East Ender accents! The second was
"Torch Song Trilogy"—good for understanding
plight of homosexuals (and very funny and touching
at the same time!)

   Today I finally got my "official" letter from
Provincial granting me my "leave." He mentioned
I have received my $5,000 from the society (I hav-
en't!). I'll have to call him on Monday.

   Less than 8 weeks my darling—I can't wait
until our lips are touching and I can tell you a thou-
sand times (maybe more) how much <u>*I love you.*</u>

Forever,

Bill

Xx

I was thrilled to see that Bill had officially notified his community. Now we could relax knowing that we no longer had to be secretive. Well, once we had shared our news with my parents, we no longer had to be secretive. Only then could we truly relax.

Finally, summer and Bill arrived. We spent a glorious week in York where Bill bought me an emerald-and-diamond engagement ring. We bonded as a family, exploring, playing, and praying together, going to Mass and Holy Communion, and becoming more affirmed in our love. The weeks in Newtown were spent more discreetly and privately.

"Now that you and Mum are getting married, does that mean we can call you dad?" Michael asked while we all sat around the dinner table.

"Well, I am happy with whatever you want to call me," Bill replied tactfully.

"Well, we want to call you dad." Sean was nodding in agreement, his mouth full of food.

"Yes, we will just have one dad in heaven and another dad here," Brian added, explaining their thought process.

"Well, I certainly love you all as a father and would be honored if that's what you choose to call me." Bill was clearly touched by their affection for him and their desire to identify as his children.

"I think it's wonderful that you all want to call Bill daddy. Let's save that name until we get to America. It will be more special then." I was concerned that people wouldn't understand. I was particularly concerned that it would cause my parents, especially my mother, distress.

It was time for Bill and Michael to head to Rainbow Cottage, Garryglass, my parents' verdant retreat in the undulating hills of Tipperary, Ireland.

"Please call me the *minute* you tell them, Bill. I'll not rest easy 'til I know that they know," I said, repeating the request.

"The minute I tell them, I will call. I promise. Now don't worry. All shall be well." He hugged me tightly and, taking Michael's hand, headed for the train station. I watched from the doorstep, excited that soon I would no longer have to equivocate when speaking with my mother.

Every ring of the telephone made me miss a breath. I wanted to hear Bill's soothing and comforting voice assuring me that everything was working out well. I wanted to hear every detail of the conversation he had with my parents: when he told them, how he told them, what he said, how they responded. Until I heard from him, I was unsettled and restless. Finally, while I was in the kitchen preparing beans on toast for the children's tea, the eagerly awaited call from Ireland came.

"Mum! It's for you" Brian's cheery tone called out. I took the phone from him as he added, "Guess who?" grinning mischievously.

"Bill!" I blurted out, keen to hear the voice of my beloved.

"Well," answered my father, with a solemn tone. I was momentarily startled not to be speaking to Bill. Even more surprised to hear my dad's voice on the other end of the line as he *never* made phone calls and, on the rare occasions he was handed the phone by my mother when we called, would be clearly uncomfortable as he floundered for the right thing to say. Now I was the one floundering. Taken aback, I hesitated, not knowing what to say. Had Bill even told them yet? I didn't know. Maybe they hadn't been told, and this was unrelated. Maybe they *did* know.

"Well," I replied, putting the onus on my dad to progress the conversation. Silence.

"Well," he repeated with a tone of resignation.

"Well?" I replied rather weakly, raising my voice in a question. Another seemingly longer pause.

"So," said my dad, as though the word *so* was a punctuation mark. A full stop.

"So," I replied, willing this agonizing phone call to move forward.

"Well," he repeated, "that's it then. You're getting married."

Relief surged through me as I detected the note of kindness in his voice. "Yes, Dad, we are getting married."

"Good. I'll pray for you."

"Thank you, Daddy. Yes, it *is* good." I willed my beaming smile to be conveyed in my voice.

The waiting and the worry was over. All I had needed to hear from them was that one word: *good.*

Chapter 23

Bill returned to Cincinnati after two months with us and with no one left to inform but the US immigration office while I, infused with a lightness of being, reveled in this newfound liberation. At last we were out in the open. No more hiding and no more secrecy.

With a potential wait time of up to two years before we could be admitted to the United States, we simply looked forward to the next visit from Bill and my planned visit to Cincinnati in February, (the cheapest time to travel), knowing that in the proper time, we would be together forever. The children seemed happier too, with something always to look forward to. In the meantime, life was waiting to be lived, and live it we did with renewed zeal and abounding gratitude. That didn't mean life was without its challenges, but I could meet them now more confidently and calmly, secure in the knowledge that God was with me every step of the journey.

> *2 Colwyn*
> *Treowen*
> *NEWTOWN*
> *SY16 1NA*
> *September 19th '89*
>
> *My Darling,*
> *Sorry for not being in touch over the past few days but I've been quite busy. My birthday went very well. I took all the children to the fete at school where both Brian and Sean won a food hamper*

each in the raffle which they gave to me as my birthday present.

In the evening a few friends came into the "Eagles" to wish me a happy Birthday and give me some cards.

At closing time I was ushered into a taxi and taken to the home of a girl I'm friendly with. She and the lads had arranged a surprise party for me. The house was decked out with balloons. There was a cake with 21 candles on it. They had all been busy during the day preparing it. I felt so honored. They had made a lovely effort even to the choice of music (Irish of course!), so there were a few jigs and reels danced. I eventually got to bed at 4:30 am tired but happy.

It is great news that you will have a whole month with us at Christmas. It will make us even more united as a family. It is such a special time. Thank you— it will be worth the extra money it's costing you—wait and see.

I have been thinking of ways to save money, obviously not going out as much in the evenings is one way—not indulging in so much chocolate is another (it will also keep my weight down!) writing letters instead of cards is another, though once in a while I will spoil myself and send you a nice card.

It will be nice to say a "Hail Mary" with you at 11pm. It will make me feel very close to you, and hopefully keep those bad dreams at bay.

On a sadder note, Theresa's Dad (you've met him) died Saturday night after a massive heart attack—he was only 59. It was a great shock for his family.

On Monday afternoon the children and I had our photos taken for the visa. I've got them back now so will post them off in the morning. Amy screamed and yelled, she didn't want to sit by herself on the stool. It took ages for us to calm her sufficiently so that the photographer could take the picture—one more step closer.

I also received a call from the shop offering me a part time job. I began today, it is not very organized, the managers are like two silly schoolboys with too much power. They don't seem to be able to hold onto their staff very long. I shall stick it out for a few months at least.

Last night our "Introduction to Psychology" class began at college. We have a female tutor who is quite entertaining. There are about 20 in the class.

The work we'll be doing is the equivalent to a degree, though condensed as we have less time to study in. I am really looking forward to it all.

Whether I learnt anything or not on the first night is debatable. Some of the words she used I could hardly pronounce, never mind understand!

So I've had a busy few days. Tomorrow evening the children and I have been invited to a barbecue—they will enjoy that—it's being held early in the evening so it won't interfere with school.

Thank you for the additional 50.00 pounds which arrived this morning with your letter. Thank you too for the offer of more if I need it. Now with this little job, the 50.00 pounds a month should be plenty.

I can hardly believe that we have <u>less</u> than three months left before you are here again. I could do with a big hug from you right now.

Ken's death upset me quite a bit as I had only been chatting with him the previous day.

It makes me appreciate every day more and especially every day spent with you. We just don't know what can happen.

I received a letter from my school friend Carol. It began "What marvelous news! Congratulations on your engagement. I'm so pleased for you." She went on to say "I was just overwhelmed with pleasure when I read your letter."

This is a sample of the sort of response I've been receiving from everyone I've told.

Bill, I do love you, more than words can express. The birthday card you sent put it so well. Trying to describe my love is indeed like trying to pour the ocean into a shell!

When we are together we can put that love into action. We will be able to live our love. I can't wait.

Looking forward greatly to our telephone call tomorrow.

God keep you safe, Darling,

<u>All</u> my love,
Julie

10/9/89

My Darling—

Here is a copy of "approval notice" for immigration petition. They gave it to me in <u>one</u> week—not the 4 to 8 weeks they claimed. Whatever! — They will notify London who in turn will notify you. Notice the petition (P1) is valid from 10/2/89 to 2/2/90—check that out with London when you are interviewed. I hope it doesn't mean you <u>have</u> to be here by then—although at this stage of the game we could handle it if we had to. If you have to (or want to) come in May, aim for the 2nd week so I'll be able to pick you up at night (I start teaching every weeknight on May 21 'til June 28). I can't believe *how quickly they approved—must like our roman-tic story! One big step closer. Now all you have to do is charm them in London.*

I just got back from Louisville—had a very nice visit. Russ's parents (from Chicago) were there. They are a lovely couple—about 5 years older than me. I went to a football (soccer) game. The boys' teams won each game. The weather remains gorgeous (60 during the day—down to 35–40 at night). Some warmer weather (what we call Indian Summer) is due at end of week.

I hope you got all my petition data by now and have sent it on to London. Maybe by some miracle you could schedule your interview to coincide with my arrival in London (Dec 15)—if not, maybe you could do it before Edel leaves so you could have a place to stay. Whatever—we can handle it. —I can't believe things have gone so well! Let's keep our fin-gers crossed and the Hail Mary's going.

I miss you madly. I crossed the Ohio River bridge today and was thinking how soon you will be doing that with me (airport is in Kentucky and we cross the bridge coming back home).

God bless you sweetheart.

All my love,
Bill
Xx

Having received the petition data for visas for each of us, I began the process of filling out forms not once but five times! It was particularly daunting because of what was at stake. If I made a mistake here, it could cost us a future together in America. I scruti-nized each question posed on the forms: questions about my political interests, my addresses, my family members, my employment his-tory, my personal history, and any criminal activity. Failure to answer accurately or completely could result in the petition being denied and/or a charge of perjury. Bill was showing great faith in my ability to complete forms for which many hire lawyers to help them fill out. That wasn't an option for us, so I sweated over the documents, reading and rereading my entries copious times before gathering up all the required documents, birth certificates, medical records, etc., and taking them to the post office. As I slid the package over the counter, I prayed silently that God guide its path to a benevolent official in the US Embassy. We were one step closer. All that was left for me now was to pray some more and wait.

10/14/89

My Darling,

Oct 14 today—on Dec 14 I will be leaving to soon be in your arms. Almost one half the time has gone by since I left Aug. 29.

Yesterday I had a beautiful time driving by myself to Brown County, Indiana. It's just over 100 miles. There is a little town there that features antique shops, handcrafted goods, homemade products, etc. It's lots of fun. I didn't intend to spend anything but did find a couple of bargains—one a set of 8 plate settings of Corning Ware—they are quite nice—each one includes large plate, small (salad) plate, large bowl, and cup.

Since I only had a set of 4 expensive place settings, I knew we would need these—in fact I will use them now to prevent breakage. It was about $20 for the set of 8. They can go in the microwave—a good feature.

The second half of the day—after lunch I went to nearby State Park—it was gorgeous! Trees were red, yellow, gold, etc. It's the largest state park in Indiana. I parked and walked about 8 miles. All the time—even shopping, I felt your presence. When I was just reveling in your love I saw some-

*thing brown running toward me far up ahead—I
thought it was a dog but it came nearer and nearer.
It was a small deer – it stopped only about 10 yards
from me—looked directly at me and (I think)
<u>SMILED</u>! It then bounded off—a beautiful moment
and another sign I think. Anyway, it was a <u>grace</u>
filled day. Even the ride home was beautiful—setting sun behind me and full moon in front. I had
dinner at a nice place—two <u>huge</u> chicken breasts,
salad, potatoes and two immense baking powder
biscuits w. honey. Only $4—we could order 3 of
these meals and feed all of us. I even checked lodge
and cabin prices in the park. The cabins can sleep
8, 2 bedrooms, living room and kitchen. Only $40
a night—not bad. The last song on the radio was
Willie Nelson singing about God being so good, how
can we repay—<u>Indeed</u>.*

I love you sweetheart.

Bill
Xx

15-10-89

Darling,

*How lovely to speak with you only minutes
ago on the telephone—at the rate we are going we'll
soon be able to dispense with such primitive means
of communication and simply "tune in" to each other's minds! (save some money too!). Fancy us both
making chocolate cake and eating brocolli, or is it
broccoli?*

*Your day out in the park on Friday sounded
idyllic, particularly the incident with the deer, it put
me in mind of "Hinds Feet on High Places," a book
that made quite an impression on me. (I saw myself*

as "much afraid" for a long time). My trust in the Shepherd is leading me so swiftly to the high places, and you are the most welcome companion I could wish for to make that glorious journey with.

We are experiencing God's love in abundance because we have submitted our wills to his will. He seems to know what is best for us. I could not imagine being any happier than I am now, secure in your love.

Thank you Darling for all you have done for me, I love you for it.

God Bless you.

All my love,
Julie
Xx

Fri, 10/20/89

My Darling,

Hard to believe but 8 weeks almost from this very minute (2:30 pm our time, 7:30 p, your time) I should be arriving at the station in Newtown. Sunday will mark the ½ way point since I left London.

Our electric power (thus heat) finally came on last evening about 6am. It had been off since about 2am the previous morning. That was the longest we have <u>ever</u> been without electricity. The weather outside remained in the 30's but my apartment didn't get too cold—down to about 60. It still is cold out but sunny and 60 is due by Sunday. Since I cook everything with electricity I was hard pressed to eat so I had cereal and milk in the morning and peanut butter and jelly in the afternoon. At night I went out and got pizza and went to the movies—the electricity was on when I returned.

I ate out twice this week (both times as a guest). Both times I had fish since I haven't had it for myself yet.

Each day Julie I am happier and more and more in love with you. The only frustration (a temporary one!) is not having you physically with me.

Don't let Mark's pettiness get you down. I guess I can understand his frustration (I'd be devastated to lose you too) but still his respect for you should preclude spreading rumors that he knows will hurt you. Don't give up seeing Ozz because of the talk either—he is a good friend and a truly nice man. It will be nice, as you said, to be freely able to hold hands in town at our Christmas visit!

My last Visa bill (Oct 15) still was getting a few English charges on it—they are slow getting them in. I can't wait to take you and the children to the Pizza place—maybe for a pre-Christmas treat—Dec 23 or 24? Or a post Xmas one, Dec 26 or 27. They'll enjoy the food and the music and the videos.

My priest friend I had to dinner couldn't get over how beautiful you were—I said the outward beauty was more than matched by the inner. I truly adore you.

Love,
Bill xx

10/22/89

My Darling <u>Wife</u>,
I just finished breakfast after coming from Mass and speaking to you briefly. This card was a good sign—I had kept it 'til last, hoping for the right moment.

I knew you would feel not going to communion a greater loss at the small group liturgy. Fr. Carson is being unkind and un-Christlike and in fact is downright <u>wrong</u>. I suppose (but wouldn't bet on it) that he thinks he is doing the right thing—perhaps with the idea that you might reconsider your decision if you are punished properly.

Try to be happy, my love, in the fact that we both are convinced (certainly <u>100</u>% in my case) that we are doing God's will—that in fact we <u>are</u> already married in His eyes, but simply have to be bogged down in some <u>man-made</u> rules for awhile.

I have never been more at peace with the Lord—I'm praying more—am happier and am radiating that to all I meet. Surely the <u>best</u> sign of all. I pray you feel the same way.

The encouraging word I heard was that the dispensations to marry are coming a <u>bit</u> quicker and with more frequency—<u>some</u> within a year or so. It still depends unfortunately on <u>who</u> you know in Rome. We'll do the best we can. Our <u>intention</u> is to marry within the Church as soon as we are able but the unofficial wedding will simply have to take place for legal (citizenship reasons) and financial reasons.

In any event—my darling be of good cheer—a song we sang this morning (another sign!!)

"And He will raise you up on eagle's wings, bear you on the breath of dawn, make you to shine like the sun, and hold you in the palm of his hand."

We <u>are</u> in the palm of His hand my love.

Let's plan on Saturday in Shrewsbury with the children where we can all go to evening Mass <u>and</u> <u>communion</u>.

I treasure and adore you. With all my love,
                              Your Husband,
                                      Bill
                                      Xx

Card: God will keep us close
So many times,
thoughts of you just seem
to whisper across the miles
between us
and bring you close
to me in heart.
I like to think it's God's way
of keeping us together...
because the warmth we've shared
together or apart,
could only be part of His plan.
And that's why,
Even though I miss you sometimes,
I'm never really sad
about being apart...
because I know
God is watching over us both.
and I know it's in His plan
to keep us close.
Ellen Brenneman

6-11-89

Darling,

I've just returned from Bristol after a lovely weekend. It seems ages since I last wrote to you though it has only been a few days.

The wedding was beautiful—I was thinking about us during the ceremony. The altar was decked in single flowers also the chairs Louise and Donald sat upon. The whole Mass was sung even the consecration, and the hymns were easy to learn. It took 2 ½ hours which was rather a long time for the smaller children to sit still. At one stage, Amy was dancing on the altar while we were singing and clapping.

I had an opportunity to speak with Dad alone on the Friday evening, he is very happy for us and very positive. I felt totally relaxed speaking about our plans.

Mam is coming down tomorrow to stay for a couple of days, she seems less enthusiastic about things in general, I think her physical condition gets her down at times.

My writing is so small because this is the only piece of paper left and I really wanted to write as soon as I returned.

The train journey was awful, but at least we got home safely.

There was a small buffet reception after the wedding—we all came back to Dyrham View and had a good get together and sing song. On Sunday evening Louisa and Martin babysat while I went out with Carron Downer and another friend to the Bristol Hippodrome for a concert with a group called MAZE. It was a lively evening. Afterwards we went for a meal in an Italian restaurant. I let Carron choose my meal as I didn't know how much he could afford. I had a delicious chicken dish cooked in a red wine sauce with tomatoes, garlic and oregano and an assortment of vegetable side dishes.

There was live music there too. A man singing with his guitar and a girl who played a saxophone superbly, and sang like an angel. You would have really enjoyed it.

It was nearly two o clock when I got in and both Mam and Dad were waiting up reading in their separate bedrooms for me.

I was very good and had just one gin, then drank orange juice for the rest of the evening.

I really missed you, it would have been so much more enjoyable if you could have been there also. Never mind, soon we will be enjoying each other's company.

The best part of the weekend for me was the receiving of Holy Communion at the wedding. It seems like such a long time since I walked up to the altar. It did feel good and right!

Well my Darling after such a hectic weekend I am exhausted so I'll be off to bed soon. Bill I love you so much—one good thing my birth certificate has been returned corrected. Not too long before we will be able to spend every day and night together, our piece of Heaven on earth.

God bless you my love and keep you safe. I'll write again soon when I buy some more writing paper.

My love forever,
Julie
Xx

2 Colwyn
Treowen
8-11-89

My Darling,
Thank you for the letter which arrived this morning, yet another four day delivery.

Well I seem to have survived Mam's visit—she too is very happy for us, we had a good long talk, mostly to clear up the doubts she had about our relationship while Adrian was alive.

She was also asking about our present situation, trying to find out whether we actually sleep together—as she didn't ask me directly, I didn't answer directly. At least I managed to speak to both Dad and Mam individually which was great. I feel totally comfortable about it all now, until I could speak with them both there was something unfinished.

My flight ticket arrived yesterday, it feels good to have it. Being with you is getting closer, I can't wait!

It was parents evening at the school tonight. I was very pleased with the progress Michael is making and the outstanding improvement in Sean's work. His teacher is very happy with him now.

I'm glad we can go back to our evening phone calls. They are much more peaceful without the children demanding my attention while you are talking to me, and much more romantic!

I hope your kitchen is back to normal now—it can become irritating when your routine is disturbed. Besides you'll be out of practice where your cooking is concerned!

Well Darling it is very late so I'll say goodnight to you now. (Mam is waiting upstairs). I love you Bill more each minute. (St. Julian of Norwich has just been quoted on the television) another sign?!

Take care Sweetheart, not long now.
God Bless,

> *All my love and more,*
> *Julie*
> *Xx*

11/16/89

My Darling,

    Well—exactly 4 weeks from this minute I should be getting ready to go to the airport.

    I like the brief sentiment on the card because I truly <u>do</u> give thanks to God every single day because He caused our lives to touch.

    I had lunch the other day with a woman who goes to the 11 am Sunday liturgy at our parish. She said that she and a number of others there are "irregulars" —not technically supposed to go to Communion but they do so. Some are divorced and remarried—other are married priests with families. The deal is that they go to the lay distributors of Communion so they won't present the priest with a dilemma. Anyway, everybody seems happy with the arrangement so maybe <u>we</u> can go to Communion here—we'll see. It's not the liturgy I'm used to attending but it <u>is</u> the most modern liturgically.

    The weather has turned cold. High of 72 yesterday—in the 30's today with lows in the teens predicted. At least there has been no snow. I hope the weather holds up for my trip to Chicago next week.

    Karen cancelled her dinner with me last night (2 times in a row she has done it!). I almost phoned you but thought you might have gone to bed. This way I can look forward to talking to you this evening. Just think—4 weeks and we can not only talk, but hug, kiss and cuddle to our hearts content. We've got 3 ½ months to make up for!!

    My love for you continues to soar and soar— and with it my love for God and life. You are a precious jewel, Julie, and I will <u>treasure</u> you all my life.

        All my love,

        Bill xx

Card: Every day,
I give thanks to God
that He caused our lives
to touch.

11/18/89

My Darling,
    A quote from a book recently read (The Hero
Within by Carol Pearson). "Consciously taking one's
journey, setting out to confront the unknown, marks
the beginning of life lived at a new level… Whether
wanderers journey only inward or also outward,
they make a leap of faith to discard the old social
roles which they have worn to please and to ensure
safety, and try instead to discover who they are and
what they want." Sounds a bit like us—doesn't it?
    They also quoted this iin a discussion guide on
the film "Wings of Desire" —a beautiful German
film about guardian angels in Berlin—and one
especially who falls in love with a woman and
chooses to become a man. I think I mentioned this
film before—it strengthened me in my decision
(along with John Huston's "The Dead"). I'll try to
get it on video—I love "The Dead."
    I've recorded a 9 hour history of Western Art
which you should enjoy. I think I've got about 1,200
hours of great programs (movies, documentaries, etc.
that we can watch at our leisure).
    I was a little sorry to hear of Brian and
Michael recounting their bad memories of Adrian
to your Mum, but perhaps it was psychologically
good for them. Let's do our very best to make up for
it with as many loving memories as possible. So far I
think we done a fair job and the best is yet to come.

The SPAR *dinner sounded nice. I should have adjusted to the time change with a good sleep or two. I'll look forward to meeting your friends.*

I saw "Queen of Hearts" the other night—a charming tale of an Italian family's 20 years in London.

By the way, what is in "Earls' Court"—I see it on the map but it's one place I never got to.

I love you to bits—stars, moons, planets, and all—

> *Forever,*
> *Bill*
> *Xx*

Chapter 24

Bill's Christmas visit coincided with a letter from the US Embassy summoning me and the children to London the first week of January for the next step in the immigration process: the visa interview. It was a shock to receive it so soon as we had expected a longer waiting period, but we were thrilled and relieved that Bill was there to accompany us and to help me with the children as we navigated the city. With only days to prepare, we had to find somewhere in London to stay overnight as our appointment was set for seven-thirty in the morning. Bill too would have to fund our travel on the train, an expense I would not have been able to cover.

Fortunately, Angela, my old primary school chum, opened her home to us without hesitation. She and I had corresponded since high school and, though we rarely saw each other, maintained a close bond. Right now she was proving a friend indeed.

The six of us descended on London, filled with a mixture of excitement and trepidation. This was not a sightseeing tour. We were there to persuade the American officials that we deserved a chance of happiness in their great country. I spent much of the four-hour train journey from Newtown wondering what sort of questions I might be asked and reminding the children of their manners. This would be a critical time for us, and we all had to be on our best behavior. Even me.

Angela and her husband had prepared well for us with couches, pullout beds, and mattresses on the floor. The children were delighted with the reception they received and, after filling their tummies, happily settled into their makeshift "camp."

Angela and Bill liked each other immediately. He was grateful for her openness to our situation and willingness to assist in any way she could. We spent a couple of relaxed hours catching up on all our news, reminiscing about our school days, and going over what tomorrow had in store—looking forward to being another step closer to becoming a family.

The waiting room at the embassy was bleak and uninviting. The unadorned grim, gray walls, apart from signs in various languages cautioning and warning, seemed oppressive. Even the chairs, made of dull metal, seemed designed to dissuade one from getting too comfortable. The reception desk was small and afforded no privacy. Every word spoken to the solemn-faced official behind the glass screen could be heard by all. I approached the glass window after directing the children to sit with Bill quietly.

"Hello. I'm here for a seven-thirty visa interview appointment," I said, mustering as much cheer as seemed appropriate for the occasion.

"Name? Papers?" The woman was curt and direct, her hand outstretched waiting. No time for pleasantries in this job apparently.

"Julie—I mean *Julia* Long," I said, correcting myself. "That's what's on my passport anyway. Julia, not Julie…" My voice trailed off as I checked my nervous rambling and slid the envelope containing our documents through the space in the glass. I was trying to sound confident. I really wanted to make a good impression.

"We don't do interviews this early. You need to get your medicals done first," she said, flipping through the paperwork I had presented.

"But we've come all the way from Wales! We have an interview scheduled for this morning." I was feeling flustered, my heart rate increasing as I considered the possibility that I may have made a mistake with dates.

"Hold your horses, lady. I'm going to tell you where to go and what to do, okay?" She was used to people being confused, it seemed, and got some twisted pleasure out of instilling panic, however mild. "You'll still have your interview today, but not until you get the medicals done." Her patronizing tone was softening a little.

"Oh, I didn't realize we needed to do that. Sorry."

"That's right. You have to go to *our* approved doctors here. So go to this address on Harley Street right away, and your children too. Then come back with the results as soon as you have them. Oh, and you'll need cash. They don't take checks or credit cards." She slid the address through the window and called out, "Next."

"How much will it cost?" I asked apologetically, feeling intrusive now, as another hopeful person hurried to the window.

"Eighty pounds for each of you."

Eighty pounds? Oh my goodness, this immigration business is expensive! I thought. I was shocked at the cost. It hadn't dawned on me that there would be any additional fees.

"It's going to cost eighty pounds, Bill, for each of us for a medical."

"I heard, sweetheart. Don't worry, we'll stop at a cashpoint on the way." Bill immediately calmed my anxiety as I gathered up the children and headed to Harley Street. We hailed a taxi, and I sat back as Bill directed the driver. I thought about the building we had just left and wondered why it was so inhospitable. I came to the conclusion that it is probably a deliberate strategy to deter those who are not serious about the immigration process. One really must want to go through all the hurdles and hardship when America is the prize.

The doctor's office, much more cramped than the embassy, was teeming with people of all nationalities and ages. Every seat was occupied, and the walls were flanked by those who could not find a seat or those who had given up their seat to another more in need. A buzzing hum of indistinguishable words in a variety of languages filled the air as family members reassured one another. This was a thriving business. Names like *Imeri, Sullivan, Briggs, Calarco* were called out at regular intervals as people leaned forward to listen for their own name.

"Mr. Shannon, your chest x-ray is ready," a voice called out, followed by, "Mr. McCoy, your blood test results are in." It seemed as though privacy was a luxury not afforded those hoping to enter the US.

I approached the counter, signed us all in, and paid the four hundred pounds. There was a clear system. Someone here may have read about Ford's efficiency and management theory. Then once again—along with half the world, it seemed—we waited.

Eventually, my name, along with a string of others, all women and children, was called. I grabbed hold of Amy's hand and told the boys to get up as I rose and followed the nurse obediently, silently, into a narrow hallway where we assembled in single file.

"Ladies, take off your tops." Some of the women did not speak English, but those of us who did hesitated, glancing at one another for clarification. Did she just tell us to take off our tops?

"Tops off!" This time, the instruction was delivered more loudly and sternly. No one in line wanted to challenge or question the authoritative figure; there was too much to lose. But it all seemed unnecessarily harsh.

"Excuse me, but where do we get changed?" I was speaking for the group. No one had yet removed any clothing. Usually, in a doctor's office, we are seen one at a time and given a private room for examination, not herded like sheep and treated as such. The nurse, clearly agitated, looked at me and said, "Here. Right here. Take off your tops!" I looked at the other women apologetically and began to remove my sweater and shirt. There was no place provided to put our clothes, no booth in which to undress, and no gowns to preserve our modesty, just a cold hallway lined with confused and embarrassed women, required to disrobe in front of strangers and young boys. I left my bra on and clutched my clothes to my chest. "Bras off too," ordered the nurse. We were clearly not people to her. We were nameless, faceless immigrants subjected to indignities, treated with disdain, shuffled through the sheep dip, prodded with needles, dehumanized, then passed on with dispatch.

Inside I was seething at the lack of basic courtesy afforded us, and yet I knew that to speak out would possibly jeopardize our immigration application. So I remained mute. An image flashed into my mind as I stood shivering in the hall, a black-and-white image I had seen as a child of bewildered and frightened naked men and women lining up in a camp during World War II.

A simple explanation that we would be having a chest x-ray and an apology for the lack of facilities would have gone a long way towards alleviating anxiety and allaying fears. That's all it would have taken to transform the mood in the hallway. Once again, I wondered at the reason for such lack of consideration.

Once the x-ray was taken, blood drawn to be tested for AIDS, and a general physical conducted, we were directed to wait for the report.

"Mrs. Long, your AIDS results are ready." I stood up, mortified. Was it really necessary to shout out anything more than my name? Head bent, eyes staring at the floor, I scurried to the desk.

"Mrs. Long?"

"Yes. That's me, and I have my four children with me too." I didn't want anything overlooked. It would be awful to get back to the embassy and discover we didn't have all the necessary documents.

"Take this report to the US Embassy right away. Do *not* open it. Also, be very careful with this chest x-ray. Do not bend it."

"Okay. Thank you very much for your help." I signaled to Bill and the children to join me so that we could leave without a minute's delay. It was almost three in the afternoon. I felt as though I had been held hostage for the past six hours.

Back at the embassy, I submitted the paperwork and was told to hold on to the x-ray and instructed to once again wait.

"Mrs. Julia Long?" a man's voice enquired a few minutes later.

"Yes, that's me," I responded, standing up expectantly.

He beckoned with his index finger. "You've applied for a fiancé's visa, is that correct?" he asked once I reached the desk.

"Yes, that's right. My fiancé is here with me," I answered, pointing in Bill's direction.

"Invite him to come in with you," he said cheerfully.

After telling the children to be quiet and behave and putting Brian, the oldest, in charge, Bill and I were escorted into an interview room where the gentleman, a US consular officer, was seated behind a wooden table. When he stood, smiled, and offered me his hand, it was the first time that day I had felt as though someone saw me as a person.

"So tell me about your relationship. Why do you want to get married?" His questions were direct. His job was to discern whether or not we were a legitimate couple or whether it was a fraudulent application. Relatively, fewer fiancé visas are granted than other types as it is by far the toughest visa to get. However, I wasn't daunted in the slightest. I relished the opportunity to share our story, and with Bill right beside me, our love for each other was evident.

"Did she seduce you, sir?" This question for Bill, after I had responded, may have been prompted by our twenty-four-year age difference, or that I had four children, or that Bill had never married.

"Well, just look at her," was all Bill said in response.

The interview concluded a few minutes later with the consular once again shaking my hand and announcing with a chuckle, "Welcome to the United States of America, Mrs. Long. The land of the brave and the home of the fee!"

"Home of the fee?" I queried. Then I remembered all the money doled out today already.

"Home of the fee," he repeated, grinning.

"That's it? I'll be given a visa?" I wanted to double-check that I had understood him. He was smiling and nodding. All the months of form filling and appointments had come to an end in this dull room, which had, in an instant, become a portal to bliss. My heart surged with joy as Bill and I hugged tightly. All the miserable inconveniences of the days and months leading up to this moment dissolved in our embrace.

"So when do you plan on going to the US?" We were being brought back to the details.

"Well, I'm going on holiday in February for two weeks, and then I'll come back and go over with the children in the summer," I explained excitedly.

"Oh no, you won't." His tone had changed. He was no longer as jovial as before. "You have been granted a fiancé visa, which expires ninety days after you arrive in the US. Once you go in February, you must marry within ninety days. If you leave the country unmarried, then the visa is revoked."

I listened attentively, processing the information. I hadn't understood the conditions of the visa until now.

"I guess we'll be a family sooner than expected now that you and the kids are all coming in February," said Bill. "We've got a wedding to plan."

I was ecstatic as we thanked the immigration official, hardly able to believe that in fewer than seven weeks, we would be starting a new life in America.

His parting words to me were, "Hold on tight to that chest x-ray. They'll ask you for it at your port of entry in the US."

Bill returned to the US a few days after the visa interview with a slew of tasks to accomplish in a matter of weeks. He had to purchase four additional airline tickets for the children, secure a home for us, plan a wedding, research primary schools, and continue to teach at the university. I had to gather medical and school records for the children, clear out my house, and say goodbye.

Saying goodbye to my friends and family would be the toughest.

I was so imbued with a renewed fervor for life that the work ahead was a pleasure to complete. My parents joined my brothers in Bristol for a couple of weeks so that I could send the children to them while I wrapped up affairs in Newtown.

I took a day trip alone to Chester, where Bill had proposed, while a friend held a comprehensive house content sale from my living room. Everything I owned was up for sale. Not that I owned much to begin with, but it was symbolic of my sloughing off the old and embracing the new. I gave our family bible to my brother Vincent, along with cherished family photographs. I posted the letters I received from Bill to the US for safekeeping, but there was nothing else I needed to hold on to. I slept on the floor with my curtains as covers once the beds were sold, knowing that each night drew me closer to Bill.

Jan 18, 1990

My Darling,

Just came back from seeing the Rector. No big surprises. If the official release from the Society doesn't come in time, a marriage would "de facto" obtain the release. He did suggest, for appearances sake, that if

*we had two official residences until we get married,
it would look better and cause less talk. So we'll see!
If I get an apartment, then I could still officially keep
John's and he (Rector) said he would pay for it. I still
could stay with you most of the time—even nights,
but on paper it would look good. That leaves the question of health insurance, which could be quite costly
if we waited say 1 month before marriage. I'll inves-
tigate the costs and figure things out. He might even
help there! So one way or the other—we're on systems
go! I'll explain all of the above on next phone call.*

    *Check #2 enclosed. Take care of yourself. I only
gained 3 pounds on the trip —not too bad. I'm determined to cut on butter—that was 3 pounds in itself.*

                     All my love,
                            Bill
                            Xx

My Darling,

    *Check #3 enclosed plus further clarification on
the wedding! The rector phoned me this morning
and said the Jesuits actually prefer that I get married
first—then the actual marriage licence sent to Rome
gets me automatically dismissed from the society. He
said it speeds things up and saves tons of paperwork!!
So we can pick a date and not wait too long or rush
things. I'm checking on churches, ministers, etc.*

    *We can still do the two residencies bit. If we get
an apartment by then, that will do. I'll keep John's
until we marry. If no apartment, then lots of possibilities. Debbie Pearce has one free bedroom (in a
large house!). Either you could stay there with Amy
and the three boys could stay with me at John's or I
could stay there and you and the kids could stay at
John's. You might prefer to be away from the boys*

for a while. Again, we could spend much of the day together—meals, etc. and even take some trips (all together during that first week). I love you madly (continued in letter #4).

Bill
Xx

My Dearest Love,
    Check #4—plus continuation of letter.
    I hope all the discussion of legalities hasn't confused you too much. It boils down to good news. We can marry when we want and the Jesuits may even pay part of insurance costs plus extra rent for apartment. Not a bad deal!
    I've heard about a woman Unitarian minister who is supposed to be very nice. When I send in the licence to get dismissed—I then ask for laicization (permission to marry in the Church) and the Jesuits pursue it.
    Other than those exciting happenings, all is well. Classes are good—peppier than last year. The weather has finally turned cooler—though still in the 40's. It should be a quiet weekend.
    I miss you tons but know you'll be here soon.

All my love,
Bill
Xx

2 Colwyn
Jan 22nd, 1990

My Darling,
    It's 10:30pm, the children are asleep so it's an ideal time to write to you.

Last night I spent two hours reading through the first letters you sent me. It was a lovely journey back in time. We have come such a long way in two years.

I read all the disadvantages (and advantages) of my choosing you as my husband, and realize now just how unselfishly and lovingly you acted towards me.

One theme so apparent throughout the letters—is trust in God's will for us. How glad I am that we were both willing to do just that, look how he has rewarded us for our faith in his providence.

I could not imagine a happiness to match that which I'm experiencing now. You are everything to me, the most wonderful human being I've ever met!

I love you madly!

The house is looking decidedly bare—it's wonderful! Every day is one day closer to being with you—I can hardly wait to see you. I think I'll collapse with joy when we get to Cincinnati. It's still like a dream.

I hope all you have to do in such a short space of time isn't wearing you out. Soon we will be able to share the responsibility—I wish I could be there to help you, then again I may well just be a hindrance.

Well my Darling man, take good care of yourself for us.

I cannot get you out of my mind—not that I want to, you are with me the whole time.

God Bless you,

All my love,
Julie
Xx

Time with my friends was now even more valued. I understood something profound about happiness since my encounter with Bill, that it can only be achieved by cultivating and maintaining loving relationships. No possession, no prestige, no accolades can substitute for a deep and reverend connection to another human being. The more I loved one person, the more I could love all people. Loving begets love. As I prepared to leave Newtown, a place where I had suffered but also rejoiced; where I was scorned but also cherished; where I had been denied access to the Eucharist but grew closer to God, I discovered that enduring suffering, an inevitable part of life, had taught me how to deeply experience joy. I began to see more clearly the beauty in all things and all people. I grew in compassion and lived more attentively in the moments, which are grace-filled, if we have eyes to see.

I loved freely and generously and received love in return. Ozz, who had been by my side since I met him only a couple of years earlier, loved in the simplest and purest way by being there for me when I needed someone. He listened as I shared my story and held quiet in his heart his feelings for me, which he shared in a poem a few days before my departure.

> *Feelings*
> *Words whispered though seldom heard outside the heart.*
> *Perplexed about the way I feel.*
> *Unable to escape the feelings moving in my heart.*
> *Honorable intentions all misguided, leaving me vulnerable to hurt,*
> *My head now preaches words that shout the hard lessons of the past well learned.*
> *But even in my head the picture of your face remains*
> *Floating at night into my dreams.*
> *In waking hours I'm drawn to where you are.*
> *So soon I'll have to love you from afar.*
> *And when you leave, my heart will bear another scar.*
>
> *by Ian Austin (Ozz)*

Although our promise to stay in touch through letters was small consolation, Ozz knew that I was grateful for his love and that we would remain close and cherished friends for life. Bill was sympathetic, recognizing in Ozz a good man.

Chapter 25

With only one month left before our departure, practical concerns consumed our thoughts and conversations. The Jesuit community was showing great kindness towards us and offered to rent us a house until we could save the money for a deposit. The house, on Xavier University campus, was in need of renovation, which would begin immediately and would be ready for us on March 19. We would need to find somewhere to stay for three weeks only, and Bill had many generous friends offering us temporary accommodation.

A wedding date was set, March 17, twenty-one years to the day we met. I thought about the fact that the only people I would know at the ceremony were Bill and my children. Everyone else that I loved would be with us in spirit.

2 Colwyn
Jan 28th, '90

My Darling,
How are you? I was thinking of you on Friday during your house-hunting expedition.
The weather here has turned to snow, the country is still recovering from the gales. 45 people died. The children have been out sledging even Amy, she loved it!
I'm not so keen, it was very slippery going to Mass this morning. Fr Carson is away, another older priest said Mass. What a treat! His sermon was lovely—he is <u>very</u> devoted to our Lady and full

of gratitude to God for all he has done, he really was lovely to listen to.

Mam has bought her ticket for February 16th and is going back after the Christening of James, she seems to want to spend as much time away from Daddy as possible. I hope that never happens to us.

I shall be taking the children to Bristol on Feb 13th by train and returning alone the same day.

Any loose ends that need sorting out then can be done before I go for good.

The house is looking decidedly bare. I've moved out of my bedroom now to share with Sean and Amy.

All the furniture from the sitting and dining room has gone, it feels a bit like purgatory, knowing there is something wonderful waiting for me but not yet within reach.

Time is passing quite quickly for me though I feel a bit sad that you have so much to organize on your own. I wish I could help you.

Some thoughts on our wedding. Brian, I presume will have to "give me away," usually the Dad's job. As he is the oldest son, he would feel so proud. (I haven't mentioned to the children any of this). Have you got a "Best Man"? maybe Michael? Just a thought. Sean and Amy will be pageboy and bridesmaid.

You have probably got a few ideas too—we will have to discuss them all. There are a lot of possibilities for the children's involvement.

Please don't worry about having a small wedding. I will just be happy to be "Mrs. Hagerty." It will be THE most wonderful day of our life, together, just the beginning, but I do want it to be memorable, magical and grace-filled, which I'm sure it will be with you there.

Please don't worry about the cost of the wedding. I shall choose a simple dress and perhaps a small bouquet of fresh flowers. It won't be extravagant, I promise.

Bill, I love you madly and feel as though we are fulfilling a part of God's plan for us both. We shall exude His love, it will be our way of saying thank you to Him for His generosity towards us.

I cannot wait to hold you close, soon for ever.

God bless you Darling,

Julie
Xx

1/29/90

Julie, My Darling,
Well at least our wedding plans are set. Sat. March 17 at 11 am in the morning. A Bellarmine (our parish) member—a very holy and great man (works for the homeless) will perform the ceremony. He is an ordained Episcopal priest and married to an ex-nun. The place will be a parishioner's home (good friends of mine). They have a <u>huge</u> castle-like home and have had two weddings of their children there already. We can have a small catered reception/ lunch there afterward so we won't have to move from one place to another. They have a gorgeous stained glass window over the stairwell. The ceremony could be on the landing with the people seated below in the main hall (big fireplace included if it is cold out). I think you'll like it. It's nice to have a friend do the wedding and be the host for the wedding.

I saw a couple of <u>very nice</u> houses last Friday. But both are in the <u>upper</u> price range (95,000 dollars). They are also 25 minutes away from Xavier.

Without borrowing, I just didn't think I could make the down-payment plus considerable other costs. Besides that the mortgage rate suddenly shot up over 10%—a bad sign. I will still look for a real bargain but it looks as if we better rent for a year (or 6 mo. If I can get that short a lease). This will give you the chance to go house-hunting with me when the time comes. I would <u>really</u> appreciate <u>your</u> input, since it will impact a great deal on your career (work, school, etc.).

Time is flying since I am so busy but it will be a relief when we have some kind of house (rental or otherwise) assured. There is no sense in getting it before mid-February at earliest as there is no sense rushing into a house purchase. I <u>need</u> your good common sense and wisdom plus <u>your</u> considerable bargaining powers.

In short, my darling, I need you. Only 4 weeks to go. I can hardly believe it. Keep up the prayers. You have created liberty and hope for me. May God keep you in the palm of his hand.

I love you to bits,
Bill
Xx

2 Colwyn
Feb 2ⁿᵈ, 1990

My Darling,
I received the photos and a lovely card from you today. Thank you.
Stephen arrived yesterday midday and left this morning. We had a lovely meal out last night in the Indian Restaurant.

It was my first "Farewell." He is off to Italy on Saturday, so I won't see him again before our trip.

I felt very sad saying goodbye. It really hit me that there is a great distance between America and here! I shall miss him.

The weather is still awful. The Severn is 14ft above normal, it rose two feet in two hours today. The Fire Brigade and Police have taken to motor boats on some main roads in Gloucestershire. It must be one of the wettest and windiest January's on record. Snow forecast for tomorrow.

I have been looking at hymns and readings but haven't chosen any yet. You are doing a <u>fantastic</u> job organizing everything.

Perhaps the Jesuits house would be a good idea for a while till you have a bit more money saved. Whatever you feel is best I am happy to go along with. Just think less than four weeks to go. By the time this reaches you we may even be closer to two weeks!

I offered up my Rosary on Wednesday night for a good result on our house-hunting.

After your phone call I received another from a friend from the Army days who is splitting up with his wife (two children). He needed someone to talk to. It was 2am before I got to bed but the Rosary still got said. My Guardian Angel didn't finish it for me, just made sure I stayed awake to say it myself!

My friend said I should have been a nun!

The children are getting excited now. It will be nice when things settle down a bit. I will be exhausted after all these months, and now sudden activity. You too will be in need of recuperation. I think we will just collapse into each other's arms (very happily).

I love you Darling and am looking forward to a life shared with you more than I've ever looked forward to anything.

We will be happy together. We are happy together.

God Bless you Bill.

We'll be together soon.

ALL *my love,*
Julie xx

2/10/90

My Darling,

Your 2nd Valentine card arrived yesterday—how beautiful! I feel exactly the same. My love for you is truly unbounded. The very thought of you brings peace, joy and a zest for living throughout my entire being. I think I was destined to love you from all eternity. I often pictured you in my dreams but never thought it could come true.

I saw "Henry V" last night—the new film version by Kenneth Branagh. Really brilliant! The speech before the battle of Agincourt is brilliant— the people in the theater applauded at the end. It's that "We precious few—we band of brothers" speech. Then after the battle picking up the dead— they sing a Latin hymn which is awe-inspiring as the orchestra comes up. "Da Nobis Domine" is the title, I think. I'll have to see it a second time so if it's still around after you arrive, let's go. Also coming in March is "My Left Foot" —the story of Christy Brown—the Irish writer with cerebral palsy. It's supposed to be excellent. Let's see that too—if you wish!

I'm going deliriously happy picturing us together—every place I go now I see you soon with me and it makes me want to dance for joy.

You are wondrous, my beloved—I thank God every day for making our life together (despite all odds) possible.

All my love,
Forever and forever,
Bill
Xx

2/11/90

My Darling,

The man in charge of remodeling the house stopped over—he's a very nice guy and seems genuinely proud of what he's doing. It looks good—on paper. The boys will be able to help us in—a family effort. I hope it's ready on time—they had to completely re-do all electric and plumbing systems. As soon as washer and dryer hook-ups are done, I'll go out and buy these so they'll be ready when we move in.

Summer like weather (or at least Spring-like) is still with us though colder temps on way. January was hottest in history. The flowers and trees are budding and will probably be killed in the next deep freeze (if we have one!)

All continues to go well—very hard to believe we're down to 2 ½ weeks!!! I'm beginning to just float on air—it all seems so unbelievable. I guess I won't believe it till I see you get off that plane – no not until I feel you in my arms.

I'm going over to Harten's house (where the wedding will be) tomorrow (sat) with the caterer.

We'll look things over. She will also provide flowers
<u>and</u> wedding cake. I keep looking at wedding list
and seeing people I <u>should</u> have invited. I'm up to
about 76 now but I'm sure that 20 or so of them
won't be able to come so I'm still confident we'll be
in 50–60 range.

I talked to Don Nastold (pastor of our church)
and told him we wouldn't go to Communion at
public Masses. He seemed relieved (he's been in trou-
ble with the Bishop over that general matter). He
reminded me I still have the key to the sacristy and
that I was <u>very</u> welcome to get communion for you
and me in private when we are alone in church—
plus, as I said, let's go to a different church once a
month and go to Communion as a family—we'll
have breakfast out on that day. Our lives will cele-
brate God's love for us.

Love you to bits.

Bill

xx

It was time to leave Newtown, but not before I paid a visit to
the cemetery and prayed for Adrian. As I stood at his graveside, reading the inscription I had chosen, "Perfected by Love," I considered
our time together and thanked him for sparing me that tragic weekend two years before. Through his dying, he had gifted me life. How
could I be anything but grateful?

Ozz arrived at my now empty house to accompany me to the
train station. We walked in silence, not knowing how to say goodbye.
I felt a mixture of sadness and peace standing on the platform, waiting, Ozz beside me puffing nervously on a cigarette until the familiar
sound of the train engine in the distance signaled it was time to say
our farewells.

"So here we are then. It's time for you to go," he said, feigning
cheerfulness and letting out a long sigh. "Be happy, okay?"

"Yes, I will. Thank you for everything, Ozz. You are my dear friend." I accepted his help putting on my backpack before leaning in for a last hug. The train pulled up, and he opened the carriage door for me. I boarded the train and leaned out of the window for one last goodbye.

"This is for you. Read it when you're out of the station," he said, handing me an envelope. The signalman's whistle drowned out my thank-you as the train slowly pulled away. I looked back until his figure shrank to a speck in the distance.

20-2-90

Missing You

It was my fate that I did wait and tarried overwhile.
I've lost my heart, now you depart and long before
    I smile.
Your eyes of green,
Your hair so black,
Of Gaelic looks enchanting,
So pure within,
Your white teeth grin of humour everlasting.
Now mountains, and rivers, and beautiful views,
Mean nothing to me parted from you.
Sunshine and blue skies, all become grey
As I think of you so far away.

by Ian Austin (Ozz)

The poem settled with me as I understood the capacity we all have to love one another. I was so grateful to Ozz for his love, which was so unselfish. He may not have known, as he handed me the poem on the platform, that I also loved him.

Five hours later, I was reunited with my children. The excitement was palpable. In a matter of days, we would be soaring at thirty-three thousand feet over the Atlantic, going where my best prayers were taking us. Though I didn't know it, my entire life had been a journey on this blessed pathway to Bill, my destiny and my home.

We were travelling light with no luggage to check in, so we each packed our own backpack containing only clothing. The children needed their arms free to hold hands and carry their favorite teddy bear. I needed my hands free to hold hands and carry my chest x-ray. Amy, aged three, had a more difficult time packing, so the boys offered to help her. Once her bag was zipped up, Michael and Sean eased her arms through the loops as Brian, kneeling, fastened the buckle securely in the front of her tummy. I loved watching them taking care of one another and especially how protective and attentive they were to their little sister.

"There you go, Amy. You're all set," said Brian, standing up as Michael and Sean clapped encouragingly. Amy, beaming, attempted to take a wobbly step forward and promptly toppled backwards, legs waving in the air, like a beetle on its back, unable to get up. At the sight of our wriggling, panting pink puffball, we all collapsed with the giggles. Her backpack weighed more than she did, so we regrouped, and the boys made room in their luggage for some of her surplus outfits.

It was time to say goodbye to my family. I hate goodbyes. I recalled how, as an eleven-year-old, I had defied my mother by refusing to say goodbye to Father Bill. "I'll never say goodbye to that man!" Now I was getting ready to say hello to him, but that required some goodbyes to others whom I dearly loved.

In the early morning of February 28, 1990, the taxi ordered to take us to the train station arrived while it was still dark. My family members drowsily gathered around in their dressing gowns and pajamas, arms folded against the winter chill in the air, until a small child appeared in front of them, arms open, offering and looking for a hug—then another and another and another. Then me. I became a small child again, momentarily, as my mother wrapped her arms around me and said, "I want you to be happy. You deserve it." The waiting was over. We were on our way.

As we boarded the plane to Cincinnati, I thought about the past two years, how my world had expanded and how extraordinary the journey had been. I had waited and planned for this time to come, but now that it was a reality. It was still hard to fathom that it was actually happening. I was looking forward with energy and hope but could not rest until I was safely in the arms of my beloved Bill. In the meantime, I was guarding my chest x-ray, ensuring it was not at risk of being bent. I was also concerned for the children, helping them buckle their seat belts and encouraging them to take a nap as it would be hours before we landed. Amy, unaccustomed to so much excitement, vomited before the plane even took off. Oh my, it was going to be the longest flight of my life.

I sat between Sean and Amy, the two youngest, knowing that they would need most attention. Sean—a creative, friendly, and endearing eight-year-old—popped his head over the back of our seat and greeted the lady behind us with a big smiling, "Hello!"

"Sean, sit down," I urged, tugging on the back of his leg gently, to no avail.

The lady graciously responded with, "Hello, what's your name?"

"Sean!" he replied, beaming.

"Hello, Sean, what do you want to be when you grow up?" *Uh-oh*, I thought, knowing what his answer would be.

"Sean! Sit down, please," I pleaded, just as he blurted out enthusiastically, "A ventriloquist!" His broad smile was fixed in place, and his jaws were clamped shut. For the remaining seven hours of the flight, he engaged that lovely, patient lady and all of us in conversation through clenched teeth. I wonder if she ever spoke to another child on a plane again.

Finally, exhausted but filled with anticipation, we arrived at Cincinnati airport and approached Customs, where I would have my last interview before being admitted. With all four children beside me, I submitted my passport for scrutiny and offered up what had received as much care and attention as a fifth child: the chest x-ray.

"What's that?" asked the Customs official.

"My chest x-ray. I was told you would need it." I was relieved to be finally handing it over.

"Nah, we don't want that. You keep it," he said dismissively. I wondered if I had been the victim of a cheeky prank by the embassy staff in London? This x-ray had caused me more anxiety since I was given it than any one of my children on this trip.

After being asked why I had a one-way ticket and my children had return tickets, I had to force myself to refrain from making a joke about how appealing that prospect seemed in this moment, especially as the boys had just been asked by the security guards, "What do children in England call policemen?" to which one of them, to my utter horror, answered boldly, "Pigs!"

"Boys!" I scolded. "I'm *so* sorry. They are usually so polite and good mannered," I said to the guard, afraid of being sent back to England on the next flight.

With a broad smile and an inviting gesture to step beyond the security line, the Customs official handed me back my passport, saying, "Welcome to the USA, ma'am. I hope you and your children will be very happy here."

"Thank you very much. I know now that all shall be well."

The children spotted Bill first and rushed excitedly at him, "Daddy! Daddy! Daddy! Daddy!" He was waiting for them with his arms open like a magnificent oak tree offering shelter in its branches, his beaming smile increasing each time "daddy" chirped through the air.

No words were needed as we held each other close in a peaceful embrace. We both knew that in the shelter of each other, we would thrive. I offered a silent prayer of immense gratitude for God's infinite love, which had led us through the darkness towards the light and given us both the courage to choose life.

About the Author

Julie Hagerty believes that she has been gifted a second chance at life and love. After marrying at eighteen and struggling to survive an abusive relationship, she discovered that love overcomes fear. Her courage, determination, and faith propelled her towards a life of authenticity and joy. She grew up in Ireland and England before moving with her four children to live in the United States to be with her soulmate, Bill. She attended Xavier University where she earned a BA and an M.Ed. She has been teaching literature and public speaking and leading spiritual retreats for twenty-five years using her story to inspire others and to give hope.

CPSIA information can be obtained
at www.ICGtesting.com
Printed in the USA
LVHW040815220719
624829LV00001B/71